Heroes of the New Hollywood

ALSO BY DAN LALANDE
AND FROM MCFARLAND

*The Drop Dead Funny '70s: American Film
Comedies Year by Year* (2023)

Heroes of the New Hollywood

Hoffman, Hackman, Nicholson, Pacino, Duvall, and De Niro in the '70s

Dan Lalande

McFarland & Company, Inc., Publishers
Jefferson, North Carolina

LIBRARY OF CONGRESS CATALOGING-IN-PUBLICATION DATA

Names: Lalande, Dan, author.
Title: Heroes of the new Hollywood : Hoffman, Hackman, Nicholson, Pacino, Duvall, and De Niro in the '70s / Dan Lalande.
Description: Jefferson, North Carolina : McFarland & Company, Inc., Publishers, 2024. | Includes bibliographical references and index.
Identifiers: LCCN 2024034676 | ISBN 9781476693552 (paperback : acid free paper) ∞
ISBN 9781476653440 (ebook)
Subjects: LCSH: Motion picture actors and actresses—United States. | Hoffman, Dustin, 1937—Criticism and interpretation. | Hackman, Gene—Criticism and interpretation. | Nicholson, Jack—Criticism and interpretation. | Pacino, Al, 1940—Criticism and interpretation. | Duvall, Robert—Criticism and interpretation. | De Niro, Robert—Criticism and interpretation. | Motion pictures—United States—History—20th century
Classification: LCC PN1998.2 L347 2024 | DDC 791.4302/80922—dc23/eng/20240816
LC record available at https://lccn.loc.gov/2024034676

BRITISH LIBRARY CATALOGUING DATA ARE AVAILABLE

ISBN (print) 978-1-4766-9355-2
ISBN (ebook) 978-1-4766-5344-0

© 2024 Dan Lalande. All rights reserved

No part of this book may be reproduced or transmitted in any form or by any means, electronic or mechanical, including photocopying or recording, or by any information storage and retrieval system, without permission in writing from the publisher.

Front cover image: Robert De Niro (as Travis Bickle) in *Taxi Driver*, 1976 (Columbia Pictures/Photofest, photographer: Josh Weiner); *background* © Atria Borealis/Shutterstock

Printed in the United States of America

McFarland & Company, Inc., Publishers
Box 611, Jefferson, North Carolina 28640
www.mcfarlandpub.com

For Rick Kaulbars, the anti-hero in my life

Table of Contents

Preface: Brando's Bastards 1

Introduction: "The Charmless Man" 5

Marlon Brando: A Budding Influence 13

Dustin Hoffman: The Graduate Graduates 38

Gene Hackman: A Sorry Son of a Bitch 64

Jack Nicholson: The Rebel King 85

Al Pacino: Forever Wired 107

Robert Duvall: A Good Soldier 125

Robert De Niro: Avenging Angel 153

1980s–2020s: The Aftermath 174

Postscript 177

Chapter Notes 181

Filmographies (1970–79) 185

Bibliography 189

Index 191

Preface
Brando's Bastards

"Lightning states"—it's how Marlon Brando described moments of histrionic electricity, including the fits of primal rage to which his on-screen avatars were prone. His feral furor sent catchphrases into the stratosphere and soaked his iconic T-shirt with testosterone-tainted perspiration. Up until Brando's emergence, movie audiences had certainly seen their heroes brought to anger but usually expressed by such comparatively tempered means as a well-aimed barb, a stern speech or a quick fist. But *this* ... this was something else. Something existential, something universal, something influential.

The outbursts from Brando's on-screen characterizations—young, marginalized, confused—spoke for an entire generation of low to middle-class teenagers silently fed up with the Brooks Brothers conformity of the 1950s. Like Brando, they had questions in their heads and chips on their shoulders; complacency came with a question mark, civility with a deep sense of betrayal. A restlessness was at work, if inarticulately, that proper American society could not comprehend nor accommodate. By expressing it as sincerely and explosively as possible, Brando brought a new, elemental naturalism to the art of acting. The effect of this technique, learned at the feet of Russian-influenced American acting gurus, created a ripple effect both immediate (James Dean, Montgomery Clift, Paul Newman) and long-lasting (Dustin Hoffman, Gene Hackman, Jack Nicholson, Al Pacino, Robert Duvall, Robert De Niro).

The latter group, the biggest brood yet of "Brando's bastards," came to the fore in the 1970s. They were creatures of a time of dramatic social and economic transition. Cities were crumbling, crime was rampant, inflation was high. The generational divide that had begun in the '60s still existed, sex and romance had grown confusing, and drugs had gone from feel-good to death-inducing—all while a corrupt president struggled to save his skin. How to find what it took to survive? And what was the point, if any, of said survival? So asked Hoffman's Ratso Rizzo, Hackman's Popeye Doyle, Nicholson's Bobby Dupea, Pacino's Frank Serpico, Duvall's "Bull" Meacham and De Niro's Travis Bickle.

In portraying characters who asked such pressing, empiric questions, Hoffman, Hackman, Nicholson, Pacino, Duvall and De Niro, in order of fame, imprinted themselves on film audiences the way their idol Brando had on *them*: by giving voice to contemporary unrest. Further, as dedicated, even neurotic craftsmen (again, *à la* Brando), they advanced, movie by movie, the art of emoting for the screen. It helped that the era in which they evolved as artists coincided with the rise of another talented and impactful generation: a collegiately trained school of directors whose virtuosic technique and culturally relevant themes brought a new energy and integrity to mainstream American fare.

These two factions combined to create a decade's worth of instant classics, films talked about as much today as they were upon their initial release.

Heroes of the New Hollywood looks at the work, lives and legacy of the dynamic male screen actors at the eye of that storm, and the period in they accomplished their best work. Not that they peaked; comparably accomplished performances ensued from each as their impressively long careers progressed. But it was over that timeline—approximately 1967–83, with the choice period being 1970–79—that they came into their own, in the last age in which the American filmmaking machine prized acting. Over that span (1967–83), using the measuring stick of the Academy Awards alone, they garnered 19 nominations and eight wins between the six of them. Fourteen of their films ranked amongst the top ten grossers of their respective years.

While the narrative focus of the book is the evolution of each career, the thematic concern is the shapeshifting nature of the male identity throughout the 1970s. With the corruption of the patriarchal model at the hands of criminal, war-mongering authoritarians, and the rise of feminism with its demand for dimensional partners over mansplaining father figures, the American male found himself in a state of considerable confusion. The six actors at the center of the book represented this ambivalence, collectively struggling to rewrite an outdated stereotype while accessing a personalized, satisfactory alternative. Hoffman starts off as the sexually judgmental Ratso Rizzo before locating a deep-seated maternalism as single father Ted Kramer; Nicholson's J.J. Gittes uses traditional tough guy roughhousing on Faye Dunaway, only to suffer a frozen comeuppance for his chauvinistic sins as Jack Torrance; Duvall is the unforgiving paterfamilias "Bull" Meacham (aka the Great Santini) until he becomes the remorseful, reformed Mack Sledge. And so on.

You, the reader, will benefit from countless hours of research, from biographies both slapdash and worthy, from the repeated scrutinization of iconic films, and the occasional revelations offered by these generally secretive talents about their shared and individual approaches to their craft. While many a book has been written on these actors as individuals, none, up until now, has considered them as a group. Further, few are interested in delving into the finer points of their practice, assessing their cultural impact, or weighing their value as representatives of their sex in adjusting times. By giving this formidable generation its full due, the present work positions itself as a unique contribution to the library of books on actors and acting.

But enough about me; back to them: We, particularly the men who attended the movies throughout the '70s, had many of our battles fought for us by those six energetic, earnest and electrifying actors. They raged for us, brooded for us, even died for us (a lot, actually). By decade's end, they were lost to us, or at least noticeably sapped of their relevance and range. Come the '80s, American films were no longer exploratory character studies, but convention-respecting re-immersions into appeasing genres.

Movies had gone from gritty and disturbing to light and accommodating, taking with them our best screen actors doing what they did best. Going forward, Hoffman et al. would be relying on signature gestures, shameless showboating and episodes of self-parody.

They could still act, of course, but their reputations would now precede them. Suddenly, nobody was casting Jack Nicholson to see him advance his craft; they were casting him to get "that Jack Nicholson feeling." Before that, though, we got to witness them at the height of their powers in, inarguably, their best films.

Read on and re-live that enriching experience.

Introduction

"The Charmless Man"

"Perhaps never before in the history of American movies have there been so many first-rate leading men doing so many different kinds of roles."
—Vincent Canby, *New York Times,* July 14, 1980

In 1978, Donald Spoto wrote in his *Camerado: Hollywood and the American Man,*

> The cinematic representation of the appealing American male may have nowhere to go at this time. As the movies' portrayal of life has more closely resembled everyday experience and a concern for recent history and pressing moral issues, most images of social appeal and approval are considered artificial, unnecessary, even duplicitous.[1]

Spoto added as an aside, "This may be why many leading male actors of the seventies—Dustin Hoffman, Jack Nicholson, Robert De Niro, Al Pacino—often portray singularly charmless men."[2]

This statement, at once an elegy for the good-natured, romantically shy, proudly moralizing everyman of the Studio Era and the acknowledgment of a new, realistic and more relevant form of American mainstream cinema, fails to take into account just how long the "charmless man" had been around. While some of the Warner Bros. tough guys had acquiesced to the good-egg archetype, others remained true to dramatic sobriety. Even when he was playing a closet romantic, as in *Casablanca* (1942), Humphrey Bogart never compromised the singular superiority that kept him sourly separated from society; Paul Muni, who brought Method Acting to the screen back when that school-to-be was primordially known as the Yiddish Theatre, retained a dark, Slavic deadpan even at his most extending; Edward G. Robinson could amuse, but it was strictly self-amusement, as is the sadist's wont.

And certainly, when Hollywood entered the postwar era, a distinctly male seriousness came to rule the roost. Many a Studio Era mensch had gone to war, only to return hellbent on a devotion to roles reflecting a more affected, confrontational persona. Top hats were traded for the ten-gallon variety, tuxedos shed for combat fatigues. James Stewart, Henry Fonda and William Holden were never the same after their time in the service, while a new generation, beefier of body and tighter of lip—Robert Mitchum, Kirk Douglas, Gregory Peck et al.—brought the war-spawned values of fortitude, taciturnity and self-examination to the screen.

Then, of course, came the big bang: Brando. Using what he had learned from America's Russian-influenced acting gurus, young Marlon took what Mitchum and company had been hinting at and enveloped it in naturalism and, bringing us back to Spoto, social relevancy. Brando's impact created a trickle-down effect that would last for decades. It climaxed, it could be argued, with the generation of male screen actors at the center of this book, all of whom had grown up ardent admirers: in order of stardom, Dustin Hoffman, Gene Hackman, Jack Nicholson, Al Pacino, Robert Duvall and Robert De Niro.

The first two, while borrowing from Brando, are not direct descendants. The others, though, fit the type: urban, angry, sexual, explosive and, above all, unpredictable. (One of Brando's acting coaches, the estimable Elia Kazan, maintained that an actor must always surprise.) To a man, they chose or rewrote roles predicated on that jack-in-the-box ethic. Nicholson wipes a table clean over a mere chicken sandwich in *Five Easy Pieces* (1970); low-key good-son Pacino stuns his family by taking over from the mobster paterfamilias in *The Godfather* (1972); Duvall the hard-ass out-hard-asses himself in *The Great Santini* (1979); De Niro doesn't say much for a long, long time, then—*pow!*—in film after film.

America at the time of their heyday, the 1970s, was an angry place. And why not? The country had gone to hell. Two Kennedys and MLK had been killed; innocent kids were being slaughtered in Vietnam and on college campuses; New York City, once the epitome of urban sophistication, had become the most dangerous place in the world; inflation was uncontrollable; labor strife was periodic; cops were on the take; race riots were a common occurrence; the generational divide was growing wider; mass murderers and serial killers were proliferating; and drugs, once a feel-good means of escape from it all, needed rogue heroes like tough cop Popeye Doyle (*The French Connection*, 1971) to curtail their epidemic abuse. We needed actors to emote on our behalf, to question, to brood, to scream, sometimes as primally as possible. We could have them at the facile level—like those taciturn urban avengers, Clint Eastwood and Charles Bronson—or, better still, at the sophisticated level, while watching them, part and parcel, advance the art of acting for the screen.

Added advantage: after cutting their teeth in half-hearted, low-budget cult films, their primes coincided with the rise of a new class of European-influenced American filmmakers. These "kids with a camera" were young, socio-politically oriented, and looking to make a mark just as much as the hungry actors who starred in their movies. Together, these pools of like-minded talents created what became known as the New Hollywood, bringing fresh energy, integrity and relevance to the inert state of American on-screen drama, even if some of the narrative exoskeletons—the gangster picture (*The Godfather*), the musical (*New York New York*, 1977), the war film (*The Deer Hunter*, 1978)—would be decidedly familiar.

And it hardly hurt that in 1966, just before these actors became major on-screen commodities, Hollywood's strict censorship system, which had kept a genuinely adult dimension from the form, gave way. At last, room had been created for freedom of subject, character and form. As Peter Biskin frames that time in his immensely readable *Easy Riders, Raging Bulls*, "It was the last time Hollywood produced a body of risky, high-quality work—as opposed to the errant masterpiece—that was character- rather than plot-driven, that defied traditional narrative conventions, that challenged the tyranny of technical correctness, that broke the taboos of language and behavior, that dared to end unhappily."[3]

These "new kinds of films" required new kinds of actors—the American equivalent of Britain's angry young man movement of the early '60s, back when that national cinema was transitioning. In his excellent *Shooting Midnight Cowboy*, Glenn Frankel described the Tom Courtenays and Albert Finneys and Oliver Reeds of that movement as "passionate, hungry, with strikingly different faces and regional accents ... they were the British version of an American generation of more naturalistic and compelling film actors ... but the British got there first."[4]

Of the American contingent, it was Hoffman who made the initial splash, in Mike Nichols' instant classic *The Graduate* (1967). That same year, Hackman left his imprint in a supporting capacity in the equally resonant *Bonnie and Clyde* (1967). Nicholson was still slumming, until he made something out of a nothing part in *Easy Rider* (1969). Then came *The Godfather*, affording both Pacino and Duvall staying power. De Niro brought up the rear: *Mean Streets* (1973) had been cult fare; when he surprised the world by winning the Best Supporting Actor Oscar for his studied, low-key turn in *The Godfather Part II* (1974), another star was added to the firmament.

They had contemporaries, of course, other actors who did occasionally worthy work but who were not, on the whole, in the same class: Warren Beatty, Robert Redford, James Caan, Burt Reynolds, Jon Voight. The disconnect between these two stratifications may well be rooted in the fact that the latter group was closer to Spoto's "endorsably appealing man," defined as "attractive to women," and made of "wardrobe, inflection, coloring, and physique."[5] No matter that they could be roguish, confused, violent or narcissistic too.

In the '70s, Hoffman, Hackman et al. also had comic counterparts, dramatic actors just as adept at comedy: Jack Lemmon, Walter Matthau, George Segal, Alan Arkin, Elliott Gould, Donald Sutherland, Richard Dreyfuss, and Reynolds again. There were also outright comic figures: Peter Sellers, Woody Allen, Steve Martin, Chevy Chase, John Belushi, Dudley Moore. These lighter entities didn't hold a monopoly on the genre ... but close. Hoffman's forays into film were comedies, Nicholson periodically played the fool, and Hackman managed to (almost) steal a pair of crowd-pleasers: *Young Frankenstein* (1974) and *Superman* (1978). But it wasn't until they aged and loosened up a bit that the others felt predisposed to try their luck at getting laughs (though De Niro had started, tepidly, as a kind of hippie satirist); hence Pacino in *Dick Tracy* (1990) and *Simone* (2002), De Niro in *Wag the Dog* (with Hoffman, 1997), *Analyze This* (1999) and its 2002 sequel, and the *Meet the Fockers* (2004) franchise (2000 and 2010). Duvall was in the darkly satirical *Network* (1976). Hackman took the plunge again in his later years, with *Loose Cannons*, 1990, *Heartbreakers*, 2001, and *Welcome to Mooseport*, 2004.

Back to their dramatic work, 1969–83. It's interesting to note that all of those testosterone-based histrionics were going on while feminism was in accelerated motion. Women, suddenly, wanted more from men: equals instead of overlords. They demanded dimension, vulnerability, open-mindedness, candor and consideration. Hence, what we got, on-screen at least, were conflicted heroes, men who struggled with staying true to an Old World–dictated identity while reaching deep within themselves for the frustratingly elusive quality it took to rewrite the stereotype.

That cast of characters included such familiar types as husbands and fathers (*The Godfather Part II, Kramer vs. Kramer,* 1979), cops and private detectives (*Chinatown,* 1974, *Night Moves,* 1975), sailors and soldiers (*The Last Detail,* 1973, *The Deer Hunter*), outliers and loners (*Five Easy Pieces, Taxi Driver,* 1976) and, if less frequently, cowboys and outlaws (*Zandy's Bride,* 1974, *Goin' South,* 1978).

Female stars too, though fewer, were coloring long-standing, gender-based archetypes with the attitudes, issues and anxieties of the feminist age: the hooker (Jane Fonda in *Klute,* 1971), the innocent (Goldie Hawn in *Butterflies Are Free,* 1972), the entertainer (Liza Minnelli in *Cabaret,* 1972), the mother (Ellen Burstyn in *Alice Doesn't Live Here Anymore,* 1974), the wife (Jill Clayburgh in *An Unmarried Woman,* 1978) and, in the case of the versatile Barbra Streisand, all of the above (*The Owl and the Pussycat,* 1970, *What's Up, Doc?,* 1972, *Up the Sandbox,* 1972, *For Pete's Sake,* 1974, *Funny Lady,* 1975). Part of the push was attributable to the release of critic Molly Haskell's seminal, much-needed *From Reverence to Rape,* holding Hollywood historically accountable for its idealization-devaluation of women in the movies. Haskell wrote of that period in the book's 1987 second edition: "If a visitor from outer space had landed on Planet Earth in the late seventies and looked at movies as a cultural indicator, he (she, it?) would have known that women were up to something only by their absence."[6]

Further, Haskell emphatically fingered the men of the New Hollywood for not picking up the feminist cause, accusing them of burrowing into "violent male-centered melodramas" or retreating into "a no less fantastic world of eternal adolescence."[7] That's giving extremely short shrift to the films of Hoffman & Co., though the more commercially minded of the helmsmen with which those actors worked, primarily George Lucas and Steven Spielberg, deserve the rap.

Haskell's critique fails to take into account the proliferation and quality of the supporting female roles in those films. Actresses including Kitty Wynn, Karen Black, Estelle Parsons, Ann-Margret, Candice Bergen, Susan Anspach, Diane Keaton, Ellen Burstyn, Teri Garr, Faye Dunaway, Louise Fletcher, Kathleen Lloyd, Mary Steenburgen, and a then-unknown Meryl Streep distinguished themselves in parts that transcended appendage and made a sizable contribution to the dramatic impact of those properties, even if those films were, in the main, explorations of the modern male mindset.

No African Americans, neither male nor female, constituted part of either pantheon. (Okay: Diana Ross, a bit.) Where were they? Relegated to blaxploitation, supporting parts and broad comedy. Sidney Poitier, one of the biggest stars of the '60s, spent most of the '70s rewriting his cultivated image, co-starring in and directing a series of jive, clownish comedies that, while fun, left many critics broken-hearted over such a willing transgression of his dignified persona. The gap that Poitier left is significant. Audiences had to wait until the '90s for the restoration of on-screen African American gravitas, with the emergence of Morgan Freeman and Denzel Washington, and even longer than that for female stars to be permitted to hold their own, like Halle Berry and Viola Davis.

Meanwhile, though, we had Hoffman, Hackman, Nicholson, Pacino, Duvall and De Niro. We got to see this generation, film by film, evolve from quirky-looking nobodies in quirky little non-films to mature working artists in legitimate box office successes. Further, from (approximately) '69 to '83, we got to see them in their prime, before they developed signature gestures, coasted on reputation, or became grand old men of the game (for the latter, see *The Bucket List*, 2007, or *The Irishman*, 2019).

There were those Academy Awards nominations and wins, and those astounding box office returns. And as another legacy goes, catchphrases, well, there are just too many to tally. Sample size: "I'm walkin' here!," "You talking to me?," "I love the smell of napalm in the morning...," "Heeere's Johnny!," "Say hello to my little friend..."

Such were the similarities between these actors that critics would occasionally complain of their interchangeability—ridiculous but not entirely crazy, as Hoffman & Co. would often find themselves vying for the same roles. Nicholson was an early choice for Hoffman's part in *Straw Dogs* (1971); both Nicholson and De Niro had a shot at Pacino's role in *The Godfather*; Pacino was up for both Hoffman's *Lenny* (1974) and De Niro's *Taxi Driver*; Hackman was an early contender for Nicholson's iconic turn in *One Flew Over the Cuckoo's Nest* (1975) and for Duvall's Colonel Kilgore in *Apocalypse Now* (1979); Hoffman was the original choice for Hackman's part in *Superman*, and even, incredibly, for De Niro's in *Raging Bull* (1980). Et cetera.

A common negotiation tactic among agents and producers was to tell whichever actor was hemming and hawing over a particular part that one of his contemporaries was also being considered. And indeed, as a collective, this generation formed a loose boys' network, though on *Scarecrow* (1973), Pacino and Hackman did not see eye to eye, while Pacino and Hoffman enjoyed a relationship of forced cordiality. Still, there'd be small jam sessions where you would see one or two or three of them together: the aforementioned *Scarecrow*, *The Conversation* (1974), *The Last Tycoon* (1976), *True Confessions* (1981), *Heat* (1985), *Dick Tracy*, *Sleepers* (1996), *Wag the Dog*, *Meet the Parents* (2000), *Runaway Jury* (2003), *Righteous Kill* (2008), *Little Fockers* (2010) and *The Irishman*.

That said, each of these actors is, of course, a singular talent, marked by distinctions that transcend their physical, familial and theatrical similarities. And dynamic as each of them, back in that formative era, was, it wasn't simply their acting that ingratiated them to audiences. Their symbolic value held equal weight. Ronald Brownstein's *Rock Me on the Water*, a look at the cultural impact of 1974, perfectly identifies the questions that the musicians, TV producers and performers of that time were asking: "What did it mean to live a meaningful life as the 1960s' dream of social transformation faded? What constituted personal contentment when political dreams dissolved?"[8]

Hoffman and the rest were not exempt from entertaining these inquiries through the practice of their craft. Each actor represented a different solution to those questions, embodying individual facets of the transition from the failed '60s to what might next be in store. To wit, starting with the establishmentarians, then those who better represented the rebellious spirit then waning:

Al Pacino: Pacino's *oeuvre* was a plea for the return to institutional order. He would make a career, in fact, of fighting for it. In the world according to Pacino, nothing's wrong with the system; the tenets of society just need to be cleaned up: organized crime in the *Godfather* films, law enforcement in *Serpico*, the justice system in *...And Justice for All*, formal education in *Scent of a Woman* (1992), City Hall in, you guessed it, *City Hall* (1996), football in *Any Given Sunday* (1999) and crime, again, in *The Irishman*.

Unfortunately, this propensity for the restoration of order would lead to a predictable climax in the bulk of his later films: long, soapbox-set speeches of volatile self-righteousness—a long way from the hypnotic brooding of his formative roles.

Gene Hackman: Like Pacino, Hackman too is a devotee of the system ... well, sort of. He's an insider but an itchy one, always looking to distinguish himself by way of personal contribution. He's all for change but change from within—*his* way. Too bad he always finds out that the system in which he operates is prone to forces, some even outside, reminding you to keep your head low, do your job, and conform: Popeye Doyle in *The French Connection*, Harry Caul in *The Conversation*, another Harry, Moseby, in *Night Moves*, Major Foster in *March or Die* (1977), Lex Luthor in three of the *Superman* films, coach Dale in *Hoosiers* (1984), Little Bill Daggett in *Unforgiven* (1992) and Captain Ramsey in *Crimson Tide* (1995).

Robert Duvall: Duvall doesn't split hairs. (I'll spare you the corny addition of "because he doesn't have many." Oops! Guess I didn't!) He's the good soldier through and through. His folly is in playing that particular card too well. It causes casualties, which creates some uncomfortable resonance within him. His stance can subsequently soften, but fuzzily: Tom Hagen in the *Godfather* films, Colonel Kilgore in *Apocalypse Now*, "Bull" Meacham in *The Great Santini*, Mac Sledge in *Tender Mercies* (1983), Sonny Dewey in *The Apostle* (1997) and Joseph Palmer in *The Judge* (2014).

Jack Nicholson: Nicholson is, of course, nobody's baby. He's not out to play ball with the system or even to cut his own path within it. The spirit of the '60s incarnate, his characters are out to tease, taunt and torture, to disrupt the lay of the land until he can outright torch it. But like his quieter predecessor, Paul Newman, Nicholson's bent always ends up being an extremely painful education. The Nicholsonian moral: Smart as you may be, the world, for all appearances, will always prove smarter: Bobby Dupea in *Five Easy Pieces*, "Bad Ass" Buddowsky in *The Last Detail*, J.J. Gittes in *Chinatown*, R.P. McMurphy (do you really need the name and year of the film?), and even the larger-than-life figures like the Joker in *Batman* (1989).

Robert De Niro: De Niro inherits the Nicholsonian agenda but makes a career of showing us the run-up to the rage. His socially alienated characters suffer in silence until they decide to take the system head-on. When they lose the battle, they lose big; when they win, a small, personal enlightenment is the ultimate benefit: Johnny Boy in *Mean Streets*, Travis Bickle in *Taxi Driver*, Jimmy Doyle in *New York New York*, Mike Vronsky in *The Deer Hunter* and Jake La Motta in *Raging Bull*.

I've saved **Dustin Hoffman** for last, even if he became famous first, because of his climactic value within this analogy. Hoffman represents the human price of this collective suffering. Unlike his contemporaries, he's not prone to boldly standing his guard, moments of explosive violence (okay, once: *Straw Dogs*), or even much scheming. The malleable quality Hoffman first demonstrated in *The Graduate* remained uncorrupted throughout ensuing identities. The plaguing uncertainty he personified held just as much relevance, if not more, as the mixed-up '60s became the what-the-hell-happens-now '70s, particularly in his career-long quest to understand the machinations of the opposite sex. And in all cases, his characters suffer a resulting comeuppance: Ratso Rizzo in *Midnight Cowboy* (1969), Lenny Bruce in *Lenny*, Ted Kramer of *Kramer vs. Kramer*, Michael Dorsey (Tootsie) of *Tootsie* (1983).

The symbolic commonality between these actors, then, is disillusionment. Each suffers it, each processes it, each resigns himself to it. The times they were a-changin' again, but to a renaissance of conservatism, domesticity and patriotism, a good-bad outcome that would solidify come the '80s.

So, for the moment—that moment being the '70s—no need for the Studio Era good guys constituting Spoto's lament. Only Robert Redford among the major male actors of that time would star in films—*The Sting* (1973), *Three Days of the Condor* (1976), *All the President's Men* (same)—affirming what Pacino's personas more nervously suggested: the notion that the system could be immediately reclaimed. The rest—Hoffman, Hackman, Nicholson, Pacino, Duvall and De Niro—busied themselves building characters who were desperately trying to find their footing. In so doing, this remarkable concentration of actors—"We few, we probing few, we band of brothers"—would reach a collective maturation before our eyes, in robust, vibrant and adversarial films that have stood, aesthetically, critically and histrionically, the test of time.

Marlon Brando
A Budding Influence

America loves a polarizing figure, even if, logically, it should love-hate a polarizing figure. No doubt, this obsession speaks to the dual nature of the culture: the proudly Puritan and the unscrupulously capitalist, tectonic plates destined to create friction. Plus, America loves the simple. Depth, contradiction, double meanings—these have been the hallmarks of other, more intellectual and artistic cultures.

And so, frustrated when a major personality reveals multitudes, America has to process it; they have to dissect the offender's character on TV panel shows, in social media exchanges, and at the dinner table. Consequently, this infatuation with duality breeds another duality. America loves that it can accommodate such figures, particularly as they provide fodder for the moneymaking gossip machine, yet it resents their refusal to conform. Playful rebellion, even expressed episodically, is a forgivable offense; sustained rebellion, particularly as a lifestyle, is outright social heresy.

Figures fueling this fire have proliferated in the past few years; people are even putting them in the White House now (President Donald Trump). But in the early 1950s, nobody was prepared for them. This was the era of plain-speaking Harry Truman, virginal Doris Day and gray flannel suits. Mid-decade, there were abrading personalities such as Jack Kerouac, Elvis Presley and Lenny Bruce, sending society into a state of schism. Before them, though, there was Marlon Brando.

Brando first appeared on screen in August 1950, in director Fred Zinnemann's *The Men*. In his Brando book for the Pyramid Illustrated History of the Movies series, René Jordan wrote of that groundbreaking occasion when the actor

> slurred his speech and stretched his silences in an ecstasy of noncommunication. He lay low, like a sated tiger, ready to pounce again at the slightest hunger pain. There was something animal, primal, atavistic in him, and everyone responded—in identification, revulsion, or alarm. Out of such fears and longings, stars are created and myths are born. Brando was both, from the very first close-up.[1]

A year later, 1951, when Brando made a bigger on-screen splash reprising his stage role as Stanley Kowalski in *A Streetcar Named Desire*, the estimable Manny Farber described him as "simply an animal and a slob, [who] screams and postures and sweeps plates off the table with an ape-like emphasis that unfortunately becomes predictable."[2]

Polarizing indeed. With his first screen appearances, Brando both elevated and reduced the art of acting.

His nickname was "Bud," the youngest child of a semi-artsy, dysfunctional family from Nebraska and Illinois. He popped out of the chute with a gift for mimicry and pranks. It earned him a one-way ticket to military school, where he was expelled due to a gift for mimicry and pranks. With few prospects, he ended up staying with his older sister Jocelyn, an up-and-coming actress, in New York. Enter the Actors Studio, enter the Method, enter Broadway.

Brando was the first public commodity formed by a Russian-influenced approach to acting. This innovative technique, known in America as the Method, was a product of post–Napoleonic Russia. In the wake of that tsardom's military triumph, Slavic pride swelled. The hunt was on for undiluted forms of domestic expression. Konstantin Stanislavski, an aspiring thespian and director struggling at that time with the artificial, almost symbolic nature of European-influenced acting, married the political and the personal by developing an approach rooted in a mix of patriotism and purity. He and his partner Vladimir Nemirovich still had to fight the state censors, who had staid ideas about acceptable dramatic content and presentational protocol.

As, in part, circumvention, Stanislavsky and Nemirovich took the experimental ensemble they had founded, the Moscow Art Theatre, to the provinces. There, to best serve its star dramatists, Anton Chekhov and Maxim Gorky, the troupe's directorial duo developed most of the conventions of naturalism that are commonplace today. As things progressed, an experimental space known as a "laboratory" was established. Within its modest confines, Stanislavski, now the movement's primary force, conducted a regime of improvisation-based études promoting the tenets of this bold new style.

In 1922, having survived the First World War and the fall of Imperial rule, a splinter group of the Art Company set out on an international tour. Along the way, they bedazzled an aspiring American intellectual with an interest in the theater: Harold Clurman. Clurman became one of the founders of the company's Western equivalent, the Group Theatre (retaining the foreign spelling of Theatre). Like its inspiration, the company both staged productions and promoted lab work. The presentations put on by Clurman & Co., whose members included Lee Strasberg, Cheryl Crawford, Stella Adler, Sanford Meisner and Elia Kazan, stunned the American theater. After the Group's dissolution in the late '30s, each member established a reputation in their own right, championing the Method as teachers, directors and authors.

One of their arenas was the Actors Studio, established in the late '40s. The venue offered classes to aspiring actors twice a week, free of charge. The only admission was one's tolerance for the despotic Strasberg, who preached his own fuzzy take on Stanislavski with a self-righteousness some considered baffling and barbaric.

The Method taught the use of one's own experiences as the palette by which an actor could convey the emotional machinations of their character. You didn't rage or cry just because the lines suggested it; you raged or cried because unbeknownst to the audience, you were subversively reliving experiences from your past at the same time you were reciting the text.

Instantly, this approach solved the actor's biggest dilemma, posited by Strasberg thusly: "Does the actor actually experience the emotion he is portraying, or should he demonstrate the emotion without experiencing it?"[3] Or, as Dustin Hoffman put it:

> Stanislavski was trying to get down what the best actors do anyway; he didn't invent anything. So, even actors who sneer at the Method, are militant against it, or, conversely, have never heard of it, when they get up and act, they use themselves. What happens when you study that aspect of acting is that you find more analogies between yourself and the material than you thought you had. The Method allows you to discover less obvious connections between yourself and the character ... it opens up a whole field of connections you can consciously bring from yourself. You bring a lot unconsciously and automatically, but the Method widens your perception: you can then add more of your own colors to the tapestry.[4]

Brando was subsequently polished by Kazan, the Greek immigrant who was part of the Method mix first as an actor, then as a director and instructor. Aside from an abiding belief in the value of naturalism, Kazan and his pet pupil shared much. Both had distant, almost cruel relationships with their fathers, had suffered scarring episodes of alienation at the hands of society (in college, Kazan had been forced to wait on tables for his fellow Yalies), and shared deeply mixed feelings about assimilation and conformity. Kazan's stage and, in particular, film work are predicated on troubled heroes suffering from all of the above, set within a context of social, occasionally poetic realism. As he once said of the values represented by his work, "I do not believe in any ideology that does not permit—no, encourage—the freedom of the individual"[5]—a contention that was tested when HUAC called him to testify as a former member of the Communist party. Looking to keep working, Kazan called out a handful of fellow artists.

Kazan's seminal *On the Waterfront* (1954), starring Brando, was a post–HUAC apologia, whose pleading nature was largely overlooked by its dramatic and technical solidity. Still, more than any of the director's previous films, it's the one that best represents the Kazanian philosophy, a thematic bent every Brando-phile would go on to hold narratively sacred. What are *Five Easy Pieces*, *The French Connection*, the *Godfather* films, *Lenny*, and *One Flew Over the Cuckoo's Nest* but that same battle cry for the accommodation of originality within a rigid and restrictive structure? Further, *Waterfront*'s style, dynamics and other elements put in motion a ripple effect that endured throughout the '70s: the neo-realist location shooting (making it one of the first entries in a subgenre known as "the New York movie"), the doomed hero, the war of two worlds, the push-pull boy-girl relationship, and the Biblical conundrum of being one's brother's keeper. All resurface in *Little Big Man* (1970), *Mean Streets*, *Chinatown* and *Dog Day Afternoon* (1975), among other titles.

Waterfront's most lasting contribution, however, was the creation of a new archetype: Kazan and Brando remade the male screen hero by making ambivalence an acceptable form of deportment. Hitherto, in the direct aftermath of World War II, having mixed emotions was okay, as long as it could be traced to exceptional circumstances. But Brando's angst wasn't war-born angst, nor, as it's often been contextualized, atomic age angst. Something bigger was visibly at work within the uniquely vexed Brando. It made him mutter, shake his head, and commit other violations of actorly protocol. Macho as he was, this inner turmoil exuded a traditionally feminine quality; it was reflected, even, in his facial features, creating a hypnotic androgyny. Not that emotional sensitivity was new for the American on-screen hero; the James Stewarts and Henry Fondas of the industry had been exhibiting that quality since the '30s, albeit in measured doses. Now, though, in Brando, it was an all-consuming capacity, complicating the sexual stereotyping of the time. As Jordan wrote in 1973, "The sensitive male type, which evolved over the next few decades, originated, at least partly, in Brando's revolutionary portraits of men."[6]

Jordan again: "[T]here was something ambivalent in the way he rebelled. … He was brutal-tender, offensive-defensive, menacing-vulnerable."[7] As such, Brando's characters could, shockingly, suffer not only ambivalence but defeat—another major break with tradition. We all know how it's supposed to go: the good guy is supposed to best the bad guy, the nebbish is supposed to get the girl, the army is supposed to win the war. These are the sacred commandments of writing for the American screen, set down by the studio heads who created the industry, immigrants who wanted to sell the romantic notion of America as a magic oasis from the socio-political oppression of Eastern Europe. But Brando popularized roles in which these victories were, at best, partial. His characters would fight for a cause, yes, but suffer anything from a horrible beating to outright death for advancing it. In this, he became "the disaffected wanderer, the synthesis of an elemental, creative force, but one who's unable to comprehend the social components of his destiny."[8]

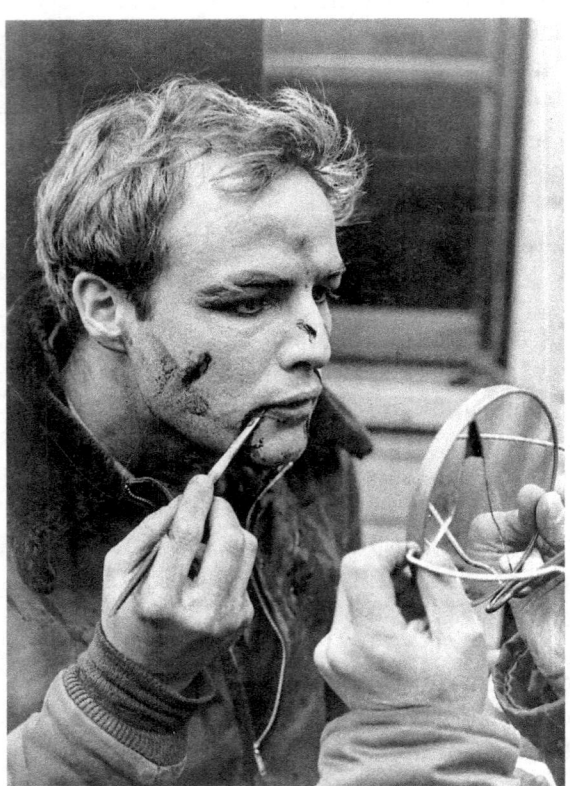

Brando prepping for Terry Malloy in *On the Waterfront* (1954). This characterization set the narrative arc for ensuing anti-heroes (Columbia/Photofest).

In so doing, Brando unleashed a new kind of screen hero: the martyr (*Waterfront* goes so far as to outright equate him with it, through the speeches of priest Karl Malden and the fallen Brando's bloodied, "crown of thorns"–style image in the film's final minutes). No doubt the religious fervor of the time boosted his cause; epics about the adventures of the fallen Christ competed, even dwarfed, Brando's smaller, sociological studies. Still, those two contrasting genres had a lot more in common than it appeared. And in Brando's case, the schtick would stick. Those religious frescoes came and went like any other trend, but the modern-hero-as-martyr thing stuck around for a very long time. Brando kept doing it until he passed the torch, in the '60s, to another edgy Method man, Paul Newman.

Like Brando, Newman bridged the gap between embodying the adolescent restlessness of the '50s and the neurotic cool of the '60s. He too played cocksure self-doubters, whose talents and swagger were ultimately exposed for smaller capacities than these crass, clued-out heroes had assumed. But where Brando hemmed and hawed until he exploded, Newman semi-silently stewed until he admitted resignation. Brando's characters rarely discovered what it was they were looking for; Newman's found their answers in the mirror, when they finally took an inventory of their warts and scars. Where Brando's Terry Malloy got back to his feet after that savage climactic beating on the docks, Newman's would have rolled over lifelessly into the drink, his floating corpse testament that in the mug's game that is life, you're the mug—a hard fact Brando's characters refused to face. This crucial differentiation made Newman more relevant than Brando throughout the ensuing decades. As time progressed, people stopped identifying with searchers and started investing in those who had solutions, pessimistic as those answers might have been. *Keep your cool 'til inevitably, it's taken away from you* was Newman's message. With the American population feeling more socially browbeaten every passing year, the constructive appeal of staying cautiously distanced and the admission of the certainty of our End of Days served as the perfect philosophical pilot light.

As a result, Newman's relevancy ended up spanning the gamut, from the introduction of the Method to that of CGI technology. Part of the generation of Brando's immediate successors, the ex–Navy man from suburban Cleveland attended the Yale School of Drama before settling in New York. There, he studied under Strasberg while performing in summer stock and live TV. After the death of James Dean, Newman assumed the tragically curtailed actor's role as boxer Rocky Graziano in the gritty-corny *Somebody Up There Likes Me* (1956), atoning for his noticeably uncertain debut in the tepid religious epic *The Silver Chalice* (1954). What succeeded was one of the most well-sustained careers in post–Studio Era history.

From biographer Shawn Levy's exemplary *Paul Newman: A Life*: "In the first films in which he made an impact, he was an unformed, psychologically delicate brooder of the classic early Method stripe."[9] A plagued, introspective man-boy, as was the Brando-esque fashion. In short order, however, Newman broke from the pack by developing a cocky, swaggering veneer, a hotshot persona by which he could bury his original, uncertain identity, only to have society crack him like an egg to reveal the raw, unformed material still in development within. As Newman matured, this quality made him "an ironist, a rascal, a scamp."[10] Throughout his peak years, the '60s, he became "a string of ne'er do wells who can laugh off both adversity and good fortune with a cynical, breezy chuckle."[11] Still, "the characters he played continually failed to mature into the responsibilities that is generation commonly associated with manhood."[12]

By holding fast to the purity of the inner bad boy Brando had overly complicated, Newman became a sort of elder statesman for the Baby Boomers, who were also out to prolong their adolescence. They saw themselves growing into him; if we ever have to play within the system, they steeled themselves, let us be Paul Newman.

The only threat Newman had for the affection of that audience was Steve McQueen, with whom he enjoyed a friendly rivalry. (McQueen had a tiny role in *Somebody Up There Likes Me*; eventually, they'd be equals, co-fronting 1974's *The Towering Inferno*.) Together, they convinced the counterculture that, as one aged, that distancing, defining quality called "cool" need not cool off—and if you were killed for it, as Newman was in *Cool Hand Luke* (1967), then, hey, it was well worth dying for.

It was thus that Newman was able to hold his own, box office–wise, with the usurping generation of Hoffman, Hackman, Nicholson, Pacino, Duvall and De Niro. That said, by the time that generation was hitting its stride, Newman had matured into mentorship roles. He lorded over the West, taught Robert Redford how to con, and ran a ragtag hockey team. His message as that succession of role models was clear: planning, pranksterism and persistence will take your limited talents as far as they can go. They'll be enough to permit you to best "The Man" now and again,

Paul Newman and Robert Redford in *The Sting* (1973). Both actors were box office draws throughout the '70s (Universal/Photofest).

though when you lose, you'll probably lose big. It'll hurt. But luck has a thing for bluster, so you've got that on your side.

This, of course, was also Newman's life philosophy. His legacy, by his own estimation, was a testament to the effect of sweat equity and good fortune on hit-and-miss ability. Cut down to size by the pain-in-the-ass of fame and his share of personal tragedies (including a lifelong battle with the bottle and the suicide of a son), his sterner stuff, in life and on screen, softened. Still, like the race cars he loved to risk life and limb in, he could never resign himself to the scrapyard. "These were tough old guys," Levy writes of Newman's final roles, "wiry, clever, hard. You wouldn't bet against them in a fight—and you *really* wouldn't want to be the one they were fighting."[13]

By the '70s, Newman's "go down swinging" defeatism, a branch of Brando-style martyrdom, was epidemic. Everyone was doing it: Hackman was sacrificing himself to save others in *The Poseidon Adventure* (1972), Hoffman was being crucified by the censors and the cops in *Lenny*, Nicholson was being lobotomized in *One Flew Over the Cuckoo's Nest,* Pacino met that climactic sucker punch in *Dog Day Afternoon,* Duvall put his lawyerly brilliance at the service of organized crime in the *Godfather* films, and De Niro surrendered to madness to save New York as that deluded *Taxi Driver.*

Kazan, referring to the protégé he'd groom right after Brando, James Dean, described that actor as a kind of grotesque: a twisted boy. It's a character assessment Kazan could have applied just as well to Brando, and that can be applied to all of Brando's successors, from the immediate—Dean, Newman and Montgomery Clift—to those who dominated the '70s.

While the latter were hardly "boys"—Hoffman was a few months shy of 30 before he became the first of the group to break through, and Hackman just a few years shy of 40—the parallel to adolescence still plays. It's a life stage marked by struggles with authority, social acceptance, the opposite sex and issues of identity. Hoffman, Nicholson, Pacino and De Niro perpetually chose characters deeply mired in all of the above, creating, for all of their integrity, a parade of overgrown boys lost in a man's world, though that world was, more often than not, misguided or corrupt.

The struggles of Hackman and Duvall, on the other hand, were, largely, to rein those qualities in, to curtail the more hysterical nature of their characters in the name of the institutions that they served. The others, meanwhile, wallowed in a lot of energetic ambivalence, not necessarily to dethrone the authoritarians in charge but to be allowed to take their place within their infrastructures on their own terms. This again is Kazan, showing us the lightweight vs. heavyweight battle between the championing of the individual and a more insular ideology.

Back to Brando. Other traits would imprint themselves on that succeeding generation, and just as indelibly: Brando's propensity for personifying marginalized people, his famous fits of animal rage, his mania for research, and his love of improvisation.

Brando didn't burst onto the silver screen riding a horse, wearing a trench coat, or charming an ingenue. He popped up like an unwanted dinner guest. He revved up, like the eponymous *The Wild One* (1953), into that sleepy California town, and announced, I'm here, at your doorstep, maybe even sticking around. For what purpose, people asked. I don't know, came the answer, just deal with it. He was looking, then, to fit in on his own terms, to create, if idiosyncratically or forcibly, a more pluralist society.

In time, this bent took on political dimensions, in the films *Viva Zapata!* (1952) and *The Ugly American* (1962) and of course in Brando's infamous support for the American Indian. Brando advocated that American society should be restless, constantly questioning its identity and example, that it should seriously think about trading its diehard complacency for an all-consuming self-reflection, that it should truly earn its mettle as an inclusive and respectful universe. His followers, Hoffman et al., would model this and make a specialty of unhappily marginalized characters at war with a rigid, self-satisfied society, a persona, in their case, serendipitously in tune with a time of even greater generational discord than the primordial clash at work in the time of Brando. By the mid-'70s, the anti-hero had become a new stereotype, though one, mercifully, made increasingly electric by an invigorating parade of practitioners.

Next, those aforementioned fits of rage. Unlike previous male stars, when Brando got mad, he got *really* mad, genuinely, uncontrollably, irredeemably mad (watch him go after mob boss Lee J. Cobb in *On the Waterfront*). It was the training, of course, which had taught him to put his finger on the pulse of his deepest, basest impulses. And so Brando's rage against his absent father, his alcoholic mother, his oppressive teachers and all the rest was encouragingly unleashed under the direction of Kazan, Kazan with his hot Greek temperament and his own bias against the well-protected world of the ruling WASPs. Teenage boys, a naturally disgruntled lot, could not believe what they were seeing. That was *their* anger being expressed on the screen, their screams of "Go fuck yourself!," their rebellion against those perpetually telling them to subsume their dissatisfaction in good table manners, chaste kisses, hard work and blind patriotism.

Andrew Dowdy, in his *Films of the Fifties*, frames that identification thusly:

> For many young people, *The Wild One* was a romantic introduction to the outsider who maintains a solid code against both society and the subculture in which he travels.... Brando's spacey style and ambiguous sensuality proved a puzzling Rorschach to a repressed time. An Eastern critic prickled over a face "excessively sensitive, almost effeminate" and a walk that "slouches, ambles, almost minces," while members of a San Francisco bike gang, precursors of the Hell's Angels, drank wine in the balcony of a Market Street theater, and "cheered like bastards" to "see ourselves right there on the screen."[14]

If Brando could so unabashedly express that discontent, so, said his young audience, can we—at least in the movies and/or on stage. So bitten, those with show biz aspirations set out for the acting schools and public venues that would allow them to follow Brando's example. They would end up making his particular form of discontent such a convention of the craft that audiences came to downright expect it. You didn't go to a Pacino picture to watch him hold it in; you went to watch what was unnerving him make its way through that Michael Corleone-like surface. You didn't go to see Nicholson keep his mouth shut (as in *The Passenger*, 1975), nor watch De Niro disappear into the more Zen-like aspects of his character. You even wanted to see the less rebellious members of that set, Hackman and Duvall, lose it, no matter if it was for the conformist side. Rage, rage against the dying of the light, we all urged them, whatever that light may be.

In this, Brando integrated a distinctly male energy and explosive form of expression into the art of American acting. If it had shades of the patriarchal oppression that would come to be labeled "toxic masculinity," it spoke, at the time and throughout the Brando-influenced '60s and '70s, almost exclusively as a cry against an unjust and often dishonorable society. It could be directed against women, definitely—consider poor, perpetually perplexed Blanche DuBois in Kazan's *Streetcar*—but more often than not, it was used to come at those who symbolically represented an inaccessible, conceited and toying world.

As Brando put it to Mary Murphy in *The Wild One*, "You think you're too good for me, and when I meet people like that, I knock them over." As that statement makes plain, it's not misogyny. It's a form of reaction that transcends gender: "when I meet *people* like that."

Not that Brando, on-screen, didn't have a troubled relationship with women (in art as in life, but let's leave that to biographers). Before Brando, the boy had always gotten the girl. Post-Brando, what the boy got was a lot of head-scratching. The reward for his romantic or sexual advances could be maternalism—the supportive if frenzied Eva Marie Saint in *On the Waterfront*—or, more dramatically, violence—the acquiescent but dangerous Maria Schneider in *Last Tango in Paris* (1973). In this, Brando was ahead of the curve, refusing to resolve relationships according to the dictates of sexual stereotyping. His disciples, too, would struggle to understand the opposite sex, especially as their work coincided with the onset of the sexual revolution and the rise of feminism.

Pacino closed the door on an accusatory Diane Keaton in *The Godfather*; Nicholson tried to slap Faye Dunaway into submission in *Chinatown*; Hoffman took Meryl Streep to court in *Kramer vs. Kramer* (1979). As Susan Mizruchi noted in one of the best books on Brando's work and legacy, *Brando's Smile*, "In drama and in life, Brando was drawn to ethical dilemmas, dramatic situations that prevented effortless affinities and solutions."[15]

But despite that complicated dynamic, women often act as the catalysts who bring out the best in Brando's characters. If these women are a source of angst, it's largely because of their innate recognition of said character's better nature. They hold a mirror up to his soul, forcing him to realize that he is more dimensional than his animal complacency is willing to acknowledge. When he tries to buy them off with love or sex, it only exacerbates the problem—and thus he finds himself, albeit ambivalently, politicized and/or prodded into action. The results cut him to the quick while making him realize that they, his nurturer-torturers, were right. We see this dynamic resurface in the films of his disco-era disciples, including *Five Easy Pieces*, *Carnal Knowledge* (1971), *Lenny*, *Chinatown* and even *Kramer vs. Kramer*.

Fathers were another famous Freudian headache of the Brando era, an area Kazan, who suffered from the same patriarchal problem, had asked Brando to delve into. Like Brando's own father, the actor's on-screen dads were either absent or represented by stuffy, enterprising substitutes. This dynamic is best represented in

Brando's most personal film, *One-Eyed Jacks* (1963), which he also conceived and directed. Throughout, protégé (Brando) and mentor (Karl Malden) endure a relationship of charged one-upmanship, culminating in the father figure's merciless whipping of his pleading-bleeding underling.

It's an announcement not just against the parental hierarchy and its stifling contempt for the brio, intelligence and restlessness of the younger generation, but against a model of authoritarian manhood hitherto considered the shining social standard. Father doesn't always, or ever, know best, the defeated Brando warned. Stop swallowing the Fredric Marches, Spencer Tracys and Lewis Stones of the world whole; they are not what they purport. And so, Brando's immediate successors find, like him, the tenacity to go *mano a mano* with their dads (most famously, Dean vs. Jim Backus in *Rebel Without a Cause*, 1955). The generation after that one, even more deeply ensconced in the search for a new male identity, continues the tradition: Hackman vs. Melvyn Douglas in *I Never Sang for My Father* (1970); Pacino vs. Brando in *The Godfather*, Nicholson vs. John Huston in *Chinatown*, etc. Like their mutual idol, this preoccupation came from an honest place: Hoffman, Hackman, Pacino, Duvall, Nicholson and De Niro were all products of broken homes, with cool to non-existent relationships with the men that they had called, through gritted teeth, "Dad."

As the last word on both subjects, Brando, shortly before his death in 2004, expressed a desire to live his life over again in a different fashion: "I wouldn't get married and I'd kill my father."[16] It doesn't get more blatant, or Freudian, than that!

Research, again born of the Method school's obsession with creating a sense of reality, was the big ideological break with practices past. Actors only had to don a costume, adopt a pose, and emote on cue to stake a claim on characterization ... until Brando. As much investigative reporter as actor, Brando rolled himself around in a wheelchair for weeks to credibly pull off the postwar paraplegic in *The Men* (1950), learned to box to play the betrayed heavyweight Terry Malloy in *On the Waterfront*, and mastered German for his portrayal of a Nazi officer in *The Young Lions* (1958). There was even a legend that early in his career, to realistically play the non-speaking role of a corpse, he lay in a bathtub filled with ice until his skin turned a dead man's blue. If that's what it took to be the next Brando, the succeeding generation bravely announced, bring it on! The practice evolved until adopters were driving writers and directors into fits of apoplexy with their molecular methodology. In "Filming a Cover-up: *All the President's Men*," a *Rolling Stone* article by Chris Hodenfield, Brando-phile Dustin Hoffman was categorized as "a fiend for research, a desperate man, throwing himself into it as if he were to be parachuted behind enemy lines."[17] Collectively, these obsessive, pressing personalities became known in the industry not as "Brando's bastards," which might have been more accurate, but as a new, production-threatening, real-life stereotype: "those goddamn New York actors."

Brando was also prone to improvisation. He respected the written word but felt that once he had a solid grasp on his character, his assessment of that persona's motives, words and actions, rooted in the actor's deep personal research, usurped that of the author.

Hence, Brando would often rewrite the script as a film continued to shoot, interpolating hemming, hawing and pausing to imbue a greater sense of actuality and a more accurate reflection of the conflicting emotions at the core of his character. Another break with precedent, and another technique adopted by his successors. Frank Perry won the Best Screenplay Oscar for *Dog Day Afternoon*, though director Sidney Lumet readily acknowledged that the scenario had been worked over on an almost daily basis by star Pacino. Hoffman too liked to ad-lib ad infinitum, in spite of his contrasting habit of putting as many writers as possible on a project, usually trusted friends. Even the foot soldiers of that generation, Hackman and Duvall, were prone to insisting on embellishing a line or two. Admitted Duvall, adopting the tone of one of his typically cut-to-the-chase characters, "If I have instincts I feel are right, I don't want anybody to tamper with them. I don't like tamperers and I don't like hoverers."[18]

By the time those actors began to dominate America's movie marquees, Brando was no longer a demiurge but a contemporary. His explosive presence in the '50s gave way to a seriously hit-and-miss career in the '60s. His methods were mismatched with middling, musty directors, and his attraction to more relevant material with tepid returns. His contempt for the industry became more vocal, and his personal life devolved into a veritable shambles.

By the end of the decade, he had become a polarizing figure yet again: revered by actors but reviled by the public. He starred in *The Nightcomers* (1971), a critically questioned prequel to Henry James' famous novella *The Turn of the Screw*, playing a more seasoned, exaggerated version of the wily, socially spurned miscreant with which he had made his name. In his Peter Quint, the lowly Irish groundskeeper keeping happy company with the manor's wide-eyed children while maintaining an offbeat sexual relationship with their priggish, troubled keeper, we have the precursor of coming Brando personas. His monkeyshines with the kids preview Don Corleone's equally playful relationship with his grandson; the sadomasochistic bent sets the scene for the controversial canoodling of *Last Tango in Paris*; and Brando's Irish lilt and self-serving devilishness resurface in *The Missouri Breaks* (1976).

The Nightcomers, a legacy story long before that became a trend, was a marginal financial success, in large part due to its carnal titillation. After that disappointment, Brando went back into semi-seclusion. Then Francis Ford Coppola, another Brando-phile from the '50s, talked an extremely skittish Paramount into letting the anthemic actor test for *The Godfather*.

The impact of Brando's performance, and that film, cannot be overstated. Overnight, both became touchstones of popular culture—forever. Cinematically, they established new yardsticks for the art of characterization and the quality of American filmmaking. Brando had made his way back to the top after a long, ignominious fall. He was again who he had been when we first saw him: An actor marked by daring, nuance and a hypnotic mix of questionable authority and surprise humanity.

The Godfather, the saga of an Italian-American crime family that implodes when it refuses to join a gang of rivals in the burgeoning drug trade, has been characterized as everything from a revolutionary take on tragic realism to (personal fave) a "celebration of Nixonian efficiency"[19] (the brilliant David Thomson,

***The Godfather* (1972) restored Marlon Brando's status as America's greatest living male screen actor (Paramount/Photofest).**

in his thoughtfully entertaining *Have You Seen…?*). It's also, through the saga of Michael Corleone, a metaphorical biography. Michael—good son, war hero, aspiring WASP—is converted, family tragedy by family tragedy, to the proverbial "dark side." With this conversion, Michael *is* postwar America, as it transitions from its good standing as the savior that settled the global conflict to the corrupt, crime- and drug-infested mess the country had become by the early '70s. *The Godfather* is a lament, then, for the good ol' days; an expression of somber nostalgia for the last time America was a functional, exemplary society.

There was a lot of that sentiment going around in 1972, in life and on screen. Much of mainstream American cinema was devoted to the romanticization of the previous decades, from the fun-loving '20s and the "we-were-poor-but-we-were-happy" '30s. (With George Lucas' *American Graffiti*, 1973, they'd be joined by a nostalgic nod to the '50s.) *The Godfather*, in its own dark way, was yet another exercise in fanciful nostalgia.

Other threads running through the film were also rooted in the zeitgeist—foremost, its examination of the value of masculinity. In the young Michael, the corrupt Corleone family's uncorrupted son, we see what was then (1972) sociologically deemed the new, feminist-influenced male, at least in larval form. Michael starts the film visibly humbled, ashamed even, by the authoritarian stock that rules the family roost, with their insistence on respect, their subjugation of women to sexual playthings and busy mothers, and their brute solutions to conflicts that *could* be solved by simple diplomacy (validating Thomson's Nixon analogy).

But as the saga progresses, Michael ironically assumes the mantle of his Old World father, making *The Godfather* one of the few films of its time in which the progress of the modern male, after having suffered a crisis of identity, is set into reverse motion. On this level, the film is about the tragic impossibility of the creation of dimensional men in implacable cultures, and the naïve and self-denying women destined to suffer as a result. (As the film unequivocally qualifies, "Women and children can be careless, but not men.")

Michael's actions are not the sudden appearance of a pre-existing disposition, brought to the fore by acts of violence committed by his family's rivals. They are inspired purely and plainly, as the Pacino-Brando scenes attest, by a son's abiding love for his fallen father. In that, the film is a kind of twisted valentine, an examination of the lengths to which familial connection can commit a person. Don't be fooled, though: It's still the anti-father stance that marks the '60s-70s generation; ultimately, Michael betrays the Don by joining the ugly business from which his father has kept him distanced. Still, Michael's blood-soaked journey up the ladder passes primarily as love. Ugly as his ends are, we understand and accept them.

Also, by that point in the film, we ourselves have become honorary Corleones. Thanks to the film's sociological bent—director Coppola vowed in pre-production that the film would be so authentically Italian, audiences would smell the spaghetti sauce—we have eaten with them, celebrated with them, talked business with them, and shared their pain. So, though we have serious reservations about their morality and methods, we go so far as to root for them. The Corleones, in our book, may be bad guys, but they are the *good* bad guys.

Plus, there's that metaphorical thing: We like what they represent. We respect their values: family, order, the righting (if offbeat) of wrongs. It's what audiences at the messed-up time of the film's release couldn't get from the cops, from the government, or even from vigilantes. And the Corleones refuse to get involved in drugs, that symbolic scourge of all that was wrong with the '60s and '70s. They're cleaning up our streets, those Corleones, and for that, we'll keep breaking bread with them.

The promotion of this deep emotional involvement with suspect heroes is also, of course, a matter of acting. While narratively, it's Michael's (Pacino's) film, it's Brando, with far less screen time (40 minutes vs. Pacino's 66 over a 175-minute film), who looms largest. Like *On the Waterfront*, the film is about the politicization of a good-hearted outsider. This time, though, it isn't Brando. Brando here is no longer the guy without any answers and just a lot of questions. That persona's relevance ended at the close of the '50s. It's the messed-up '70s now. The world needs hard and fast solutions. He's aged out of his existential angst and into a prescriptive surefootedness. People come to *him* now with the questions. Brando is no longer the shit-stirrer; he's the guy who's been worn down by stirring it and who leaves the dirty business of solving the world's puzzles to others. Brando's Godfather, smart, seasoned and sly, is a figure of dubious respect, which is what Brando had become by 1972.

Coppola cleverly introduces Brando's Godfather *à la* Shakespeare, building up suspense about his titular character by opening the film with a long, pleading monologue delivered at the character's feet (the baker Buenoserra's famous "I believe in America" speech, also making clear the film's editorial intentions). How many filmmakers, at least once or twice during that speech, would have inserted a reaction shot of the subject being addressed? Coppola, however, holds fast. Further, we hear Don Corleone's voice before we see his face. We recognize the voice and yet we don't. It has that garbled, indifferent quality that we know, but it's older, more seasoned. It's Brando, pushing the ubiquitous criticisms about the incoherent nature of his pipes.

Then, finally, we see him, in close-up. Immediately, we are struck by the jowls, the protruding jaw suggesting lazy defiance, the tired, regal quality at the heart of the character. Brando even gives us a little mannerism (he loved those): a small brush of the hand on the side of his face, suggesting a manufactured man of class, one who has had to work at the appearance of respectability.

Then, in an over-the-shoulder shot, we note the cat on his lap, with whom he's lovingly warring. It's a detail that suggests a bent for looking after things but also a predisposition for messing with the savage element—a telling touch, speaking to Brando's love and use of props (the cat was his idea).

Then the Godfather rises, giving us a Frankenstein walk. As he sagely pontificates, he alternates toughness with gentility. This interpolation continues throughout the film: Don Corleone will order a hit, then waltz with his daughter. He'll offer an ultimatum, then play the clown. He'll endorse his successor, then initiate a game of hide-and-seek with his grandchild. Brando's trademark fuzziness has settled into a firm duality, equal parts demonic businessman and doting paterfamilias.

In the end, though, it's the human side that wins. If Brando's performance has reached iconic status, it's because it calculatedly manages to cut through its overtures to caricature to give us a resonantly vulnerable persona. In this, Brando again leads by example; Hoffman & Co. later served up characters we would underestimate, only to be won over by their core humanity (Ratso Rizzo, anyone?)

And how ironic is it that in a film about the male's inability to grow more human at the pull of the Old School (Michael's story), we have the Old School growing increasingly sensitive? Brando's performance, for all of its reinvention of his image at the time, is a resolute affirmation of what we knew that had been obscured by his messy work in the messy '60s: that this is a brazen, defiant actor with a fresh approach, not afraid to flirt with the ridiculous but in complete, nuanced command. Check out the palpable anguish on his physically restricted face when Don Corleone, in hospital, is told that good son Michael has become a common Mafioso. Plus, there's another reminder of the Brando of yore: the scene in which the gunned-down Godfather falls to the ground. It's impossible for the film-savvy not to equate it with the image of the battered Terry Malloy at the conclusion of *On the Waterfront*.

As far apart as those characters appear, these images twin in our minds, reminding us that both personas, in their own way, were simply victims of trying to do the right thing, of calling others on the carpet for the dirtier aspects of their business, and who, in boldly playing the nobility card, found themselves near-paying the ultimate price.

Two of Brando's young worshipers got to work with him in the picture: Pacino and Duvall. Though their collective relationship remained, essentially, distant, occasionally they would form an impromptu boys' club, reigniting Brando's adolescent love of mimicry and pranks. And on-screen, Pacino and Duvall admirably hold more than their own with him, exhibiting his influence while exercising their respective approaches.

After reviving his career with *The Godfather*, Brando went on to shock audiences yet again; this time not by showing what you can do by subscribing to the Method, but by betraying it.

At the time of his next film's release (1972 in Europe, 1973 in America), the pornography industry, a byproduct of the sexual revolution, was in full flourish. Theaters once devoted to commercial fare were filled with patrons eager to see Debbie do Dallas, Linda Lovelace perform deep throat, and what was going on behind the green door. Just as the music industry once knew that whoever could combine black rhythm and blues with clean-cut Caucasianism would create the next pop superstar (Elvis won that one), the film industry, by 1972, knew that whoever combined the no-holds-barred nudity and mechanical sex of pornography with the emotive force and technical artistry of legitimate cinema would be hailed as the world's next great filmmaker. Bernardo Bertolucci got to the pole first, with *Last Tango in Paris*.

As Molly Haskell wrote in *From Reverence to Rape*, "*Last Tango* is about Brando, is Brando, and our reaction to the film will depend, directly and chemically, on our response to Brando."[20] While equal time is devoted to the film's female lead, the grossly gamine Maria Schneider, it is indeed Brando's picture. He rescues it from what might have been, with a suave European lead as was the director's initial inclination, a careful melodrama interrupted by crass episodes of physical exchange. But by bringing, literally, his all to it—his obtuse, ugly wit, his fuzzy misogyny, his autobiographical rantings and, of course, his acting—Brando creates within the story an acutely common and ultimately moving pronouncement on the easy corruptibility of love.

Brando is Paul, an ex-pat American at loose ends in Passy, part of Paris' 16th arrondissement, after the surprise suicide of his wife. As the portraits by Francis Bacon that adorn the film's opening titles inform us, this will be a multi-sided male character study, teeming with operatic lasciviousness and pensive brutalism.

The latter is exactly what we get in the film's first close-up: Brando's raw, reeling face, emitting a Munchian scream brought on by the exaggerated roar of an overhead subway car, symbolically suggesting the intrusion and oppressiveness of everyday life. At once, Brando looks young and old. With Brando released from his *Godfather* guise, we rediscover his blondness and his beauty; but now, he's balding and browbeaten. He drifts despondently through a flat, gray Paris (one of the few times film has portrayed that uber-romanticized city in such a manner), like the French equivalent of the tortured souls from *Midnight Cowboy*.

From there, we are immersed in a simple story: Paul meets a nubile free spirit, whom he beds before they even get to know each other. He spends the rest of the film cocooned with her in a shabby, barren apartment, trying to keep their relationship as anonymous as their surroundings. It's a strictly physical arrangement, as Paul, through various forms of controversial sex, attempts to transcend the pain set within him by the tragedy of his late wife. Said Bertolucci,

> In the film, sex is simply a new kind of language that these two characters try to invent in order to communicate. They use the sexual language because the sexual language means liberation from the subconscious, means an opening up.[21]

Over the course of the sexual revolution of the '60s and '70s, many filmmakers presented May-December romances, usually between a stuffy establishmentarian male and a young, bohemian female. It was a skittish attempt to examine the generation gap, ending either with the former pronouncing his generation's chaste ways the better model for living or the latter managing to charmingly convert her father-figure stick-in-the-mud.

But *Last Tango* brazenly employed that dynamic to a whole new end, stripping it of any Puritan veneer or other notions of Hollywood temperance, even of the more mature, poetic approach to sex that had become the European standard. While yes, the film deals with the ubiquitous '60s-70s theme of free love vs. marriage, it does so strictly as subplot: a pretentious union between the female lead and her filmmaker boyfriend, which, with its endless, labyrinthine hastiludes, plays like discount Godard. *Last Tango* is instead about the easy corruptibility of affection and the effort to eschew its complications through a commitment to sex, a back-to-basics tack that in one scene, has Brando and co-star Maria Schneider grunting like primates.

When Paul, purged at last of his soul-eroding feelings over his wife, attempts to start a proper romance with his longtime plaything, he is accidentally killed the moment she surrenders her name. In the end, then, men and women are destined to forever dance a tragically ironic tango, much like the couples in the ballroom near film's end—a truly surrealist union.

In *Tango*, Brando brazenly turns his back on his training. He doesn't just affect a look while privately accessing his own emotional experiences and investing them in the character's expressions, but outright uses his own person and persona. This is Brando without makeup, mannerisms or anything otherwise actorly. Some of his close-ups, in fact, have an almost documentarian reality to them (especially his final one, as Paul breathes his last). Brando doesn't just blur the line between actor and character here; he flirts with erasing it entirely.

For all of the stylishness that's invested in the film—Vittorio Storaro's fluid cinematography, Gato Barbieri's fiery saxophone, Philippe Turlure's artfully grubby art direction—Brando's performance is what dictates the feel and rhythm of the film.

Midway through, as Paul continues on his complicated journey, you become aware that at a moment's notice, Brando can take you in any conceivable direction: He could be kind, he could be cruel, he could be kooky, he could be all of the above. He breaks out his sour, obtuse wit, his brute sexuality and, of course, his uncurbed exasperation—but never when you expect them. It's the Kazan battle cry—"The actor must always surprise"—expressed at its highest possible volume.

As a result, *Last Tango* takes on the suspenseful nature of a horror film, a notion supported by the grace notes of Grand Guignol that are added throughout. Brando, though, is exempt from this agenda; his behavior is consistently organic. No artifice for him, thank you. This is deeply sincere work. In fact, Paul's (Brando) crying fit in the famous long take before his wife's corpse will go down as the most serious and sustained reactiveness the father of on-screen male sensitivity ever offered.

Given Brando's lifelong premium on privacy, one is forced to wonders: What on Earth possessed Brando to so expose (physically and emotionally) himself? Perhaps, after his comparatively theatrical turn in *The Godfather*, he was determined to

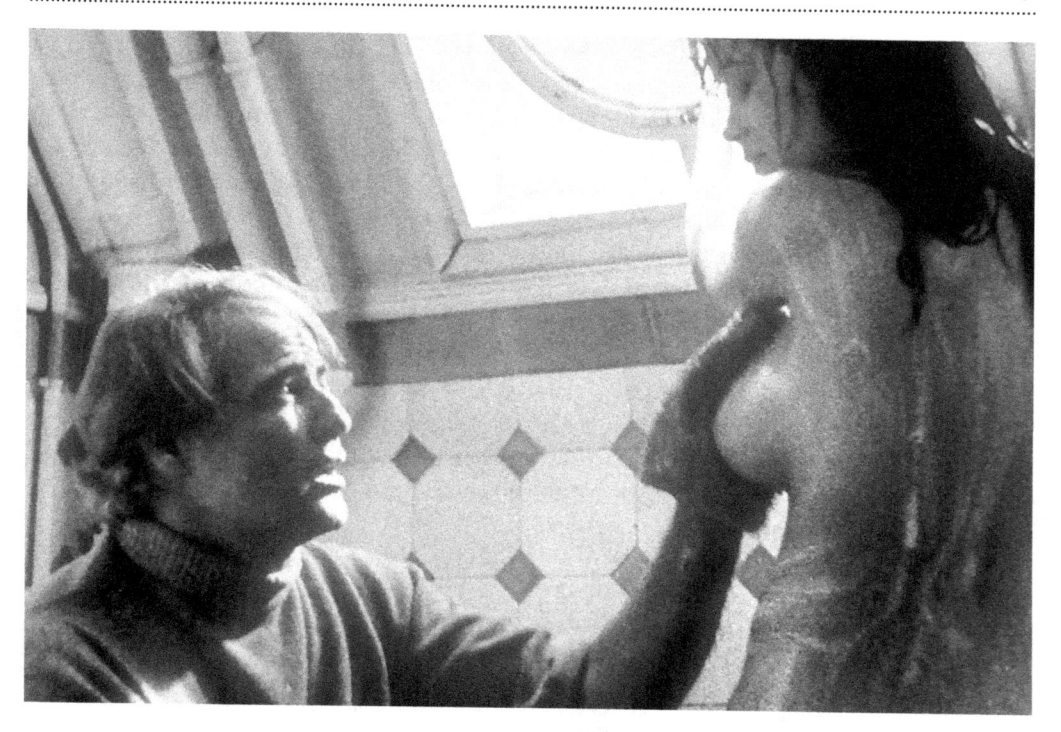

Brando and Maria Schneider baring body and soul in *Last Tango in Paris* **(1972) (UA/Photofest).**

go boldly in the opposite direction. Perhaps, growing bored with acting and increasingly uncomfortable with the burden of memorizing lines, he decided to throw caution to the wind. Or perhaps, an irrepressible instinct for public self-examination was at work, like the monologue he improvises about a humiliating episode from his bucolic adolescence? After all, many men his age (Brando was 48) were, at the time, experiencing midlife crises, giving themselves a thorough Freudian once-over to adjust to the changing social values of the times.

We'll never know. We only know that for Brando, this international *succès de scandale* (the film was rated X in most countries; Italy even tried to prosecute the above-the-line talent) left him with a deep sense of self-betrayal. When the film was over, he walked away feeling that he had put too much of his true self on screen, a persona he had been trying to hide from public view since his first false answers about his upbringing to hungry publicists.

As a consequence, he would spend the rest of his spotty career trying to atone by baffling audiences, choosing roles and making dramatic choices that would re-establish a healthy separation. Enigma meant safety (something another pop culture god, Bob Dylan, has subscribed to), just as it had for *Last Tango's* Paul. Going forward, Brando developed a talent for weirdness—and even *that* would have its imitators, like Johnny Depp (who insisted on casting him in his film *Don Juan DeMarco*, 1994). Plus, approaching 50, blonde, beefy Bud was losing his looks, while his family life was taking on aspects of Greek tragedy. And the press, long a sparring partner, delighted in this.

But he remained a deity—and so he played deities: the exalted gunman in Arthur Penn's *The Missouri Breaks*, the celestial Jor-El in Richard Donner's *Superman* and the God-Devil Kurtz in Coppola's *Apocalypse Now*. He was also looking to shock, a habit veteran actors take on once they feel they've exhausted all of the roles in which audiences expect to see them. Brando, in the 1970s, had but one rival in this department: Laurence Olivier, who, like Brando, would collect huge paychecks for small roles in films that were crassly commercial and generally beneath his dignity.

In the '70s, Olivier was one of two challengers for the distinction of the World's Greatest Actor, the other being George C. Scott. Like Brando, their appearances in a film were often more of an event than the film itself. One knew, in all cases, that one would be rattled, shocked, manipulated and awed. Olivier, at this late stage of his career, was high on his own happy histrionics, amusing himself by leading his faithful, foofy followers on, daringly flirting with caricature. His was a mission to go from class to crass, from cold to bold. After years as an object of universal respect, he now tried to be an acquired taste.

Scott was another matter. Mistaken, by virtue of his weighty style, with the Method generation, the Detroit-raised Scott did his apprenticeship in industrial films. He graduated to the New York stage, making a reputation, like Brando, by introducing America to a specimen of rage it had never before witnessed (even in classical properties). His impact on film was almost as instant, as he moved up from character parts to an all-too-brief period of stardom.

By the time of Scott's virtuosic incarnation of *Patton* (1970), whom he parodied-revered as a kind of killer clown, the huzzahs were deafening. Twinned with his Eugene O'Neill–ian follow-up as the deeply troubled Chief of Medicine in Paddy Chayefsky's brilliant *The Hospital* (1971), Scott eclipsed the then-fallen Brando and the pop-up Olivier as screen acting's undisputed *nonpareil*. Scott was a deeply insecure individual; his periodic explosions, delivered through that mad owl's face in his distinctively sandpapered voice, were not, unlike Brando's or Olivier's, acts of contempt for the audience but of contempt for the self.

Scott specialized in dedicated professionals at war first with circumstance, then with themselves, men trying to hold up the whole world, brought to crumble under its weight into the abyss of their debilitating shortcomings. Sometimes this was done comedically (his insistent warmonger in *Dr. Strangelove*, 1964, his doomed impresario in *Movie, Movie*, 1978), sometimes dramatically (his uppity gangster in *The Hustler*, 1961, his clued-out father in *Hardcore*, 1979), and sometimes, both (again, his *Patton*).

Scott's primary audience were the members of his own generation, the hard-working, Depression-raised optimists who had fought World War II (Scott had been a Marine) and had established the Dick-and-Jane '50s, only to see, by the early '70s, all that they had painstakingly built come to decay. *What's the world coming to?*, his characters would continually ask. *Why are my intentions suddenly so ridiculous? Why soldier on?* In this, Scott was publicly positing the gnawing resignation of America's much-malaised midlifers.

As proof that all of his thunderous self-pity came from a real place, Scott's battle with directors and demons grew. He either directed himself or opted for the less

The dynamic and difficult George C. Scott briefly joined the pantheon of Brando and Olivier (Pan Canadian Film Distributors/Photofest).

fussy, time-is-money arena of television, minimizing the mano-a-mano matches of actor vs. auteur that had become too much for all involved. By decade's end, Scott was a spent power, allowing Brando, through hyped appearances in the blockbusters *Superman* and *Apocalypse Now*, to regain America's heavyweight acting crown.

That path was set, after a five-year hiatus, with *The Missouri Breaks*. Brando's participation in this revisionist Western (a third for director Arthur Penn, after the equally offbeat *The Left Handed Gun*, 1958, and the classic *Little Big Man*, 1970) came at the suggestion of longtime admirer Jack Nicholson, then at the height of his popularity.

Top-billed Nicholson plays Tom Logan, a wishy-washy, and unwashed, rustler operating with his equally grubby gang on the breaks of the Missouri River in Montana, familiar territory for novelist-screenwriter Tom McGuane. When Braxton, a wealthy land baron, hangs one of Logan's brethren, Logan appropriates the adjacent property, near-steals Braxton's daughter, and silently plots revenge. Wise to him, Braxton hired an eccentric gunman, Robert E. Lee Clayton, to pose as an area "regulator." Lee's hidden agenda is to spy on, then kill, members of the Logan gang. As revelation of Lee's masochistic character, the *crise de conscience* Braxton suffers halfway through matters not at all to the determined gunman, who continues to hunt, as it were, for sport.

On the surface, this is a post-classical Western in the manner of *The Wild Bunch* (1969), the aforementioned *Little Big Man*, *High Plains Drifter* (1973) and other entries in the subgenre that were, by the mid-'70s, *de rigueur*. When the Hays code relaxed in the late '60s, filmmakers took it upon themselves to de-sanitize the Old West. Just as the Method had revolutionized acting with the introduction of naturalism, so too would the Western be remade by that same premium on authenticity. Cowboys would be unshaven, unkempt and, worse, subscribers to an unformed morality, in a psychology-based break from the white hat-black hat stereotypes of yore. Further, they would be framed differently. VistaVision romanticization of the landscape was replaced by a less forced, more organic appreciation of the geography; the towns would look smaller, shabbier, and more unabashed about their basest amenities, including the houses whore and out.

Then, of course, there was that new take on violence, pioneered by Peckinpah, Leone, Eastwood and, before them, Penn himself, via the equally venerable genre of the gangster picture (*Bonnie and Clyde*). The point, during those days of the immoral Vietnam debacle, was to re-introduce audiences to the ugly reality of gunplay, an effect reinforced through ear-popping foley, overloads of squibs, and long, slow-motion death throes. The third act of *Missouri Breaks*, for example, is little more than a "turkey shoot," as Brando's Lee knocks off character after character. But each murder must top the last—so we have a central character equal parts Shane and Torquemada.

This novel violence was, in part, Brando's idea, as were his idiosyncratic costumes; his Lee, something short of a master of disguise, dresses mainly like a thrift shop fop. And his dialogue was ad-libbed in the sing-song Irish lilt first essayed in *The Nightcomers*. Clearly, Penn had allowed Brando to run amok; critics still scratch their heads wondering why. Perhaps even a director as estimable as Penn had been intimidated by the actor's inflated reputation ... or perhaps Penn didn't have the nerve or energy to go head to ideological head with his temperamental star. Whatever. The Brando that Penn got was a Brando reluctantly out of exile, still reeling over the embarrassingly excessive praise he had received from the double-whammy of *The Godfather* and *Last Tango in Paris*—and still deeply regretful that he had put so much of his real self on the screen in the latter.

So he showed up looking to estrange himself from audiences, to have them grow uncomfortable with him, to have critics take him down from their pedestal and to be as perplexed and frustrated by him as they had been over his initial on-screen appearances. He was out to smash the idol.

In this, *Missouri Breaks* becomes an important film. It's the one in which Brando created a new identity, his last, and the only one by which a new generation of filmgoers would know him: the larger-than-life weirdo. As his spotty career progressed, while his personal life took on aspects that were bizarre even by tabloid standards and his weight grew to Wellesian proportions, he became a figure of public fun. In part, though, he had asked for it, beginning with his *Missouri Breaks* performance. He rides into this exercise in historical authenticity like a visitor from another planet. In that, he's a cubist figure in a landscape painting.

Reviews of his performance weren't just mixed, they were *about* the mix: "Depending on your viewpoint, Marlon's performance as a schizophrenic lawman who grows into more of a fruitcake with each passing scene is either a darkly comic tour de force or operatically self-indulgent."[22] How 'bout a third alternative: a showy, self-amused star turn in which the actor draws on the most idiosyncratic aspects of his character, just as he had in *Last Tango*, replacing the autobiographical subtext with histrionic tricks of a playful, if insular, variety?

He has a few scenes with Nicholson—which, after all, is why we're watching—and they're good; Brando behaves himself (he seems to be sticking to the taut script) and Nicholson holds his own while standing out of his idol's way. It's a reflection of the respectful relationship the two enjoyed both on and off the set. (Brando and Nicholson even became neighbors on L.A.'s tony Mulholland Drive.)

And despite the star presence of two such volatile men, the film makes room for a strong-minded, independent and sexually liberated woman, played with likable authority by the underrated Kathleen Lloyd. Just as Penn had been a friend of the counterculture long before it had become a recognized force—even *Missouri Breaks* plays on the dirty hippies (the rustlers) vs. the clued-out capitalists (Braxton) dynamic—he was also a champion of feminism, giving us determined heroines who carved their own paths, from Annie Sullivan in *The Miracle Worker* (1962) to *Little Big Man*'s Lulu Pendrake.

After *Missouri Breaks*, Brando disappeared again. Going forward, he could only be coerced out of his rabbit hole with money. And so, he began to make headlines for reasons other than controversial performances and family issues: record salaries. The roles would get shorter and the checks would get bigger. For his next film, a chancy big-budget revival of the iconic Superman character, Brando received a then-unprecedented $3.7 million salary and 11.75 percent of the gross profits. He ended up suing over the latter, a situation that resulted in the deletion of the scenes he had shot for the sequel (it was a double shoot).

Not only wasn't Brando cheap but he was also a location liability: the production couldn't shoot in Italy, as planned, because the actor was still up on charges for his participation in *Last Tango*. So, *Superman* was shot in London, where Brando, as the eponymous character's heavenly father, put in 12 costly days in a snowy Marcelle that made him look, according to a send-up of the film in *Saturday Night Live* (1975–present), like then-popular country singer Charlie Rich.

By the mid-'70s, Nixon was out of office and Vietnam had ended. A clean slate. America was ready to return to traditional values. The 1976 Bicentennial helped, prompting the on-screen return of the familiarly simplistic hero, a familiar face that had gone missing after *The Graduate*. His new name was Rocky. He was a product of the streets, a boxer with a garbled voice who was resigned to his lack of success, biding his time by canoodling with gangsters ... uh, sound like Brando in *On the Waterfront*?

But this boxer wasn't be politicized; he'd be coerced into fighting a battle he could actually win. He'd be the triumphant underdog in a heavyweight bout against a Muhammad Ali parody named Apollo Creed, in a storyline out of the Joe Palooka flicks of the '30s. As in *On the Waterfront*, though, there'd be (some) authenticity to his story: a genuine feel for the mean streets of Philly and the working-class bums who populate them. An urban fairy tale, then. America loved it. As such, it served as the first salvo in the usurpation of the anti-hero movement, spelling the slow but sure end of Hoffman & Co.'s Brando-influenced halcyon period.

The next old-but-new hero in the queue was the all-American Superman (though a Canadian creation), cut from the same populist cloth as the beefy Mr. Balboa. Unlike the low-budget *Rocky* (1976), however, this would be a costly, chancy production. Producers Alexander and Ilya Salkind had purchased the rights to the titular character for 25 years, with a grand design to make no fewer than five movies, the first two being shot simultaneously. So, if the first film flopped...

It was a hell of an arrangement to stake on an unknown. After everybody and his dentist (literally) were tested, the part of the Man of Steel went to a humble, handsome Juilliard graduate, Christopher Reeve. To hedge their expensive bets, the Salkinds surrounded the newbie with an all-star cast (the opening credits take a lifetime!), headed by the biggest star of all, Marlon Brando.

Brando is just shy of visibly disinterested here. His primary responsibility, as Superman's Krypton-based father Jor-El, is to set the scene: relegate the trio of villains who've jerry-rigged the destruction of the planet into exile, in a kind of "Nuremberg in outer space," then give his newborn son his blessing before sending him to planet Earth as a measure of safety. For this, Brando adopts an upper-class English accent—to better blend in with his British co-stars perhaps?—and reacquires the haughty earnestness of the *agent provocateur* he played in Gilo Pontecorvo's *Burn* (1969).

Instead of calling attention to his costume or the sets, or otherwise making fun of the proceedings, Brando remains on his best behavior. He seems dutifully aware that he was cast to add gravitas to such silliness, to legitimize the frippery the way Alec Guinness did the equally far-flung and lightweight *Star Wars* (1977). So he surprises us this time by not surprising us. He plays the good soldier and sticks to the script. There's a small trace of emotion, as Jor-El must surrender his baby son to an unknown destiny, but on the whole, not much that's showy. Brando had gone for broke in *The Missouri Breaks*; now, it was time to get back to basics. The sage, monotone dignity he brings to the role is almost exclusively devoted to expository dialogue. When a great actor is reduced to that, you know that you're in the presence of a diminished power, albeit in this case, one willingly castrated. As further proof of his irrelevancy: It's only when Brando leaves the screen that the picture gets going, director Richard Donner (with some Richard Lester thrown in) delivering a combination screwball-romcom-slapstick-crime caper.

The film, as it should be, is Reeve's, though Gene Hackman is a welcome addition as a campy, giddy Lex Luthor. Brando appears to be through stealing the spotlight or otherwise hijacking films. He had clearly entered the emeritus phase of his career, even if his name continued to bear clout.

Who better, then, for a small but crucial part in Francis Ford Coppola's ambitious and troubled take on Vietnam, *Apocalypse Now*? With 'Nam, that long, bloody embarrassment, over, filmmakers began examining the conflict's absurdities and legacy in earnest. In time, it would become a veritable subgenre. Coppola was one of the first to board the bandwagon, using the power he had acquired via the success of the *Godfather* films to make good on a crazily ambitious script he and a few colleagues had been working on since the height of the conflict in '69. It was a great hook: a transposition of Joseph Conrad's 1899 novella *Heart of Darkness* to Southeast Asia, providing the Vietnam experience in travelogue form.

But the Philippine-based production was plagued with logistical problems, painstakingly detailed on paper in poor, suffering Eleanor Coppola's *Notes* and on film in the equally revelatory documentary *Hearts of Darkness: A Filmmaker's Apocalypse* (1991), which also offers amusing outtakes of Brando's notorious ad-libbing.

The film's opening images: napalmed jungles double-exposed with close-ups of a sweaty Captain Willard, the CIA-trained assassin who will soon be tasked with a journey upriver to cut down one Colonel Kurtz, a poet warrior running his own fiefdom in the heart of the Cambodian jungle. Right from the start, the film makes clear that we are in the realm of nightmare. According to Coppola, Vietnam was not only a shitshow, it was also a horror show (hence the new application of Conrad's iconic epitaph recited at film's end by Brando's Kurtz: "the horror … the horror…"). As such, it was almost impossible not to get with the program. "In this war," we're informed, "things get confused out there: power, morality…"

Apocalypse Now is about the fuzzy line between good and bad, and our susceptibility to accept, to use the title of Hannah Arendt's famous book on Adolf Eichmann, "the banality of evil."

Brando's Kurtz brings this thesis home with a carefully recited monologue about seeing the severed arms of a group of South Vietnamese children he and his one-time unit, back when he was a good-hearted soldier, had inoculated. After

As Brando aged, he became a deity—and so he played deities, like Colonel Kurtz in *Apocalypse Now* (1979) (Photofest).

confessing his tortured response to witnessing those actions, he goes on to express an appreciation for the novelty of the violence, lauding it as a veritable act of genius. 'Nam then, with its no-holds-barred savagery, is the proverbial brink, the precipice over which good men, like the once exemplary Kurtz, can descend. No matter that a year earlier, Michael Cimino's *The Deer Hunter* had already made the statement.

Given Kurtz's stature and value within the story—he's the film's engine, its climax and its moral; quite a load!—only an actor of a certain standing could have fit the bill. A larger-than-life figure, at once reclusive, controversial, sensitive, mad, mysterious, idiosyncratic, repulsive and admirable. Sound like Brando? Coppola thought so, and so pegged him as first choice.

Despite Coppola's vision of Kurtz as a hirsute ectomorph, however, Brando showed up with a shaved head and an expanded waistline. From there, albeit—though yes, he played his usual overgrown bad boy, refusing to learn his lines, complying to a limited number of takes, etc.—he appears to have been on generally good behavior. He owed Coppola, after all, for having revived his career with *The Godfather* and respected him too as an "actor's director." So Brando here (unlike in *Superman*) is trying again: he's acting.

Good thing too: There's a lot, narratively, staked on it. From the film's opening forward, Brando-Kurtz is posited as a big man. He's built up to, piece by piece, revealed in small, mounting revelations the way that Don Corleone was: a photograph here, tidbits of biographical info there, and definitions including "brilliant," "outstanding" and even "God." Anticipation for Brando-Kurtz's presence energizes the film, and allows it, otherwise a clothesline upon which absurdist episodes are hung, to transcend the picaresque.

Brando's Kurtz was modeled, on paper, on a number of officers known to have staged their own wars within the war, often using primitive acts of violence to gain attention. Some even enjoyed, as a result, "pagan idolatry" (the film's words), as does, in *Apocalypse Now*, the religiously worshipped Kurtz. And indeed, Kurtz resembles an Eastern religious figure, clearly the vision cultivated for the character by Brando. With his bald head and philosophic musings, he's a reverse Buddha, endorsing not pacifism but its antithesis. He waxes, when confronted by hit man Willard, about the quality of judgment, specifically, the irrelevance of moral standards in an ethically deracinated universe.

In this, Kurtz represents the ultimate price of Vietnam: the loss of the warrior's humanity at the hands of the surrounding savagery. It's an "author's message" Brando puts forth with whispery, meditative reflection, akin to the confession of his adolescent embarrassments in *Last Tango*. Kurtz lets Willard carry out his mission by passively submitting to Willard's sword, because, as a sycophant has stated, Kurtz, while promoting madness, is also its victim, and thus "sick of the whole thing."

For Brando, that "whole thing" was acting. *Apocalypse Now* represented his last good kick at it. He'd do a gas-crisis two-hander with rival George C. Scott the following year—a tepid thriller called *The Formula* (1980)—then resurface but on occasion, either to support political causes like the anti-apartheid movement (*A Dry White Season*, 1989), to try his hand at self-satire (*The Freshman*, 1990), or, embarrassingly, to indulge in slapstick comedy (the deservedly obscure *Free Money*, 1998).

Like Kurtz at the hands of Willard, the mighty had fallen.

In the end, though, for whatever he put audiences through, the adulation endured. Marlon Brando, actor and man, was best eulogized by biographer William J. Mann in his bulky, forgiving *The Contender*: "Marlon should be remembered for his unwavering commitment to his own vision, for insisting on excellence but also on authenticity, and for forever being wary of the dehumanizing cost of fame."[23]

Not to mention his mass influence.

Dustin Hoffman
The Graduate Graduates

Everybody was once a nobody. Some everybodies were once *real* nobodies. To wit: Dustin Hoffman. Such was Hoffman's physical appearance and personal vibe—short, bird-nosed, nervously innocent—that even after his turn in one of the biggest box office successes of all time, *The Graduate*, he was classified by the same dead-end adjective by which he had been previously marked: un-castable (poor Hoffman, post–*Graduate*, even ended up collecting unemployment benefits). The kid had "gotten lucky," had been the pervading thinking. He had fit the one bill that had suited his gawky, waffling demeanor. How was that diminished stature, those proletariat looks, that obtrusive ethnicity going to suit other roles? It wasn't until the advent of *Midnight Cowboy* that the industry, and audiences, collectively realized just how erroneously they had judged him. What they had on their hands was not an incongruous-looking ingenue, they were brought to know, but a prematurely seasoned character actor—further, one who, while balanced with equally potent presences (Anne Bancroft, Jon Voight), could outshine them to the point of suggesting he could carry a picture by himself.

The truth, unknown to movie audiences, was that Hoffman had been honing his craft on the stage for years. In spite of his Brooklyn looks and voice, he was a Los Angeleno; his introduction to audiences had taken place at that famed West Coast playground, the Pasadena Playhouse. In the early '60s, he and a pair of fellow Californians, Gene Hackman (Midwest-raised) and Robert Duvall (parts Texas and Virginia), each made a pilgrimage east; that's where the *real* actors were, not the pretty boys being primed for TV and the movies. They all ended up at the famed Actors Studio. Hoffman subsequently fell into summer stock and off-Broadway, garnering good reviews and an Obie. In 1966, he was cast in his first film: a lowbrow crime comedy shot in Spain, *Madigan's Millions* (1966). Two years after that picture tanked, it was re-released with a new, opportunistic ad campaign: "Dustin Hoffman in a hilarious post–*Graduate* role." Next, it was a mere 45 seconds in a film fronted by the husband-and-wife team of Eli Wallach and Anne Jackson, *The Tiger Makes Out* (1967), an amalgam of two short off-Broadway plays written by Murray Schisgal. (Hoffman and Schisgal had collaborated on the stage, the genesis of a lifelong friendship. In time, the former would prompt the latter to work on many of his films, most famously *Tootsie*, 1982.) Finally, Mike Nichols threw his aspirational casting to the wind and, based on a wonky screen test between Hoffman and an uppity Katharine Ross, gave the former the eponymous role of confused Golden Boy and generational spokesperson Benjamin Braddock.

The Graduate partitioned America. Older audiences saw a snappy, naughty Broadway comedy compromised by concessions to trendy European cinematic technique and music-heavy bows to the youth movement. The kids, meanwhile, saw their fundamental dissatisfaction with the billy club of middle-class success reflected in the nervous ennui of the title character—a new variation on Brando's itchiness.

Further, they fell in love with Braddock's Oedipal folly. The character's confused amorism represented a small, dangerous attempt to rewrite proper society: let's turn our backs on professional expectation, show up our stuffy, self-occupied and unhappy forebears, and make love a knee-jerk affair. Like Braddock and his paramour-convert at the end of the movie, both smiling uncertainly on that inner-city bus to nowhere, those who fell in love with the film would worry about the consequences of having emulated the behavior of the central characters later.

It's safe to say that almost none of that would have come across without Hoffman. Had the original choice for the role, blond, square-jawed Robert Redford, been cast, would anybody have swallowed Braddock's breaches of behavior, particularly the climactic one? Redford, yes, played underdogs, but underdogs who spoke for a clean, new-old order, for better versions of long-standing institutions. And so, even as he was fighting, he seemed rooted. Wishy-washiness was not his game. As director Sydney Pollack, a frequent Redford collaborator, said of the actor, "He holds his ground, and you either enter his turf or you don't get it. Period. He will not court you."[1]

With Redford, a clear, implacable agenda was visibly (often too visibly) at work. It was as true on screen as it was in life. Like Paul Newman, with whom he had co-starred in two of his biggest successes, the physically blessed Redford was never comfortable in his own magnetic skin. If another contemporary, Steve McQueen, was out to use the movies to perform stunts of derring-do and race sports cars and motorbikes, the brainier Redford's focus was the enhancement of America's environmental consciousness and the promotion of small-scale auteurist cinema.

In that, he extended the interest in social causes promulgated by the '60s and the spirit of personal moviemaking that had dominated the '70s. His films, as best as he could help it, always had something to say—even if that message had to be imported into crass, commercial star vehicles underwritten by the major studios. Further, Redford encouraged ensuing generations to do the same. Putting his money where his mouth was, he financed the Sundance Film Festival, a hotbed of cinematic creativity whose low-budget art films counterpunched the blockbuster mentality of the '90s.

Hoffman, on the other hand, has always been all tightrope, no net. Life, according to the dark-haired, diminutive anti–Redford, is a series of eggshells Man is drawn to traverse. Being as ill-equipped as he is to take the journey is what elicits instinctive audience sympathy.

For the ultimate affirmation of the Redford-Hoffman contrast, see Alan J. Pakula's *All the President's Men* (1976) in which they play the famous journalistic tandem of Bob Woodward and Carl Bernstein. Redford, as Woodward, is the rookie on the beat, while Hoffman-Bernstein is the more experienced hand. And yet Redford demonstrates the firmer grip on the wheel. Struggle as he does to be allowed to pursue The Big Story, we never once root for Redford-Woodward as we might a more classic underdog—and yet we remain constantly unsure about Hoffman-Bernstein, though that character is the more reliable persona. The fact that Redford produced the film while Hoffman assumed the passive role of co-star is also significant.

All the President's Men, by the way, also speaks to Hoffman's premium on same-sex friendship, a leitmotif of his work throughout the '70s (and a major commonality with Robert De Niro). A healthy percentage of his films belong to the popular '70s subgenre of buddy films, as they were known before the catch-all cognomen "bromance." It's a testament to Hoffman's ego, while legendary, that he never minded sharing the screen with another actor. And if, in these situations, he always played the Costello and not the Abbott, that was fine by him too. It permitted him to keep in touch with his roots as a character actor and promoted the interplay he prized.

Benjamin Braddock, on the other hand, stood alone. As such, with *The Graduate*, Hoffman not only captured the spiritual emptiness of the young, he rewrote American film's leading comic archetype. Hitherto, that had always been the bumpkin, the socially awkward man-child trapped in a universe of mature, oppressive establishmentarians. No doubt Hoffman biographer Ronald Bergan considered this when he wittily called the actor a "nebbish without a cause."[2] Undersized and overmatched, the comic hero would triumph over his betters and get the girl but almost always by sheer accident—a narrative template that ran from the days of the silent comics through to Jerry Lewis. But for Hoffman's *Graduate*, cut from the same behavioral cloth, those rewards were not, in the end, enough. They did little, in fact, to quell his fundamental uncertainty. Hence, a new comic hero was born: the seeker, traveling just as indelicately through a hermetic, self-important world but in search of something bigger than material or romantic reward. The floodgates were open for Alan Arkin, George Segal, Charles Grodin and other neurotic heroes of the late '60s and early '70s, all victims, as was Hoffman's Braddock, of the spiritual itching powder under the decade's collar.

It would have been easy for Hoffman to replicate that part, with slight variations, for the next few years—and indeed, here and there, he did. *The Village Voice*'s Andrew Sarris even feared that Hoffman might become "the Andy Hardy of the sixties and seventies."[3] But Hoffman, to his credit, was also looking to act. And so, we come to his startling follow-up, the one that convinced movie audiences that they were privy to a talent more malleable than they had assumed, with staying power to boot: director John Schlesinger's *Midnight Cowboy*.

In 1965, New York's newly crowned civic overlord, John Lindsay, created the Mayor's Film Office of Film, Theatre and Broadcasting, established to increase film production in the Big Apple. Up until then, producers needed up to 50 permits to access real-life locations within metropolitan confines. With these barriers dismantled, a new cinematic category was born, one that would monopolize screens throughout the '70s: the New York film. As the dream of social progress that had inaugurated the '60s fell apart, so too did the nation's most populous city. New York, once the world capital of commerce and culture, fell to crime, labor strife, corruption and penury. It became, literally, the most dangerous place on the planet. Politicians told its citizens not to venture to particular areas or to set out after dark. Filmmakers, on the other hand, were invited to avail themselves of the whole shambolic shebang—and they wanted in. What better avenue to hard-core drama, social relevancy and dark, angst-based comedy than this den of inequity? The result was almost a decade's worth of gritty, realistic tales of conflict and alienation that would catapult Hoffman and his generation to fame. The first of these was *Midnight Cowboy*.

John Schlesinger had been a member-in-bad-standing of Britain's Angry Young Man movement, England's postwar shift from drawing room melodrama to working-class character studies. While that movement had made the reputations of fellow filmmakers Tony Richardson, Lindsey Anderson and Karel Reisz, Schlesinger remained a minor figure, even after the smash successes of his *Billy Liar* (1963) and *Darling* (1965). His status changed when he became the first to apply that movement's sensibility, with its sour sociology, devalued heroes and complicated sexual entanglements, to the American cinema.

In his British films, Schlesinger's heroes either longed to break from their provincial circumstances but found that they couldn't, or accomplished the feat only to discover a great big world eager to eat them up. *Midnight Cowboy* is part of the latter tradition, using Schlesinger's wide-eyed but jaundiced impressions of New York to reinforce the heartbreaking myth of cosmopolitan success, or as it's known on this side of the Pond, the American Dream. *Midnight Cowboy*, a kind of John Wayne in Wonderland, is about the city: its low tolerance for innocence and decency, its bias against wish fulfillment and in particular, its creation of a crippling ennui.

As relief from the latter, title character Joe Buck (Jon Voight), a shit-kickin' country boy looking to make easy money as a sexualized Marlboro Man, pairs with a mealy-mouthed street rat, Enrico "Ratso" Rizzo (Hoffman). To atone for trying to swindle him, Ratso allows Joe to share his grubby, unheated, rent-free hideaway in a condemned tenement. From there, their pimp-prostitute relationship progresses into a series of dark adventures, over which time Ratso grows deathly ill and his tenuous friendship with Joe movingly dimensional.

The film is full of cinematic sidebars, including a McLuhan-esque take on media, a look at the self-indulgent showmanship of the counterculture, and *cinema verité* montages of quotidian street life. For all of its documentary pretensions about capturing the soul of America circa 1969, *Midnight Cowboy* is essentially a two-hander. Schlesinger and screenwriter Waldo Salt agreed that while in the source material, James Leo Herlihy's semi-autobiographical novel, Joe and Ratso subscribe to an unabashedly homosexual relationship, mainstream America was not yet ready for a central dynamic of that controversial variety. That said, gayness would definitely be in the air via a variety of supporting characters, most forcing a desperate and disillusioned Joe to compromise himself for the sake of survival. That was the best the self-consciously homosexual Schlesinger could do, via the film, to vicariously come out of the closet. If confronted, he could always say what he had made was a film about the salvific nature of friendship as remedy for urban alienation, plain and simple.

Voight and Hoffman had worked together in the theater and enjoyed a relationship of frictionless one-upmanship, which they use in the film to good avail. That aside, contrasting styles are clearly at work: Voight the naturalist vs. Hoffman the showman. At times, it's as if Voight is acting for film while Hoffman is acting for the theater. Mind you, that was exactly Hoffman's agenda: to inform film audiences of his roots. His Ratso is an affected concoction, from his Bugs Bunny voice and his exaggerated limp (Method Man Hoffman had walked the streets of New York for weeks with pebbles in one of his shoes) to his shabby wardrobe (shredded socks included) and that gummy mouth of stained teeth set within his sallow, pursy visage. It has allusions to caricature, testing, particularly in contrast to the more believable Voight, our level of credibility.

Then Ratso gets sick. It's not a subtle transformation—the makeup department pours on the sweat, and there are signs as unsubtle as a fall down a stairway. And yet, it's the catalyst by which Hoffman humanizes his creation.

For all of its obviousness, Hoffman's Ratso does his best to suffer in silence, allowing the actor to take his club foot off the gas and let his internalist take over. We are made painfully aware that the specter of death is the one bad break that low-life Ratso, whose entire existence has been nothing but bad breaks, is not capable of shrugging off. It exacerbates his isolation, of course, as now, even his thin thread to fair-weather friend Joe Buck is under threat of being cut. With this bait-and-switch, Hoffman pulls when you expect him to punch, as do Voight and the script, never milking the sentimentality of the situation. By the time of the film's final cruel irony (Ratso's quiet death on a redemptive bus trip to Florida by which Joe and Ratso have a fool's plan to begin new lives), Hoffman's earlier histrionics have not simply been forgiven, they've been forgotten.

Critics were divided over the film's pretensions—the aforementioned sociology, as well as the fuzzy flashes of backstory and the odd fantasy sequences that tear us away from the central story. But everybody loved the Joe Buck–Ratso Rizzo relationship, some pronouncing it a modern *Of Mice and Men*. The film's smash success despite a baffling X rating furthered the popularity of the buddy movie—the male-on-male subgenre that had kicked off with the enormously popular *Butch Cassidy and the Sundance Kid* (1969). It also made a star of Voight and opened the door for Hoffman to play a wider variety of roles. No more fear of Andy Hardy-ism.

That said, there was a return to his original image, with a slight upgrade, just a few months later: *John and Mary* (1969). Essentially a two-hander interpolated with cinematic snatches of backstory, the film was a stunt-casted love story pairing Hoffman with America's other young, unconventional new star, Mia Farrow. They play two young singles who, throughout a protracted one-night stand, spar diplomatically over the status of their burgeoning relationship. In so doing, a lot of questions about sex, love and fidelity are considered as, in 1969, the sexes were stutter-stepping their way toward aspirations of equality. Clearly, the influence of French cinema was at work, with its films full of young, hip couples sitting around chic, spacious apartments talking in melodramatic, existential overtones about the nooks and crannies of *l'amour*.

On its own terms, *John and Mary* plays as an interesting timepiece: a look at the fragile state of sexual politics in a confused age of gender redefinition. In its day, though, different story (*Time* magazine's review: "*John and Mary* is as empty as a singles' bar on a Monday morning"[4]). While you can't blame the critics for collectively calling it a setback for the above-the-line talent—Hoffman was coming off *Midnight Cowboy*, Farrow off of *Rosemary's Baby* (1968) and director Peter Yates off of *Bullitt* (1968)—the film is not without its merits, particularly the caliber of the central performances. Farrow, with her skeletal sensuality, Disney heroine-sized eyes, and soft, semi-affected voice, is at once innocent and intuitive. Hoffman, meanwhile, makes a lot of his shy, gap-toothed smile and his cautious inquisitiveness. His John is a slightly seasoned, slightly saltier Benjamin Braddock, a little more confident but still fundamentally adrift in the world of sexual politics. That said, it's evident that Hoffman was back on dangerous ground. He was being refitted for the sticky skin of a young, clued-out neurotic-romantic, the heir apparent to Jack Lemmon. Fortunately, *John and Mary* was the slimmest of box office successes, its presence failing to derail the precedent of versatility that had been set by *Midnight Cowboy*.

To reaffirm the depth of his talent, Hoffman next devoted himself to a role that encompassed myriad identities: Jack Crabb in Arthur Penn's *Little Big Man*, a man at once a 121-year-old sage, a Western dandy, and a Cheyenne brave.

By 1970, the Vietnam conflict was in full swing. Penn, long its critic, would use the slaughter of the Cheyenne leading to the Battle of Little Big Horn as a metaphor for America's brutality against the innocent civilians of Southeast Asia. Many a critic, in fact, noted a physical similarity between Penn's Indians and the real-life Vietnamese, a situation that prevented the literati from seeing the forest from the trees. What many missed was a sweeping, picaresque character study chronicling the cowboy–Indian conflict at the heart of the Old West, brimming with larger-than-life characterizations, amusing ironies and, courtesy of Hoffman, a master class in the art of acting.

Crabb, for which Hoffman subjected himself to agonizing layers of makeup and constant screaming to achieve the right hoarseness of voice, is the lone survivor of Custer's notorious Last Stand. He recounts his life through a series of flashbacks, adventures in which he switches affiliations from the cowboys to the Indians and vice versa. This sets an agenda within Hoffman's *oeuvre*. Going forward, he will periodically posit himself as a citizen of two worlds: cowboy–Indian here, humble folkie-paranoid superstar in *Who Is Harry Kellerman and Why Is He Saying Those Terrible Things About Me?* (1971), stand-up comic–social advocate in *Lenny* and man-woman in *Tootsie*.

Throughout his long life, Crabb meets every Western stereotype Hollywood has ever created, turned inside-out: the schoolmarm, the gunslinger, the preacher, the medicine man, etc. Best of all is his relationship with his Native grandfather, played by the emphatically sagacious and quietly bemused Chief Dan George, who is Crabb's Yoda. George, in fact, would have stolen the film—no easy task when the cast includes Martin Balsam, Jeff Corey, Faye Dunaway and Robert Mulligan—if it hadn't been for Hoffman's virtuosity.

Hoffman here is clearly cast against type, a challenge he periodically welcomed. He's hardly "tall in the saddle" and far too urban–Jewish to play a Cheyenne tribesman. And yet, it's a limbo state that works in the actor's favor. As I wrote

Dustin Hoffman (middle) on the set of *Little Big Man* (1970) with Arthur Penn (left; other unidentified). Throughout the 1970s, he played products of contrasting cultures (National General/Photofest).

of Hoffman's performance in my *The Drop Dead Funny '70s: American Film Comedies Year by Year*, "Crabb is a man who belongs to no culture.... Who better than a versatile talent not handsome enough to be a traditional leading man nor cartoonish enough to be a supporting actor?"[5]

Crabb is also a survivor, a scrounger, hitching his wagon to whichever camp will have him if that's what it takes to save his hide. It's a trait he shares with other Hoffman characters, from the swindling Ratso in *Midnight Cowboy* to struggling actor Michael Dorsey in *Tootsie* who, like Crabb, trickily maintains dual identities to find acceptance. A struggling actor for years, Hoffman no doubt developed a kinship with personalities forced to fight for approval, as well as those who lived, for better or worse, off of the avails of guises.

Little Big Man made Hoffman, fittingly, a big man. With the acclaim he and the film received, he had realized his dream: that of being a top-billed commodity as a bona fide character actor. As the old saying goes, however, be careful what you wish for. With this success came pressures, deals, responsibilities and advantages that would wreak havoc over Hoffman's finances and personal life. Perfect. He would use all of it in his next film, the story of a successful folk-rock singer immersed in the dark side of fame, personified by a mysterious muckraker named Harry Kellerman.

Who Is Harry Kellerman and Why Is He Saying Those Terrible Things About

Me? was directed by Belgian import Ulu Grosbard, whose relationship to Hoffman went back to a 1964 off–Broadway production of Arthur Miller's *A View from the Bridge* (Hoffman was its stage manager). They remained tight as Hoffman's star rose and Grosbard enjoyed a modestly successful stage and screen career. *Harry Kellerman* was their first cinematic collaboration, based on a screenplay by another theater alumni and crony, Herb Gardner.

Hoffman, in curls and a Fu Manchu, plays Georgie Solway, a Dylan-esque deity whose image graces the cover of *Time* magazine (as had Hoffman's, sharing it with Mia Farrow for *John and Mary*) while he jams with Dr. Hook and the Medicine Show and agonizes over the spoils of stardom in his ivory-colored penthouse. Worse, there's this elusive Kellerman character, a mud-slinging phantasm who messes with Georgie's career and drives him to a quirky psychiatrist. But while this free-flowing comedy-drama is, yes, about the sticky, prickly world of status, about the intersection of Hoffman the icon and Hoffman the person, it holds larger thematic intentions. Like Benjamin Braddock's angst in *The Graduate*, Georgie Solway's discomfort reflects something universal: a malaise that is equal parts aging, divorce and the oppressive effects of urban decay—in other words, the shit a significant portion of America was going through in 1971, as long-standing conventions of everyday existence were crumbling at the hands of sociological and economic transformation.

You might remember an earlier Gardner hero, TV writer Murray Burns from Gardner's hit play-film *A Thousand Clowns* (1965), whose remedy from the ache of modern bullshit was withdrawal from society. Solway is cut from the same solitary cloth; further, there's the pull of nostalgia for a simpler, better time, represented by flashbacks to his hungry years as a Portnoy-esque nobody. These episodes constitute many of the film's best scenes, displaying Gardner's easy talent for Jewish-American humor and the winning mix of despair, gentility and brashness Hoffman first displayed as Benjamin Braddock.

Harry Kellerman tried hard to ingratiate itself to the younger, cinematically savvy audience that was fast replacing its Studio Era–weaned forebears; with its meandering narrative, a lot of the film aspires to the work of Federico Fellini. And it develops its own ambling, low-key if ultimately vacuous charm. Still, it and Hoffman's performance failed to push the envelope the way the film had obviously hoped. Perhaps that was the reason why, for his next effort, Hoffman chose something decidedly explosive.

First, the arcane title: "Straw dogs" is a Chinese reference (per Lao Tzu) to anything discarded after use—and Hoffman's 1971 film is, in part, about the devaluation of our reason and humanity. The story, as retooled by director Sam Peckinpah and co-writer David Zelag Goodman from an undistinguished novel, places a humble American astrophysicist at the mercy of his sexy, flirty English wife, who brings him to her quiet childhood home in West Cornwall to make good on a research grant. But the place isn't so quiet. It's populated by leering, brawling bullies intent on emasculating this eggheaded *arriviste* while laying sexual claim to the local he's been insultingly bedding. Brought to the brink, Hoffman's low-key liberal-intellectual surprises himself by climactically accessing his inner Rambo.

Straw Dogs was the first shot (pun intended) in a cinematic movement promoting a controversial idea: violence as an act of redemption. The people of the troubled late '60s and early '70s were fed up with the all-out corruption of civic life. With no honorable bodies to turn to other than indifferent governments and unscrupulous cops, they could only find relief in acts of personal vengeance against society's worst elements. In 1971 alone, such controversial films as *A Clockwork Orange* and *Dirty Harry* promoted this style of DIY vigilantism, as did Jules Feiffer's brilliantly black comedy *Little Murders*.

As the decade progressed, there'd be more of this kind of thing, a veritable subgenre's worth. As Quentin Tarantino reflected, the closest thing to a feel-good movie in the early '70s was revenge films. As a result, an appetite for on-screen violence developed, first to add the ugly, explosive reality of violence to the gangster films, war pictures and Westerns that had rendered it acceptably toothless, then to homogenize it again in sync with the rise of shoot 'em-up video games. America's highly polarized stance on guns has helped, the anti-gun lobby endorsing these kinds of films as polemics on the dangers of firearm ownership and the Right labeling them cinematic endorsements of the bullet-based behavior that had built the country. As for Peckinpah ... uh, I'm pretty sure you can guess which side of the fence that squib-happy hellraiser was on.

By 1971, the volatile Peckinpah had burned his bridges in Hollywood. Studios were fed up with his notorious addictions (alcohol, cocaine) and his constant insistence that his films, often running over three hours in length, remain untouched. Fortunately, he had distinguished himself back in 1966 on a TV project with a British producer, who lured him back to the U.K. seven years later to put the distinctive Peckinpah spin on an undistinctive 1969 paperback, *The Siege of Trencher's Farm*.

In the film version, Peckinpah's strengths are all there, the aspects of his talent critically overshadowed by his pioneering take on on-screen violence, as demonstrated in his reputation-making *The Wild Bunch*: his feel for the milieu (you can almost sense the autumnal chill of Southwest England), his playfulness (there are amusing, loving moments between husband and wife) and his ability to sustain tension (which, throughout the entire film, is positively palpable). Unfortunately, so is Peckinpah's obviousness, leaving much of the complexity of the scenario unexplored. Many, as a result, viewed the film as a simple-minded affirmation of testosterone-fueled territorialism. To the critical eye, though, there's no overlooking the interesting questions it asks about the fundamental make-up of the male identity, a major realm of thematic exploration throughout the cinema of the '70s.

As Neil Fullwood properly stated in *The Films of Sam Peckinpah*, *Straw Dogs* is about "the question of whether a man's predisposition to violence is latent or deep-rooted, or something at which he must demonstrate his capability before he can call himself a man—in other words, a rite of passage."[6] In this, Hoffman's astrophysicist-brought-to-the-brink is both the traditional all–American male and its post-sexual revolution re-invention. He's a Jekyll-Hyde persona, at war over which identity might serve himself, and the world, best. Hoffman's character, then, represented the troubling dichotomy being suffered by men at that time, and still, for better or worse, today, in our less-than-progressive age of "toxic masculinity."

Hoffman's character is also, of course, a fish out of water, an American in a quintessentially English setting. There was a lot of anti–American sentiment at the time, which the film interpolates into some of its dialogue. Vietnam, race riots and gun violence had reframed America as the international epicenter of modern evil. As such, though his quiet, nervy demeanor belies it, Hoffman is "the ugly American." The film being a product of the proudly philistine Peckinpah, however, that designation elevates Hoffman to heroic status. *Straw Dogs* is then, in part, an American revenge fantasy against that country's socio-political critics.

It is also a semi-disguised Western, as all Peckinpah films are, conforming to a traditional Western storyline—in this case, the humble, good-hearted white hat reluctantly coerced into taking on a goading gang of black hats after all else fails (*High Noon*, 1952, anyone?).

And *Straw Dogs* is a bit—careful qualification here: *a bit*—of a feminist tract. Bra-lessness was the leading public symbol of the formative years of the women's liberation movement. So the Lolita-esque Susan George, as Hoffman's toothy, nubile wife, goes about with her mammories freed for much of the picture (she's even intro'd tits first). This hardly goes unnoticed, especially in a village of drunken, drooling sexists; but unlike the increasingly put-out Hoffman, George doesn't seem to care. She's a new breed of woman, out to express herself as she sees fit. Peckinpah, of course, questions the value of this: Is this kind of personal freedom ethical in a world in which men are, fundamentally, ruled by their basest instincts?

He answers that question with a confusing rape scene that critics, all these years later, are still trying to sort out. The sex begins at the brutal behest of an old beau for whom the victim, George's character, holds some attraction. After this Yes-No, an interloper forces his way into the proceedings, prompting a decided No. On the one hand, then, the sequence promotes the dangerous myth of the female rape fantasy, until, ultimately, it posits the act as a clear criminal offense. Further, while Peckinpah goes on to sympathetically devote time to the victim's post-traumatic stress, he moves on to explore the pushy, budding sexuality of a young village girl.

What attracted Hoffman to this property, with its disturbing sexual politics and its relentlessly violent climax, is both easy to see and hard to grasp. His on-the-record contention is that the lure was the dissolution of the marriage at the heart of the story (brought on by his character's refusal to read the riot act to the encroaching villagers, an act of faith and pacifism to which his wife objects). Hoffman himself was then having marital difficulties (though divorce wouldn't come until a more fitting time: when he was prepping *Kramer vs. Kramer* in 1979), so yes, that was no doubt a part of the mix. Plus, that storyline was already proving to be his preferred male-female dynamic; Hoffman's characters enjoy playful relationships with women, until his partners inevitably turn on him. Then, in the end, the two reach an uneasy truce (at least in the films within the purview of this book, from *The Graduate* through to *Tootsie*).

By this time, Hoffman had also begun to show another career-long habit: a thing for roles in which he would play products of two worlds. Peckinpah's low-key intellectual, brought to a no-holds-barred boil, certainly conforms to the type. And as an undersized, less-than-sightly adolescent, Hoffman had no doubt suffered the slings and arrows of his condescending contemporaries—so maybe, too, he liked the idea of avenging himself against his oppressors. (The Jewish Hoffman does it again by standing up against antisemitism in 1976's *Marathon Man*.) The real answer to what he responded to, however, might be the film's fundamental query: As men, are we the possessors, for better or for worse, of an innate instinct for extremism? Or was the film, per Hoffman's politics (as opposed to Peckinpah's), an important examination of the corruption of the good-hearted liberal at the unrelenting hands of simple-minded might-makes-right types? Are our fundamental humanity and ability to reason, the picture asks, capacities destined to be corrupted? Many at that time, with the Vietnam conflict being brutally prolonged by the Nixon administration, certainly thought so.

Whatever the reason, Hoffman pulls off an admirable balancing act, waffling throughout between shaky self-assurance and latent assertiveness, with grace notes of ironic humor. It's Benjamin Braddock, darkly reframed.

Looking for balance, or maybe distance, Hoffman next threw himself into a comedy, albeit not of the mainstream American variety. *Alfredo, Alfredo* (1972) was the last film co-written and directed by Pietro Germi, the Italian neo-realist who, after switching to satirical sex comedy, scored an international hit with *Divorce Italian Style* (1961). Germi was on familiar ground here, using Hoffman as a timid banker unable to leave his comically co-dependent wife for his cool-headed mistress due, in part, to Italy's outdated anti-divorce laws.

In the late 1940s, Hollywood formed the Motion Picture Export Association of America. This body permitted the U.S. to flood Western Europe with its movies (those countries had been deprived of Hollywood fare for throughout World War II). Concerned with the subjugation of their national film industries, France, Italy and other countries fought back, imposing quotas and other restrictions. This protectionism eventually fathered "runaway productions," deals that called for a mix of American and foreign talents to work together on European soil to make films of cross-cultural appeal. The practice, which gave us everything from those Steve Reeves *Hercules* movies to Sergio Leone's spaghetti Westerns, included a series of broad, popular sex farces starring Sophia Loren and Marcello Mastroianni.

For all the spirit of collaboration, the language barrier remained a big, unsolvable problem. On set, everyone spoke in their native tongue, making the taxing art of acting an even more difficult process. The films were then dubbed into a single language for designated markets, a necessity American audiences and critics had difficulty accepting. Many American actors found themselves diminished as a result; see poor Robert De Niro in Bernardo Bertolucci's *1900* (1976).

Despite this barrier, Hoffman distinguishes himself nicely as the lucky-unlucky Alfredo. No doubt it helped that he was playing an archetype, the nebbish, with which he was deeply familiar, and that most of his lines were expressed via voice-over. As for looking Italian, he leaves that to a little tan makeup, a slick comb-over and a few exaggerated hand gestures. An expert comic, Hoffman recognized the value here of downplaying (even his voice-over is in a confessional monotone), leaving the bombast to the supporting players, particularly the striking Stefania Sandrelli as his incurably neurotic wife, whose job is to energize the central joke of this oversexualized psycho chick's uncontrollable physical appetite for her nondescript nudnik of a husband.

Like a lot of European cinema, the film is about the magical, sometimes dangerous aspect of each gender's incurable vulnerability to the other. It's a perfect subject for Hoffman: From the get-go, he had made American films largely devoted to that same exploration. You can argue, in fact, that almost his entire thematic throughline in the '70s was the nerve-wracking quest to comprehend the opposite sex, a mission that culminated in *Tootsie*. Anyway, *Alfredo* works. It's just broad enough to dodge obviousness, and just delicate enough to eschew sentimentality. It didn't do much for Hoffman's career, however, and was soon labeled a curio, a status the film maintains today.

Frustrated with the overall quality of his most recent work, Hoffman signed on to be a partner in First Artists. The independent production company had been founded a few years earlier by Paul Newman, Sidney Poitier and Barbra Streisand, the three biggest stars in America at that time. Now, two newly weighty presences, Hoffman and Steve McQueen, were joining.

First Artists offered each signatory the opportunity to exercise greater control over select star vehicles, along with a substantial salary, in exchange for certain commercial concessions. How could control freak Hoffman resist, even if First Artists' initial efforts had proven self-indulgent flops? Besides, it would quell his fears that being, looks-wise, no Newman, no McQueen, would negate future star parts; now, he could settle comfortably into the role of character actor and not suffer the constant headache of trying to find major showcases.

Hoffman investigated potential properties and creative partners while fielding the usual Big Studio offers. One, a role that would be written just for him which would pay great money and allow him to work with the other recent First Artists signatory, had European roots but desperately needed a pair of American names to make a splash on the other side of the Pond.

By his own admission, director Franklin J. Schaffner specialized in displaced heroes, idiosyncratically exemplary characters who found themselves dramatically jostled out of their rightful milieus and into the thick of strange new environments, worlds subscribing to unfamiliar, often brutal mores and folkways. Among that group were those time-space victimized astronauts who found themselves surrounded by sophisticated simians in *Planet of the Apes* (1968), the eponymous old soldier fallen out of grace in the new touchy-feely army in *Patton*, those Russian aristocrats who fell prey to that uprising in *Nicholas and Alexandra* (1971), and the hammy Nazis looking to make a disco era comeback in *The Boys from Brazil* (1979).

Papillon (1973) belonged to the same tradition. The title character, so named because of that artful tattoo of a butterfly on his chest, is Henri Charrière, a French lowlife framed for the murder of a pimp in 1931. He is sent to a notorious penal colony in the heart of French Guiana, from which he tries to escape repeatedly, succeeding only after 14 interminable years.

When Charrière's chronicle of this real-life adventure story became a best-seller in Europe and North America, the Vietnam conflict, which had been started by the French, was hitting fever pitch. As such, much interest developed in the history of atrocities committed by the French. That said, neither the book nor the film held any such metaphorical intentions. One doubts contemporary socio-political criticism ever even occurred to the strait-laced Schaffner, who, in the era in which he worked ('60s and '70s), was a glaring anachronism: a widescreen entertainer in a time of smaller, socially conscious cinema. What he and Warner Bros. saw in the book was an old-fashioned prison film, a big-budget version of the kinds of pictures that studio used to grind out with Humphrey Bogart or James Cagney, combined with the over-the-top action elements that had made Steve McQueen's *The Great Escape* (1963) one of his iconic hits.

Small prob: While the book boasted a sufficient quota of adventure, it offered virtually no character development—and McQueen, despite being a great minimalist who knew how to get the most out of his limited range, was not the kind of actor you let carry two and a half hours. Otherwise, *The Magnificent Seven* (1960) would have played as *The Magnificent One*.

McQueen was yet another actor of the post–Brando generation who had grown up fatherless. Nevertheless, the senior McQueen, a stunt pilot who had barnstormed the Midwest, left a sizable imprint on his son, instilling a deep-seated thrill seeker's mentality. This quality, coupled with a Freudian instinct to wage war against authority figures, made a juvenile delinquent of the growing McQueen, whose behavior was ultimately curbed by the Marines. Looking for his next kick, McQueen parlayed his stipend from the G.I. Bill for a ticket at the feet of a veritable Who's Who of American acting gurus: Meisner, Hagen and Adler. Meanwhile, he raced motorbikes, sports cars and small aircraft. The stage was set for another "twisted boy" *à la* James Dean: a combination of the introspective unrest of Marlon Brando and the death-defying bravado of John Wayne.

McQueen made his name as part of the TV Western craze of the 1950s (*Wanted Dead or Alive*, 1958–61), then became one of the first personalities to successfully transition from the little screen to the bigger one. He fronted casts of a new, Kennedy-era generation of action stars in two highly successful epics, *The Magnificent Seven* and *The Great Escape*, until it was deemed that he could carry a picture by his lonesome. Once he garnered clout, McQueen acted less and stunted more, helping to make the car chase a major convention of the American screen. By the late '60s, he, along with pal-rival Paul Newman came to epitomize "cool," a new sensibility predicated on self-reliance, taciturnity and a cultivated separation from the mainstream. Newman, in his films, would be forced to betray that quality and walk away a broken man; McQueen would instead play "chicken" with it, leaving his oppressors in the dust.

By the time of *Papillon*, McQueen had become the highest-paid movie star in the world, a situation that "twisted his melon," in the hipster *patois* in which he spoke. And he could have had more, much more; the opportunity was there for him to eclipse even the sizable success he had enjoyed in the '60s. In the '70s, McQueen turned down *The French Connection, Dirty Harry, Close Encounters of the Third Kind* (1977) and *Apocalypse Now*, among other iconic hits. Movies, clearly, had stopped providing the thing that he prized most: a rush of adrenaline. The thrill now, according to McQueen, was in turning your back on it at the height of your fame, in letting your once sculpted physique go to pot, and in re-doing your iconic visage in facial hair and granny glasses. It was the ultimate act against authority, plus, it made the world stand up and take notice of your bold, adolescent audacity. Perfect.

Before that, though, he would play Papillon. The source material provided the action he was looking for, but it was baseless. So Warners threw the best writers they could afford on the film, a veritable A-list of names now screenwriting deities: Dalton Trumbo, Lorenzo Semple Jr. and (unbilled) William Goldman.

The film seems to owe the most to the latter. With the addition of a sidekick—myopic counterfeiter Louis Degas, played by Hoffman—much of the film echoes Goldman's *Butch Cassidy and the Sundance Kid*, another hit McQueen had turned down. Goldman adds some much-needed interplay, a little humor and, most of all, a beating heart to this otherwise routine exercise of escape attempt after escape attempt after escape attempt.

Steve McQueen peaked in the '60s and petered out in the '70s (First Artists/Photofest).

That said, try as both performers might, no spark between McQueen and Hoffman is allowed to ignite. Their scenes together are limited affairs, sometimes existing strictly to accommodate expository dialogue. Just as the film itself is a kind of exercise in genre nostalgia, both McQueen and Hoffman seem to be exercising nostalgias of their own: McQueen is trying to replicate the success he enjoyed in the aforementioned *Great Escape* while Hoffman is cashing in on *Midnight Cowboy*. Like that film, for Hoffman, it's another case of him dwarfing himself in the presence of an all–American male.

Where Charrière-McQueen is impressively chiseled, magnetically tense and indefatigably courageous, Degas-Hoffman is laughably slovenly, comically nervy and incurably cowardly. Just as he had with Jon Voight in *Cowboy*, Hoffman in *Papillon* enjoyed a friendly rivalry with his co-star both on and off the screen. Again, this is a case of Hoffman being attracted to a tale of constructive friendship. In most of these cases, he plays the boy-in-the-back-room, the trusty, semi-comic reliable who supplies the swords or the arrows to the hero (here, Degas financially subsidizes Charrière's attempts at going over the wall). His reward for this is tolerance, which spills over into affection.

What was the periodic attraction to these kinds of roles, when the much-esteemed Hoffman could have been making star vehicles? The Freudian explanation might be that Hoffman was the product of a failed father, a Willy Loman type (whom Hoffman would draw on generously when he played that role in Volker Schlöndorff's 1985 film version of that classic play). As such, Hoffman would occasionally appear in narratives in which his characters got to express a sincere, heartfelt sympathy for Alpha-type hard luck cases. It could also be that these films were, at least in part, a kind of "day at the beach" for him—albeit in *Papillon*, one surrounding a jungle fortress. Characterize them as "breathers," respites from the crippling toil of carrying a picture by himself, a chance to keep up the acting chops while preparing to plunge once more into the all-consuming breach of stardom. Hoffman followed up *Papillon*, in fact, with *Lenny,* which, to this day, he considers his most intense and difficult characterization (quite a pronouncement when you consider the rigors of *Rain Man*, 1988).

That said, he does get to act in *Papillon* a bit: when he tearily comforts McQueen after the latter's near-death time in solitary; when he has a tainted ankle treated with a steaming knife blade; and in the closing scenes when he bids his longtime partner adieu after McQueen finally accomplishes, yes, the escape he's been attempting since the film's first frames.

Despite the limited McQueen-Hoffman chemistry, *Papillon* the film proved as successful as *Papillon* the book. In time, the latter's authenticity would come into serious question; no such problem for the film, which, from the first mile-wide frame, smacks of Hollywood artifice. The beats are big and forced, the usually chancy Jerry Goldsmith's score is derivative and bombastic, and the atrocities, which carry the emotional impact of the story, are stagey and amateurish (there's a guillotined head that looks like it was on loan from a hat shop). Oh, and have I mentioned the makeup? When a white-haired McQueen emerges after five years in solitary, he comes out looking like the experience turned him into Buddy Ebsen.

So, on to one of Hoffman's iconic roles: *Lenny*....

Lenny Bruce (*née* Schneider) was America's first hip comic. Hitherto, stand-up comedians, most of them reared in vaudeville, spouted tired one-liners about nagging mothers-in-law and the town drunk. Suddenly, here came a trim, oily sharpie who talked about race, sex, religion, death and other taboo subjects, in an exploratory, conversational style akin to jazz. A creature of the lower show biz depths— amateur nights, burlesque, strip clubs—Bruce was slowly but surely adopted by the chic, until his excesses—liberal language, hard drugs, a hate-on for authority—got him repeatedly busted and wore him down. In the end, he was classified a modern-day martyr, a counterculture numen who died (at 40) for our sins by exposing institutional hypocrisy and promoting recreational self-abuse.

As the Baby Boomers began to attend the movies more often (though they wouldn't become the dominant demographic until the '80s), studios began to look for properties that celebrated their idols. The '70s would see biographies of Bruce,

Janis Joplin, Buddy Holly and other figures whose art, be it comedy or music, rattled the establishment before their star was prematurely snuffed out, affording them legendary status. *Lenny* was one of the first out of the gate; at the wheel was smokin' hot Bob Fosse, coming off a magical year in which he became the first artist to win three-quarters of an EGOT (an Emmy, an Oscar and a Tony) in the same year.

Why Fosse, hitherto known as a director of groundbreaking stage and screen musicals? Because much of Fosse's pedigree paralleled that of Bruce: Both were products of the nightclub scene, Fosse an up-and-coming dancer, Bruce a comic emcee; both fought wars over censorship, Fosse from Broadway producers put out by the concupiscent nature of his dance numbers, Bruce from the law for his use of blue material; and both were incurable addicts: Fosse died too young from his cigarette habit, Bruce from his dependency on heroin.

Then, there's sex. Fosse had become famous for introducing it into the otherwise chaste stage musical and enjoyed an equally creative sex life in his off-hours; Bruce was an admitted philanderer, who had had his share of strippers on the nightclub circuit. As for long-term relationships, both Fosse and Bruce perpetuated troubled, on-off liaisons with, respectively, Gwen Verdon and Honey Harlow, the first a legitimate dancer, the second ... uh, not so much. In the film, the latter is portrayed by the striking, surprisingly versatile Valerie Perrine (sad to say, never assigned a better role), embodying, at once, both women. So, Bruce is Fosse and Fosse is Bruce; it's as if the director is telling, in effect, his own story, with the famed comic as his public defender. Call the film, then, a run-up to Fosse's more autobiographical *All That Jazz* (1979).

For the all-consuming eponymous role, Hoffman accessed his inner investigative journalist (ironic, as the film is structured as a series of journalistic interviews giving us, in retrospect, a piecemeal Bruce; it's a Watergate-era *Citizen Kane*, 1941). He interviewed over 60 people who had known Bruce personally, a tally rivaling that of Albert Goldman, who released his best-selling, Bible-thick biography of the troubled comic that same year. Further, Hoffman diligently studied Bruce's comedy albums and TV appearances. There are only six of the latter, the controversial comic having been considered too hot for the tube. And Hoffman looks and sounds the part: There's the hooded eyes, the lamb-like pompadour and the reflective posture—plus, Hoffman nails Bruce's cadences with such accuracy, the actor's own tell-tale voice almost disappears, something he had found almost impossible to do in prior parts.

But though it's a perfectly studied and palpably energetic performance, perhaps the most high-octane of Hoffman's career, Bruce ultimately comes across as a nice, conscientious and indefatigable Jewish boy, out to liberate button-down society out of the goodness of his own heart. In life, Bruce was a much more hard-boiled character, a slick opportunist who only championed civil liberties when it took on aspects of personal vendetta. Bruce was not out to save the world, at least not foremost; his own skin took precedence.

Still, the audience for which the film was intended made *Lenny* a sizeable hit. They were happy to have a Christ figure whose legacy stood for the human cost of the battle against institutional oppression still raging as, in 1974, the last wave of the counterculture continued to confront the corrupt and condescending squares. The left's new combination stand-up comic-patron saint was George Carlin, the bearded goofball then at the height of his fame lauding "the seven words you can't say on TV," a bit clearly influenced by Carlin's idol Bruce.

The role of Bruce exhausted Hoffman. He took 1975 off, leaving the debate over who was America's greatest living screen actor to followers of Jack Nicholson (*One Flew Over the Cuckoo's Nest*) and Al Pacino (*Dog Day Afternoon*). Then, Hoffman came back to enjoy not one but two successes in America's Bicentennial year.

The bulk of his colleagues were either appearing in flops or making flops-to-be: Hackman was filming *March or Die* (1977), Nicholson was appearing in *The Missouri Breaks* and *The Last Tycoon*, as was De Niro (though De Niro also had *Taxi Driver*), and Pacino was prepping to fall from grace with *Bobby Deerfield* (1977). While this was happening, Hoffman's reputation was buoyed by two resounding hits, one released in the spring, the other in the fall. Both were thrillers, if of different styles, and both shared the same screenwriter: William Goldman.

The first was the film version of *All the President's Men*, the non-fiction chronicle of the Watergate scandal that was considered unfilmable: too many characters, no physical action, a story that the public was sick of hearing. They had lived with President Nixon's covert attempt to undermine the competition in the 1972 election for two solid years, as this country-shattering scandal had monopolized newspapers, TV and dinner table conversation. Nixon was gone now, mercifully, so why relive that international embarrassment—particularly so soon, and particularly in what should be a celebratory annum?

In part because people, particularly filmmakers, were still processing Nixon. As Jonathan Kirshner wrote in *Hollywood's Last Golden Age: Politics, Society, and the Seventies Film in America*,

> It is almost impossible to overstate the influence that the presidency of Richard Nixon had on the context, or the subtext, of the movies of the era. Scratch any story about power, privacy, or paranoia, not to mention endemic institutional corruption, and Nixon would be revealed just below the surface.[7]

Besides, the clever Goldman had intuitively recognized the movie-esque in the first half of journalistic tandem Bob Woodward and Carl Bernstein's straight-ahead best-seller. Therein, Goldman discovered, lay the elements of two old-fashioned movie genres: the newspaper film and the detective story.

Once upon a time, at the height of the Depression, cynical, wisecracking beat reporters stood up for the little guy by taking down their stuffy, underhanded oppressors (a natural, as most Hollywood screenwriters had come from the newspaper racket). A decade later, in the postwar '40s, the gumshoe was the avenging angel of choice. He was just as jaundiced and judicious, only he fought with a Smith & Wesson instead of a Smith-Corona. By the '70s, nostalgia for Studio Era fare like the films that had featured such heroes was widespread, as a "They don't make 'em like they used to" mindset, spawned by the comparatively complicated nature of modern times, set in. Goldman, with *President's Men*, recognized an opportunity to appease that appetite under the guise of a relevant, real-life narrative.

And the property fit him in a more personal way: Hitherto, he had specialized in stories of foolish courage. His central characters, from Western outlaw Butch Cassidy to flying ace Waldo Pepper, were preternaturally disposed to the kind of chance-taking destined to end in elegiac disaster. (They would always go, as Goldman's dutifully doomed soldiers did in his 1978 war epic, "a bridge too far.") Who more foolishly courageous than Woodward and Bernstein, staking the reputation of one of America's most respected news voices on the absurd notion that the president, of all people, was an incompetent crook, or for that matter, Nixon, the ballsy paranoid who punched simultaneously below the belt and above his weight?

It was the politically conscious Robert Redford who had bought the book, cast himself as Woodward, and set the production into motion. Hoffman, picked to play Bernstein after Al Pacino turned Redford down, would ultimately call the film "Bob's movie." After an inauspicious incubation in TV, and reprising his Broadway role in the film adaptation of Neil Simon's *Barefoot in the Park* (1967), the blonde, eagle-faced Redford had been one of the first of a generation of big names to boldly mix films predicated on their pretty-boy image with those reflecting a personal social interest. This was another precedent that had been set by Brando, with worthy but failed attempts like *The Ugly American* (1963). But the more savvy Redford bested him by moonlighting as a bona fide producer. Contemporary Warren Beatty, another modern-day matinee idol with an implacable social conscience, was doing same, even if, unlike Redford, his films just as often relied on self-examination or nostalgia.

But Redford was a political animal through and through. As such, he helped Warner Bros., the company that underwrote most of his properties, return to form as a maker of "message pictures," once a point of studio pride. He championed the plight of the American Indian in *Tell Them Willie Boy Is Here* (1969), the environment in *Jeremiah Johnson* (1971) and political integrity in *The Candidate* (1972). Call *The Candidate*, then, a precursor to *President's Men*, with Redford combining his bent for the polemic with another of his favorite genres, the spy film (from *Three Days of the Condor*, 1976, through to *Spy Game*, 2001).

In *President's Men*, Goldman takes Woodward and Bernstein's pursuit of a simple, botched "robbery" at National Democratic headquarters during the run-up to the 1972 presidential election and converts it to a series of swift, successive scenes, each offering the next clue in the ultimate revelation. We're in the trenches as the driven, undaunted duo, nicknamed "Woodstein," make countless phone inquiries, scribble the names of leads on steno pads, stage secret rendezvous with underground (literally) sources, and fight with their journalistic betters for the right to stay on the story. It's all coated with an appropriately shadowy veneer, thanks to director Alan J. Pakula, who had come to specialize in lurid, atmospheric films preying on post–Kennedy cover-up paranoia, and the tasteful, chiaroscurist bent of cinematographer Gordon Willis. (Kudos, too, to the art direction team for their painstaking, depth-of-field replica of the offices of *The Washington Post*. The film, as a result, serves as a timepiece: the last living example of a pre-digi newsroom.)

Redford, an actor of limited range, is especially good. No doubt it's his greater stake in the story, and his appreciable awareness of its importance. But it's also a matter of staying in his wheelhouse. Traditionally, Redford forces himself on audiences; in so doing, he has to be delicate. He is here, expertly varying his weight on the gas pedal. His scenes on the telephone—he has many—are especially impressive. That task is a fine art. It's all reaction, to which the tireless Redford brings a versatile authenticity. Hoffman, too, is damn good at it.

For once, Hoffman doesn't shrink in the shadow of a more handsome presence. He's not out to pull a Ratso Rizzo or a Louis Degas. In fact, he studied hard, shadowing the actual Bernstein and spending so much time at the *Post* that they practically had to kick him out of the place. But like Redford, he's primarily out to serve the story, which he does with chain-smoking zealousness. It helps, too, that the real-life subject he is playing was something of a ladies' man. (Bernstein and his wife, auteur-to-be Nora Ephron, had even taken a crack at the script, in which they had played up the former's sexual allure.) And yes, even in the umbra of Redford, Hoffman manages, on occasion, to be sexy, a new capacity. So, while no, it's not a star vehicle, it's not another case of Hoffman taking it easy either. He stretches here and there, and ends up, in some small measure, re-inventing himself.

It's also interesting to note that a few years earlier, Redford-Hoffman/Woodward-Bernstein would surely have been posited as suit-and-tie hippies out to cock a snook at their Old School superiors. They certainly ruffle the feathers of their elders, a veritable Who's Who of middle-aged character actors: Martin Balsam, Jack Warden and Jason Robards, plus Hal Holbrook as whispery whistle-blower "Deep Throat." But what they're seeking, and are ultimately awarded, is that venerable generation's benediction. They even enjoy a paternal relationship with the gruff Robards, as *Post* editor Ben Bradlee. As such, the film served in its time as an affirmation that the war between the young and the old that had been in motion since the mid–60s was clearly on the wane. The counterculture was "selling out," looking to embed itself in traditional occupations after having crashed and burned as hedonistic bohemians. If you were young and masculine, you didn't simply stick to your own kind any more; male bonding was expanding into an all-ages brotherhood.

That said, by contemporary standards, the film also plays as a lot of IBM Selectric "clack-clack-clack" over the trading of the names of back room bad guys long forgotten. You're also stunned by what an Old Boys network the good guys constitute. In the war room, there isn't a feminine presence among the white dress shirts, weighty reading glasses and worn-out loafers. Outside of it, there's the odd female reporter on the floor and the odd female witness in the field. The most substantial female role belongs to the earnestly doleful Jane Alexander, as a conscientious bookkeeper who breaks an editorial impasse. Her presence affords Hoffman one of his best scenes, when his inquisitive Bernstein is forced to dance and jab at her in kid gloves, a mix of tact, guile, nerves and charm.

As for ethnicity, there's a single black reporter but he's afforded no lines. Given the film's painstaking authenticity, one can only roll one's eyes over the limited diversity of journalism circa 1976.

The success and respect garnered by the film reinstated the reporter as America's cinematic social savior (something Pakula had promoted in his previous film, the equally involving if less important *The Parallax View*, 1974). And why not? The cop on the beat was corrupt, save for Serpico, and the self-appointed vigilante or rogue lawman who'd been cleaning up the streets was beginning to appear tired (gun-wielding Charles Bronson seemed to have a film out every other week). What the film did for Hoffman wasn't much, other than to maintain his rep for appearing in properties of quality and integrity and to boost his box office clout. It would be boosted even further in his next release, based, too, on a best-seller but one with pulpier appeal.

Marathon Man was posterized simply and declaratively as "A thriller." Pauline Kael called it a Jewish revenge fantasy, which it certainly also is. (While this was relatively unique at the time, there'd be more, most notably Steven Spielberg's *Munich*, 2005.) Throughout the '70s, rumors and discoveries of hiding Nazi war criminals began to surface regularly. The same year that *Marathon Man* was released, the best-selling paperback was Ira Levin's *The Boys from Brazil*. William Goldman, though, had been the first pulp novelist to play with the notion, before adapting it to film.

In the film, Hoffman is Babe Levy, a Columbia history major working on his dissertation, which touches on the 20-year-old suicide of his blacklisted father. When Babe's jet-setting older brother Doc gets in too deep with a coterie of mysterious middlemen abetting hiding war criminals, the dark circle in which Doc operates begins to close in on his younger brother, leading to a new twist on the old Western showdown: Jew vs. German.

The work, while a thriller, is semi-autobiographical. Goldman was working out a lot of his issues through the proceedings: the suicide of his father (a failed salesman), the pain of operating in the shadow of a successful older brother (the playwright James Goldman), and, of course, his Jewish heritage. All of this is embodied in the central character of Babe Levy, who, throughout the story, plays victim (a lot!), hero, *naïf* and mastermind.

The role of marathoner Babe fit Hoffman as naturally as the sweaty jogging outfit he wears throughout most of the film. It touches on many of the bents he, as an actor, had long been cultivating: the underdog persona, the quiet, winning flirtatiousness, the plain man–handsome man dynamic, the collision of contrasting worlds, the romantic betrayal and, most obviously, the unassuming liberal-intellectual put in touch with his inner capacity for vengefulness (back to *Straw Dogs*).

It's the latter that critics were most vocal about, some appreciating that the film allowed the Jews to exact revenge on their one-time oppressors, others calling the idea offensively fanciful. And there was division about director John Schlesinger's ability to create suspense, some feeling that the crosscutting of scenarios and locations disrupted the film's overall momentum. (This same criticism that had been applied to his *Midnight Cowboy*.) Others were perfectly satisfied with the percentage of incidents to which the director gave his full Hitchcockian attention, suitably enhanced by Conrad Hall's dark cinematography and Michael Small's modern, minimalist score.

Hoffman got to display his full range in the film. And while there's plenty of opportunity for self-indulgent showiness, he consistently opts for low-key authenticity. As a result, while he has his share of big moments—many affirming what a great *re*actor he is—it's one of his least bombastic yet most accomplished performances.

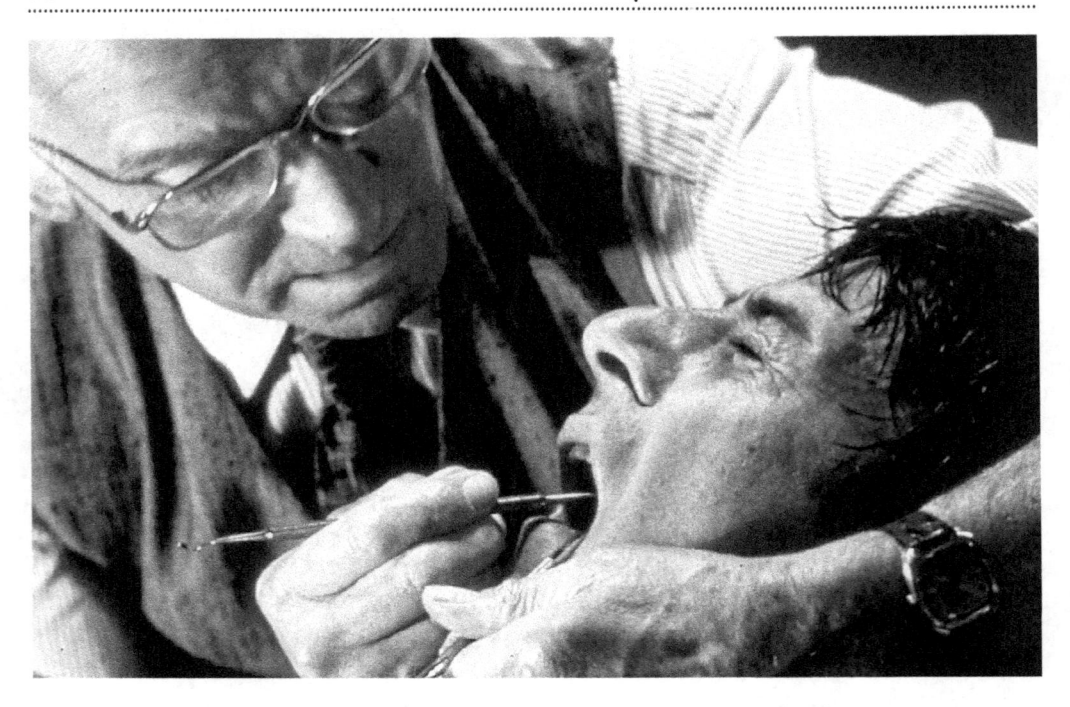

Laurence Olivier and Dustin Hoffman in *Marathon Man* (1976). At the time, Olivier rivaled Brando for the title of world's greatest male screen actor (Paramount/Photofest).

Hoffman was paired with Laurence Olivier, by that time a revered Old Master of the classical tradition having a high personal time collecting sizable salaries in unabashedly commercial films. And for all of the action, Olivier almost steals this one. His septuagenarian Nazi is at once avuncular, chilling, histrionic and nuanced. He and Hoffman enjoy a handful of strong scenes together, exuding mutual respect and mercifully eschewing one-upmanship.

After the twin successes of *President's Men* and *Marathon Man*, both of which had been projects into which Hoffman had been parachuted, Hoffman finally made good on that deal with First Artists. At last, he would be imposing his control over self-selected properties, giving audiences (at least that had been the hope) Hoffman in toto.

He would even direct the first film himself—or so he had planned, until he had come to feel, early in the shoot, that the added responsibility was taking away from his performance. Enter Ulu Grosbard, the old, trusted bud with whom Hoffman had worked on *Who Is Harry Kellerman?*

Six years earlier, Hoffman had bought the rights to the novel *No Beast So Fierce*, the tale of an L.A.-based career thief and his struggle to assimilate into society after a prison stint in Folsom. You can imagine the prep: Hoffman not only hung out with ex-cons, he went so far as to have himself incarcerated—all of this to access his inner tough guy. Studios were never going to cast him in that role, so here was a chance for Hoffman to reassert himself as a character actor capable of anything, this time by playing a disco-age James Cagney. With his greasy locks, drooping 'stache and Billy Martin temperament, Hoffman, as the paroled and perplexed Max Dembo, struts his way through a revealing polemic on the dead-end life of ex-cons.

The good-hearted Dembo operates in a universe where nothing is truly pardonable; he's stigmatized by his parole officer, the working world, even his own kind. The woman who enters his life, played by a young but impressively genuine Theresa Russell, has her doubts about his ability to reform. She compartmentalizes her feelings until Max has had enough of society's lack of faith in his rehabilitation. He not only returns to his original ways, he takes them to dangerous new heights.

The role was a clear, decided departure for Hoffman, in more ways than simply converting himself into a menacing presence (convincing as he is, though, we never fear him physically). In *Straight Time*, as opposed to his earlier films, it is Hoffman who is the inciter of violence, repeatedly. It's as if he's still in *Straw Dogs* but this time, as one of the villagers. His relationship with women is different too. Hoffman is the aggressor this time, playing it cool instead of nervy, and, in the end, the betrayer, when he leaves Russell's character instead of taking her on the lam, an act of latent protectionism. Like the more traditional male heroes Hoffman helped dethrone, he's the lone wolf here, self-reliant, distrustful of even his closest associates, operating by his own inviolable code.

One has to think that while Hoffman had procured the source material much earlier, his attraction to the part increased with the shift in the cultural zeitgeist. By 1978, disco was king. It was a movement not simply rooted in catchy, repetitive dance music, but in a renaissance in physicality. The '60s had been about being part of a group; "United, we can change the world" had been the thinking. By the late '70s, those battles were in the rearview mirror; it was time to kick back and indulge in personal pleasures: dancing, drugs and especially sex. Cultural critics called practitioners of this lifestyle "The Me Generation"—and indeed, the films that Hoffman and his contemporaries were making are anchored on singular characters. For men, disco's premium on the body manifested itself as a showy return to "the macho ethic" (the Village People's "Macho Man" was one of the year's biggest pop hits). Fed up with being formed by feminism, men went back to their pre-sexual revolution roots. They worked out (note Hoffman's impressive body in the film), donned unbuttoned shirts and tight pants, and prided themselves on their sexual prowess, usually with "love 'em and leave 'em" one-night stands. This phenomenon shot shallower actors like Burt Reynolds and John Travolta to the top and suggested that the more substantial Hoffman and those of his generation had grown too complex for such superficial times.

So here was Hoffman, getting with the program, among a dynamic cast of supporting players: Russell, M. Emmet Walsh, Gary Busey, Harry Dean Stanton, even a young Kathy Bates. It's a solid, underrated piece of work. Looking at it today, it's difficult to discern why Hoffman ended up so disgruntled with it, aside from the limited distribution it received. His ire would result in an image-tarnishing lawsuit, but not before the release of his next First Artists film.

That film was the equally maligned *Agatha*, a European product which, for all of its troubled history, would prove a modest hit. For Hoffman, it was another case of a character specifically fabricated to bag American distribution. As in *Papillon*, his job, like writer Kathleen Tynan's, was to make something of this afterthought of a part. (Tynan was the one-time wife of bad boy theater critic Kenneth, perhaps a model for Hoffman's role.)

It certainly helped that Hoffman's company was producing the picture, affording him a lot of say.

In December 1926, murder mystery maven Agatha Christie, then at the height of her success, disappeared without a trace for 11 days. Tynan's book and screenplay have her running away from an unhappy marriage and hiding in a spa. There, while secretly plotting against her husband's recently revealed mistress, she's wooed by a dapper American. Unbeknownst to her, he's a reporter, out to blow the whistle on her whereabouts … until, of course, he develops a personal interest in her.

It was another opportunity for Hoffman to break type. This time, he'd be a dashing, mysterious figure, relegated to the shadows where he would pensively blow clouds of cigarette smoke and cultivate an old-fashioned air of ambiguity. In a daring and curious break from habit, Hoffman doesn't act through much of the film so much as pose; he seems strangely satisfied to be operating in the realm of ideal. Further stunting the development of his character, Hoffman's Wally Stanton, star reporter, is a single-minded obsessive. He wants his story; any expression of anything else is simply a ruse to procure it—so much so that when the film asks us to believe that he has developed real feelings for the woman he's stalking, it's a tough sell.

Perhaps that's also a product of the chilly offset chemistry between Hoffman and co-star Vanessa Redgrave. During production, trade papers were crowded with tales of their mutual dislike. Redgrave was a vocal supporter of the Palestinian cause, a position that understandably rattled the Jewish Hoffman. Their relationship grew worse, until their incompatibility was as dramatic as their differences in height.

The film, then, like Hoffman's performance, is well-intentioned, interesting, yet ultimately unconvincing.

It's easier to see Hoffman's issues with *Agatha*, however, than it is his objection to *Straight Time*. Still, the willy-nilly quality of the two films was enough to prompt Hoffman to file a multimillion-dollar lawsuit against First Artists. He accused the company of seizing control of both movies, a violation of his contractually recognized creative prerogative. Hoffman asked for an injunction against editing, distribution and exhibition. He lost and was countersued by a First Artists co-conspirator, Jarvis Astaire, Hoffman's former business manager.

Fortunately, the actor's time in the woods was short. Despite his reputation as a frustrated renaissance man, he was invited to participate in someone else's project beyond the capacity of actor. Contractually, he would be awarded generous input on the script, the right to request additional takes and/or improvise, and approval of the final cut—not to mention a then-hefty million dollar salary plus a substantial piece of the profits.

That film was *Kramer vs. Kramer*, an examination of the burgeoning "house daddy" movement. The sexual revolution of the late '60s and early '70s had created a spike in the North American divorce rate, and with it, single parenthood. And while women still did the bulk of the child-rearing, as custody battles were largely decided in their favor, more and more men were assuming the kinds of parental duties that had hitherto been considered "women's work."

Ted Kramer is a busy ad executive with scant time for his young family. When his wife sucker punches him with the news that she's leaving both him and their only child, Ted's thrown into the topsy-turvy world of work-life balance. In time, however, he grows comfortable with his new domestic duties—so much so that he battles his wife in court for the right to rear their perpetually pouty seven-year-old.

From the moment he was presented with the first draft of writer-director Robert Benton's script, adapted from Avery Corman's obscure novel, Hoffman recognized much of his own life in the story. By this time, he was a freshly divorced single father sharing custody of two young daughters. Given his substantial creative stake in the production, Hoffman set out to ensure that the narrative accurately reflected the emotional reality of single parenthood. He wanted to be able to draw from his own recent experiences as much as possible; no script had ever been so conducive to his subscription to the Method.

Kramer represents a major step on a thematic path Hoffman had been following, on and off, throughout his career: the effort to understand women. When Hoffman-Kramer whispers to his heartbroken son that his mother's absence is attributable to his father's inability to rightfully accept her dimensionality, then reiterates that contention in the Third Act courtroom battle, it's Hoffman himself finally getting the proverbial message. As such, Hoffman-Kramer spoke for the archetypical '70s male, whose long journey from confused patriarch to obliging partner was, by 1979, aspiring to completion.

For writer-director Benton, *Kramer* was another work anchored on a complicated central relationship between colorful but common people, a dynamic he'd been

Dustin Hoffman's work in the '70s constituted a progressive investigation into the opposite sex. He unleashed his deep-seated maternalism in *Kramer vs. Kramer* (1979) (Columbia/Photofest).

relying on since his *Bonnie and Clyde* screenplay; it would continue through successive efforts such as *The Late Show* (1977), *Still of the Night* (1982), and *Nadine* (1987).

And indeed, the sincere proletarianism of *Kramer* is what ingratiated the film to audiences. The film validated much of the middle-class experience at that time, spawning equally successful reflections of familial dysfunction (for example, Robert Redford's *Ordinary People*, 1981). As such, *Kramer* upstaged the much more ballyhooed *Apocalypse Now* in 1979 both at the box office and on the awards circuit, the latter providing too otherworldly to bring its ugly reality, the Vietnam conflict, home.

And Hoffman is terrific in it, making the film a rare instance of an actor exercising large-scale interference and having the picture end up the better for it. For a performer obsessed with authenticity, this was Hoffman's most realistic portrayal to date. Try finding a trace of the sometime-character actor who adopts poses or affectations to imprint himself on an audience. And unlike his other go-to persona, the unsettled ingenue, Hoffman's Ted Kramer, while just as vexed as those personalities, exudes a maturity and confidence throughout his tribulations; these are new additions to the actor's arsenal. *Kramer*, then, is Hoffman's *Last Tango in Paris*, the film in which, like his idol Brando in that controversial classic, he unabashedly exhibits the most of his true self (but unlike Brando, suffered no post-production regrets).

Not to say that this was a new Hoffman in all ways. So vested was he in the film that he ran roughshod over his fellow actors. Meryl Streep, a wan, freckled newbie playing the other Kramer, was consistently taunted by the actor, all in the name of promoting the on-screen tension between them. Streep, soon to become a legendary craftsperson herself, went on record labeling Hoffman's behavior as excessive. She wasn't the last of his co-stars to make such pronouncements.

The Best Actor Oscar Hoffman received for his performance (his first) gave him the clout to press his professional agenda even further. Now, there would be no stopping his insistence on rewrites, directorial input and other forms of aesthetic control he'd been trying to procure since his messy litigious days as part of First Artists. It would make the production of his next film a veritable nightmare for his co-creators—also, a smashing success, one so big it even topped *Kramer*: *Tootsie*.

America, where, it was long said, "men are men and women are women," loves to switch genders. At least for laughs. The joke of the cross-dressing all–American man goes back to the days of vaudeville and extends through to Billy Wilder's *Some Like It Hot* (1959), still considered the single best film comedy ever produced. But by 1982, after the advent of the sexual revolution, the rise of feminism and the growing integration of gay culture, the joke had lost its potency. Yes, a serial practitioner of gender-bender comedy remained at large, writer-director Blake Edwards, but his work, while still popular, was considered old-fashioned and forced. *Tootsie* breathed new life into that age-old comic convention.

The film, per Hoffman's dictates, was an examination of two distinctly Hoffmanian matters: the life of the working actor and the inability of men to achieve synchronicity with women. With *Tootsie*, Hoffman's avatar takes the latter issue head-on, his Michael Dorsey going so far as to try on a woman's skin to definitively comprehend the opposite sex.

Dorsey is a struggling New York actor who, because of his smallish body type and inextinguishable intensity, can't get a break. (This is clearly Hoffman recreating his hungry years.) Desperate, he disguises himself as a frumpy, spirited, middle-aged woman. As such, he scores a cult following on a TV soap opera. Unfortunately, he then falls for a co-star (the tense, angular Jessica Lange), unleashing a light-hearted bedroom farce that became so appreciated, *Tootsie* ended up as the highest-grossing comedy of the 1980s (a decade that included such comic juggernauts as *Back to the Future*, 1985, and *Ferris Bueller's Day Off*, 1986).

While Hoffman is to be commended for continuously trying to bridge the gender gap, particularly in both *Kramer* and *Tootsie*, feminist critics had a different take on this career-long commitment. Wrote Molly Haskell, lamenting the absence of star vehicles for women throughout the '70s,

> Oh yes, we finally did get a couple of mainstream feminist films. One, about the three-ring circus, familiar to working women, of trying to hold down a job, raise a kid and run a household all at the same time, and who got the role? Dustin Hoffman, in *Kramer vs Kramer*. And the other, the story of a woman "of a certain age" and homeliness struggling to make her way, and fighting off harassment, in a man's world. And what was it? *Tootsie*, with (yet again) Dustin Hoffman as the actor who has his consciousness raised and his sexual complacency punctured, in the course of his travails as a very plain woman.[8]

That said, Haskell lauds the odd aspect of the latter for providing what was so sorely missed:

> The scenes in which Jessica Lange and Hoffman become friends, then intimates—those moments in which two very different kinds of women discover a bond in their mutual vulnerability—set off with infinite grace the image of "sisterhood" that we expected to be the grand theme of the decade.[9]

Then there's Susan Dworkin, in her excellent chronicle on the making of the film: "Hoffman was not looking for the truth about women. He was looking for the woman in himself."[10] Nevertheless, when graded against his contemporaries, it is Hoffman who evolves most over the '70s in his attitude toward women, embodying the feminist era man as he struggles to make the adaptations dictated by the fight for an egalitarian universe.

By the time of *Tootsie,* Hackman had temporarily retired, Nicholson's career was in anticlimactic mode, Pacino was making flops, Duvall was still largely a supporting actor, and De Niro had fallen into smaller, more idiosyncratic work. So *Tootsie* served as another type of climax for Hoffman: the summit of his career.

The film's instant iconic status firmly fitted the crown of America's Greatest Male Actor atop Hoffman's head. But tabloid tales of his neurotic intensity both at the development and shooting stages added tarnish to that headpiece. It showed America his process, revealing him as the Method Actor's Method Actor. In so doing, it solidified his growing reputation as an overzealous, self-righteous, perennially dissatisfied meddler. Method actors had always been extremists, doing all kinds of things for the sake of creating credibility. Hoffman had now upstaged them all. It made him both highly respected and detrimentally feared.

Gene Hackman

A Sorry Son of a Bitch

He always maintained that he looked like a potato. And for the duration of his formative years as an actor, his proletariat visage, coupled with his admitted immaturity, afforded Gene Hackman few professional favors. Mind you, his closest buds in the acting racket—Dustin Hoffman and Robert Duvall—were no pretty boys either (though the three did occasionally chum around with the then equally unknown Robert Redford). This circumstance was partly responsible for their exodus, one by one, from California to New York and the more physically forgiving world of theater.

Before Hackman was bitten by the acting bug (he had been a field radio operator in the Marine Corps), the military taught him to work hard; besides, he was out to show that institution up, after a one-time superior had written him off in civilian life as "a sorry son of a bitch." Hackman would use the military's own sweat 'n' blood ethic, then, against them, lauding their professionalism, yes, but just as often exposing their questionable extremism (*March or Die,* 1977, *Uncommon Valor,* 1983, *Bat*21*, 1987, *Crimson Tide*, 1995).

If contemporary Hoffman was always out to display confusion, and Duvall the burden of properly playing the game, Hackman was on a career-long mission to prove himself. His characters, while operating in a highly structured environment, go zealously rogue within the system. The "above and beyond" is their concern, often incurring reprimand, heartbreak, even death. You don't go around manhandling drug dealers in New York City, even if you're a narc (*The French Connection*); you don't save innocent hides by sacrificing your own life, noble as that may be (*The Poseidon Adventure*, 1972); you don't let the town drunk take over your basketball team, especially not in buttoned-down Indiana (*Hoosiers*, 1986).

Hackman was a rebel then, if an older, more self-serving one. Still, it was enough for movie audiences in a rebellious time—the '70s—to elevate him to marquee status. They fell for other aspects of him too: his grounding simplicity, his folksy fieriness, his Henry Fonda–like moments of taciturn Midwestern self-reflection. (Though Hackman was a native Californian, he had been raised in Illinois and Iowa.) Hackman was common, in both senses of the word: base yet decent.

Like his brethren, it was the discovery of Brando that had convinced him that there might be a place for him on screen. "I saw in Brando some kind of kinsmanship," he admitted, "not because of the way he looked but something inside him that let me say: *I can do that.*"[1] Previously, Hackman's hero had been James Cagney, the quintessential street tough whose on-screen persona, like Hackman's in both actuality and the movies, was perpetually propelled by personal vendetta. As Gary Giddins put it, people came to watch Cagney "assert and defy authority."[2] And like Brando, Cagney radiated a plebeian authenticity.

Cagney- and Brando-inspired, Hackman embarked on that now famous pilgrimage, with Hoffman and Duvall on his tail, from LaLaLand to The Big Apple. He'd spend the early '60s honing his craft in top-rated television series and off-Broadway productions—this, chancily, while raising a family. In time, there'd be a hit-and-miss career on the big stage: One production ran over 900 performances; two others closed after a single night. These were interpolated with the odd stint on the big screen. Such was the Hollywood–New York divide at the time that to *real* actors, i.e., those in the East, film was a poseur's medium. It meant easy, dirty money that would allow you to keep working in more legitimate circumstances. It was a popular philosophy to which Hackman unabashedly subscribed. Then, on a recommendation from Warren Beatty (with whom Hackman had worked in his second film, 1964's *Lilith*), Hackman was cast in *Bonnie and Clyde*.

I'll spare you yet another chronicle of that seminal film's history, as books, documentaries, essays and blogs continue to recount it. The short version is that Robert Benton and David Newman wrote it, Warren Beatty nurtured it, Arthur Penn directed it, Jack Warner hated it, Bosley Crowther panned it, Pauline Kael defended it, and audiences loved it. Oh—and it made a dependable character actor out of Hackman. So much so that in its aftermath, Hackman, by his own admission, took almost everything that came through the door. After years as a struggling actor, here was an opportunity to enjoy a sustained period of good, steady income; he would exploit it while it lasted. What ensued was a lot of crap, which, in the end, would mercifully constitute career footnotes. These were mid-sized parts in middling films: *The Split* (1968), *Riot* (1968), *Marooned* (1969), *Doctors' Wives* (1970) and *The Hunting Party* (1971), though that list does include a couple of curios considered cult classics: *The Gypsy Moths* (1969) and *Cisco Pike* (1972).

In the middle of the muddle was a part that, while not sizable, planted the seeds for the signature persona Hackman would develop throughout the '70s: *Downhill Racer* (1969).

The eponymous character is Dave Chappellet, a taciturn hotshot on the U.S. ski team preparing for the Winter Olympics. Chappellet, who posits himself above his teammates, mixes it up repeatedly with his no-nonsense coach, whose job is to keep the boys in line during their collective quest for gold. Aside from a half-hearted love story that takes up too much of the film, that's it. Then again, it was written by novelist James Salter, renowned for his elliptical style, and directed by Michael Ritchie, then an accomplished documentarian transitioning to drama.

The film belongs to Ritchie and the man who gambled on him, star Robert Redford. It was Redford's first opportunity to show off his much-loved Colorado and Utah to mainstream audiences (though there are scenes set in Austria, France and Switzerland), with another of his low-key, driven heroes composed of shaky certainty playing host. And he and Ritchie shared a greater agenda: to capture the subworld of competitive downhill skiing as realistically as possible.

For Ritchie, a master of milieu, this meant countless cameras, copious cuts and stupefying sound design. This hybridization of documentary and dramatic form would serve him well over the first, and best, part of his career, most notably in his revisionist family film *The Bad News Bears* (1976).

Hackman's *Downhill Racer* character—Eugene Clair, Chapellet's coach—is a limited, obligatory affair, almost thankless. Nevertheless, it established a persona he was asked to replicate repeatedly. In a significant break from high-flyin' Buck Barrow in *Bonnie and Clyde*, Hackman here is a cold-blooded authoritarian, the Alpha, the mentor, the example. His primary tasks are to read people the riot act, contextualize their circumstances in no uncertain terms, and lead the charge in a difficult, sometimes impossible pursuit, often at great reputational, personal or collective cost. Sounds like a throwback, particularly to past patriarchal personalities like Spencer Tracy. And indeed, for all of his love of Cagney, there is a trace too of Tracy in Hackman, particularly the former's succinct summation of the art of acting: "You just look the other actor in the eye and tell him the truth." But Hackman updates the archetype, subtly but significantly. For all of Coach Claire's focus and bluster, a humanist instinct seeps through. Going forward, many of Hackman's characterizations will be people not entirely convinced that what they're so zealously advocating is the proper cause; a secret doubt is at work within the recesses of their souls, not only about the dire nature of the situation or task at hand but about their abilities to rise to the challenge and inspire others to do same. There's an existential doom about these characters, which they have to work hard to suppress to practice the practicality they preach. In this small, palpable way, Hackman quietly augments the A-type American man—not with a lot of shouting and sweating and emoting *à la* Brando, but by craftily revealing small cracks within the armor. He recalibrates an old type for a new, angst-ridden era.

Some of this was, no doubt, rooted in—you guessed it!—Hackman's relationship with his father, the primary role model in his life. Hackman's paterfamilias left the family when Gene was all of 13, making way for Gene's inclusion in the post–Brando pantheon of actors who, like their idol, would repeatedly argue with authority figures on-screen and off. In that, these performers would find themselves in sync with their audience, who, too, in those years, the '60s and '70s, were in the heated throes of a generational divide.

No film in the collective catalogue of Hackman and his brethren explored this dynamic so directly and at length as the modest melodrama *I Never Sang for My Father* (1970). It's a small film, never daring to stray too far from its off–Broadway roots; play and film, in fact, shared a producer-director, Gilbert Cates. The project was given the green light based on the success of a previous play-movie father-son dogfight, *The Subject Was Roses* (1968). And still it was a hard sell.

In 1970, the critic was king. Film had become an intellectual chew toy, elevating newspaper hacks and ivory tower pundits with high to middling cinematic I.Q.s into a make-or-break judge and jury. If your picture got the gold seal from tough cookies Pauline Kael, Andrew Sarris or John Simon, the highbrows were sure to go; if the populists like Roger Ebert, Rex Reed or Charles Champlin liked it, the common element would attend. The nervous, pushy campaign for *I Never Sang for My Father* borrowed from both camps, devising a poster that was nothing but print media superlatives from across the critical spectrum. But it didn't work. A mile-high pile of cross-audience encomiums could do little for an old-fashioned drama in an era of edgy relevancy (*Five Easy Pieces*) and satirical spectacle (*Patton*).

Hackman here is another Gene, Garrison, a teacher and writer under the thumb of his oppressive father. Both are widowed. Gene longs to start his life over in California but cannot get himself to separate from his Machiavellian father, a suburban New Yorker in failing health. Things come to a head in a sanitized version of the father-son confrontations then epidemic across America. (Pop folkie Cat Stevens even had a hit album cut about it.)

Play-like as the film is, it offers a glimpse of Hackman the stage actor. While he's miscast—he's too old and too naturally savvy for the part of the infantilized son— he does his best, feigning innocence through his sad, open face and wallowing deftly in mixed emotions. Melvyn Douglas, with his hawkish bluster, plays an age-spotted version of the kind of role otherwise synonymous with Hackman: the authority figure brought to face his limitations. They spar until, spurned in part by his sympathetic sister (a tempered Estelle Parsons), they come to their climactic confrontation.

Aside from the opportunity for an old movie fan to work with Studio Era survivor Douglas, Hackman classified the making of the film as a deeply depressing experience. Its central dynamic was very close to the bone, aggravating a deep Freudian wound. He'd play the oppressed party again in *Night Moves* (1975), but that character would remain his own man. Gene Garrison, conversely, could only dream of becoming one.

After the integrity of *I Never Sang*, and the surprise Oscar nod that came with it, it was back to the surer bets and easier paychecks: Hackman was asked to rescue a cop picture inspired by the mega-hit *Bullitt* (1968). The film's director, a Chicago wise guy with four wonky pictures to his name, was having problems with the first-time actor he had insisted upon for the central part. Further, he was struggling to make something more out of the film than a mere excuse for a car chase.

At the time of William Friedkin's *The French Connection*, the cop on the street was garnering a bad reputation. Too many were proving ineffectual or corrupt, while others were violently doing the bidding of the Nixon-voting generation determined to put down the counterculture. *French Connection*, mind you, wasn't out to right that reputation but instead to show its necessity. There was only one way to clean up the streets, especially as drugs were becoming international big business. That was by letting America's most presumptive, pro-active policemen propel the paddy wagon. In so doing, however, the line between the criminal and the cop was blurred—the thesis, according to Friedkin, of *The French Connection*. And indeed, many a critic upon the film's initial release complained of not being able to clearly delineate the white hats from the black. Stereotypes, they had yet to realize, were out. American film was transitioning to a new, dimensional kind of hero.

Hence, Popeye Doyle, the porkpie-hatted hothead played by Hackman (his next nervy narc, after *Cisco Pike*). Popeye and his partner "Cloudy" Russo (Roy Scheider) tail a Brooklyn candy shop owner for kicks, only to discover he's the middleman in an international transaction that will import $32 million worth of heroin into New York City. A non-stop game of cat-and-mouse is put into motion, with the volatile, unstoppable Popeye chasing down the operation's elusive mastermind (Fernando Rey, in a take on the suave Hitchcockian villain).

In translating this true account of New York City's then-biggest drug bust to the screen, Friedkin, who had a background in news and documentary, set out to authenticate the life of the street cop, feeling it had been tragically sanitized by prime-time TV. He met a kindred spirit in Hackman, the devout Method man, who'd been parachuted into the production to replace *New York Post* columnist Jimmy Breslin. (It's impossible to imagine Breslin in the role, given its high degree of physicality.) Hackman and Scheider based their performances on real-life detectives Eddie Egan and Sonny Grosso. (Egan is in the film as their superior, and soon appeared in a few more, including the even more autobiographical *Badge 373*, 1973.). The actors shadowed their role models for weeks (as had Friedkin before them), even appropriating their insider's verbalisms. Said Scheider of the film after shooting, "We didn't know how good it would be, but we did know it'd be the most authentic cop movie made up to that time."[3]

Hackman's first reaction upon scrutinizing the script: "When I first read the part, it seemed like a chance to do all those things I watched Jimmy Cagney do as a kid."[4] And Hackman does, throwing ripostes and roundhouses repeatedly. It was a capacity, for all of his admiration of tough-guy Cagney, that did not come easily. He had issues with the more psychotic aspects of the character, as well as his racism. (The film, with its victimization of black citizenry, foreshadows the age of Rodney King, TV's *Cops*, 1989–2022, and the George Floyd tragedy.) But Friedkin, a kind of Machiavellian, Popeye-style character himself, clearly helped his star unleash his inner demons.

As a result, Hackman's Popeye is a zealous philistine, redeemed only by the fact that he happens to be on the side of justice. Declaring a one-man war on the drug trade the way he does, Hackman-Doyle served at the time as urban America's id, its primal instinct to clean up the streets with a personal primitivism.

While the film targets America's black population (excusing itself via the addition of a black informer and a villainous, Bondian mastermind who is a white European), it owes a lot to the then-popular blaxploitation pictures: the same conventions and locations (over 80 of New York City's drug-dealing hot spots), the same primal violence, the same urban energy. Friedkin, in his autobiography, likened the film to that genre's Studio Era predecessor: the B-movie. And that's exactly how it was treated by Fox, which gave it an underwhelming release, in some cases as the add-on in drive-in–designated double features. But audience response exceeded expectations, necessitating wider distribution. The film went on to surprise its detractors even more by winning the Best Picture Oscar. Hackman received a Best Actor Oscar for a portrayal he had mixed feelings about—then, over time, be classified it as a classic.

Both the film's premise and the behavior of its central character helped popularize the vigilante genre, street-set revenge fantasies that dominated screens until the mid-decade mark. As for Hackman, never again would he present the persona he had established in *Downhill Racer* in such impactful, unadulterated form.

Previously, while his characters could be stern, they prided themselves on keeping a cool head. In Popeye Doyle's New York City, however, a cool head would have let criminals walk. Let the higher-ups dispense the kind of cautionary advice that prior Hackman characters might have; Popeye operates on a level above decorum, a place where redemption, both the personal and the social, is synonymous with radicalism.

Another interesting aspect of the film: In an industry where the leading narrative is the little guy defeating the big guy, here, it doesn't happen. The big guy gets away with the crime, creating that American cinematic rarity in a hit: an anticlimax. (Sequels weren't a thing yet, so an open door like that was a rarity.) Doyle's effectiveness is a matter of serious question. We cheer for him as he hunts down his prospective assassin in a car vs. El train race (which indeed outdoes the centerpiece of *Bullitt*), but in the end, particularly given his indifference to having accidentally killed a colleague, we question the emotional investment we have afforded him. Film was, in 1971, growing up. Until the return of classical genres and values in the neo-con '80s, heroes would remain complicated and justice a tricky affair.

The French Connection's surprise success catapulted Hackman to star status. Suddenly, he was that most improbable of personas, one he was certain his everyman's looks would prevent him from attaining. (An English critic once described him as having the mad, ill-assembled features of "a puppet carved from packing-case wood."[5])

Hackman joined colleague Dustin Hoffman, as well as the up-and-coming Jack Nicholson, as part of a new breed of bankable male stars. The following year, Pacino and Duvall joined the ranks, then, in 1974, De Niro.

Let John Wayne ride into the sunset and leave Steve McQueen's cool to cool. Big-screen American manliness had a new spokesperson, one shaped by the times: urban, angry, and conflicted.

Stardom both gratified and worried Hackman, an admitted waffler. Convinced of success' ephemeral quality, and subscribing to a working actor's mindset, he threw himself into too many pictures, striking while the iron was steaming. First up, a decidedly offbeat comedy-adventure that had been in production before *French Connection* was released: the Lee Marvin vehicle *Prime Cut* (1972). It reunited Hackman with director Michael Ritchie.

Marvin, the lanky, wintry toughie who had surprised audiences and critics alike with his comic turn in the patently playful Western *Cat Ballou* (1965), was in the dying days of a win streak that had included *Point Blank* (1967) and *The Dirty Dozen* (1969). As an actor, Marvin never had much in his arsenal—a condemning glare, a lazily direct baritone and a masochistic mien—but it had been enough. (Let's face it: Careers have been built on less. Vin Diesel?)

Unlike the genre films in which the Old School Marvin had made his name, American movies were growing more personal, more relevant, more offbeat. Hence Marvin the anachronism found himself in *Prime Cut*, a dark, idiosyncratic action-comedy wherein a Chicago-based gangster breaks up a sex slave operation run by a group of greasy Kansas City meat producers.

The film was Ritchie's follow-up to his inaugural feature, *Downhill Racer*. And

Gene Hackman as a new kind of cop in *The French Connection* (1971). Critics complained that you could no longer distinguish the good guys from the bad (20th Century–Fox/Photofest).

while his documentarian pedigree remains in evidence—the film is part travelogue through the American heartland—Ritchie was transitioning to quirky satirist, as attested by his succeeding pictures *The Candidate* (1972), *Smile* (1975) and *The Bad News Bears*. In all cases, Ritchie's primary target is celebratory America:

- its iconic public rituals (county fairs in *Prime Cut*'s case)
- political rallies
- beauty pageants
- baseball games

—all with their spangly, *e pluribus unum* spirit on the outside and their divisive, dangerous dynamics on the in. *Prime Cut* is the first, and least successful, of these examinations. While there are certainly comic highlights—a play on Hitchcock's *North by Northwest* (1959) in which Marvin and the wide-eyed maiden-in-distress (Sissy Spacek, in her film debut) are pursued through an open field by a combine harvester—too many of the others miss the cockeyed mark.

Hackman put a mere six weeks in on the film, relying on his knowledge of the crass Midwestern types with whom he had grown up. Echoing Buck Barrow, he heartily gladhands and roughhouses as the story's unabashedly capitalist-sexist baddie, upping his natural *bonhomie* and relying on his signature chuckle of self-satisfaction.

Like the string of films in which he appeared between *Bonnie and Clyde* and *The French Connection*, however, *Prime Cut* was but a footnote. Hackman was an Oscar winner now, affording him the unexpected opportunity to participate in the gamut of American film production. He'd start with a handful of personal indulgences: the chance to head an unabashedly commercial entertainment, *The Poseidon Adventure*, and the opportunity to recommit to his mettle as a character actor on a bigger scale than *Prime Cut* had allowed, with films like *Scarecrow* (1973) and *The Conversation* (1974).

Nineteen seventy saw the film adaptation of Arthur Hailey's *Airport*, the melodramatic best-seller about a hijacking gone awry. At the time, a skyjacking craze was in effect. Disgruntled American dissidents were laying claim to commercial airliners, bringing them to Fidel Castro for military re-purposing. There was no such Communist sympathizer in Hailey's book, however; the "baddie," like a lot of U.S. citizens circa 1970, was a middle-aged depressive fed up with the times, looking to kill himself (and, incidentally, others) to make good on an insurance policy. The novel's mix of soap and suspense served as a microcosm for the sorry circumstance of Nixon's "great silent majority," a hard-working generation that, thanks to the topsy-turvy zeitgeist, was watching the world they had built go to Hell. The country was in a disastrous state—so why not disaster movies?

Over the rest of the decade, planes and boats and trains, even roller coasters, would suffer improbable technical injuries (in 1974 alone, Universal was simultaneously building such booby traps as the doomed cityscape for *Earthquake*, the ill-fated zeppelin for *The Hindenburg* and the shark for *Jaws*). Only the brave—i.e., those with top billing—would stand a chance.

The chief architect of the "disaster picture" was Irwin Allen, the successful TV producer behind such homogenized sci-fi as *Voyage to the Bottom of the Sea* (1964-68) and *Lost in Space* (1965-68). After the success of *Airport*, Irwin entered the fray by purchasing the rights to *The Poseidon Adventure*, novelist Paul Gallico's allegorical tale of a capsized ocean liner and the messianic macho man who leads a small band of passengers to the promised land—aka safety. If *French Connection* had allowed Hackman to be Cagney, the film version of *Poseidon* permitted him to don the carapace of another of his heroes, Errol Flynn. (Hackman, the resilient ex-Marine, would even perform his own stunts in the film, including the underwater sequences.)

It's crass, oversized entertainment—full of sweaty, soot-stained faces breaking out into hysterics as they climb rusting scaffolding and squeeze themselves through secret passageways—in which Hackman seems happy to appear. And why not? His paycheck was the size of the eponymous boat, plus, he got to hang with a Who's Who of Hollywood relics (making the *Poseidon*, then, the original Love Boat). While his contemporaries looked down on that generation for its more superficial acting style (Robert Duvall in particular), Hackman reveled in it; he would rub shoulders with Studio Era royalty again in *The Domino Principle* (1977).

In this waterlogged Biblical allegory, Hackman's modern-day Moses lords over his people, preaching a homegrown philosophy of self-reliance and brotherly respect over dependency on institutional safekeeping—basically, the then-fashionable hippie ethic. Much of his dialogue, and he's not alone in this, is brazenly expository and unabashedly histrionic, but the undaunted Hackman takes it as seriously as he can, putting paid to old actors' adage, "They don't pay you to make good lines sound good—they pay you to make *bad* lines sound good." In fact, as the best (and most modern) actor in the cast, he brings a gravitas to the proceedings that makes the whole misadventure swallowable. He even redeems one of the film's corniest moments, Shelley Winters' death scene, with his plausibly teary reaction.

Having happily sold out—*Poseidon* was one of Hackman's all-time highest grossers—it was time to get back to legitimacy. A succession of character studies ensued, starting with *Scarecrow*.

To this day, Hackman considers the part he played in *Scarecrow*, an ambitious drifter who teams with a fellow vagabond on a catch-as-catch-can pilgrimage from Denver to Pittsburgh, his favorite. While the role lacks depth and dignity, anyone with biographical knowledge of the actor could well comprehend his appreciation. Hackman's hobo represents the proverbial "road not taken." It's who Hackman could have, might have, been had acting not come along. His was a nomadic existence full of loose ends and menial jobs, until the inspiration struck to try his mettle on the stage. It's no surprise, then, that the part seems to come to him with noticeable facility, fitting his bulky body like one of the countless, ragtag underlayers his myopic drifter dons in a constant obsession with bodily warmth.

Plus, Hackman had help: director Jerry Schatzberg, of *The Panic in Needle Park* (1971) fame, with his background in still photography. The film is mostly comprised of static takes, with minimal camera movement or cutaways—a long leash for an actor. As a result, Hackman gets to flex his stage chops. Paired with fellow powerhouse Al Pacino, Hackman and his co-star banter, feud, laugh, cry and scheme together, in a mix of pliable narrative and periodic ad-libbing. The surprise is their compatibility; off set, Pacino's inextinguishable intensity and Hackman's nine-to-five approach became, reputedly, a matter of friction (much like the characters they were playing who, mid-film, suffer a dramatic rift).

Critics correctly traced the central dynamic's roots to the lineage of road movies and buddy films that had immediately preceded it: *Butch Cassidy and the Sundance Kid*, *Easy Rider* and *Midnight Cowboy*, though it more obviously owes to something a lot older: John Steinbeck's novella (later play and twice, a film) *Of Mice and Men*. Hackman's the sharpie who calls the shots; Pacino's the innocent who gets in his way. Together, they chase a pipe dream, a journey marked by tragedy and sentimentality.

The ultimate consensus is that the film fell decidedly short of admittance to the dramatic pantheon that had inspired it. European critics disagreed, awarding it the interim equivalent of the Palme d'Or at the Cannes Film Festival. The film, particularly its first act, was very much in tune with the vapidness still fashionable in international cinema (a hangover from the popularity of Michelangelo Antonioni) predicated on barren, industrial landscapes (shot here, Italian-style, by Vilmos Zsigmond), off-point dialogue and existential ennui.

After the American failure of *Scarecrow*, Hackman began to suffer doubts about the fading nature of his star. So panicked, he clung to the classic show biz remedy for a flop: more work, fast! The next few years were Hackman's most prolific of the '70s. In '74, '75, and '77, he appeared in three releases a year (there was but one in '76). Nineteen seventy-four was a mixed bag, with the critically embraced *The Conversation*, the box office disappointment *Zandy's Bride* and a scene-stealing cameo in *Young Frankenstein.*

The best of the lot, *The Conversation*, is an existential spy thriller, written by Francis Coppola in the late '60s. Serendipity saw that the film wasn't realized until '74, just as the Watergate scandal was developing. As such, the film's milieu, the weird world of wiretapping, caught a cultural wave. Otherwise, it might have been classified as an example of Coppola returning to his pre–*Godfather* roots: a small, solemn personal piece in the manner of his melodramatic miniature *The Rain People* (1968).

When left to his own devices, Coppola's films suffer from thin narrative, staid momentum and incurable earnestness; when working at the behest of a Big Book, doing service work, or juggling multiple storylines, these flaws are rewardingly minimalized. But *The Conversation*, perhaps due to its Hitchcockian influence, perfectly combines Coppola the auteur and Coppola the hired hand. We get the best of both worlds, in a taut combination character study-murder mystery. Hackman, the film's unlikely star, is Harry Caul (okay, there's the obviousness of the nomenclature), a legendary surveillance man who eavesdrops on the part of big, mysterious clients. When his latest assignment puts him wise to the prospective murder of an innocent young couple, he experiences an uncharacteristic *crise de conscience*, propelling him into personal involvement.

As in *The Godfather*, Coppola is again dealing with the blurred line between the professional and the participatory. The other commonality is the Catholic premium on "sin," the weight of having wronged others either passively or actively. Michael Corleone conditioned himself into a veritable state of immunity from it and went on to head an empire; Harry Caul cannot eschew it and goes on to embroil himself in a scarring, self-revelatory misadventure. No stop at his neighborhood confessional, no objection to any flip use of the Lord's name can assuage the nagging discomfort of Caul's involuntary violation of the distance he so cautiously keeps from those on whom he spies.

The Conversation constituted an impressive departure for Hackman. Prior, most roles had depended, in part or in whole, on his natural gregariousness. Here, he takes on the kind of part tailor-made for Robert Duvall (who makes a thankless cameo): a respected, anonymous-looking outsider, invisible to all but his closest confidantes, who hold him up as a figure of suspect respect and who suffers his own small, mounting pangs of regret over the necessity of his actions. Caul's carefully constructed repression was at serious odds with Hackman's organic extroversion. Said Hackman of Caul, "He was really a constipated character."[6] Further, Caul's look—recessed hairline, horn-rimmed glasses, bushy mustache—put the actor in mind of his much-reviled father, adding to his discomfort. Nevertheless, Hackman delivers a masterfully nuanced performance, arguably his best of the decade.

Relying on his moody, self-reflective quality, Hackman slowly and systematically humanizes Harry. Each scene, whether a quiet episode with the few women in his life, a sweet'n'sour exchange with a co-worker or colleague, or the odd, climactic fit of temperament, builds a man in full, piece by piece. Framed within Coppola's creepy classicism, it's a subtle, hypnotic portrait of the price of our inviolable humanity.

The film won the Palme d'Or at Cannes—two in a row for Hackman films. He was becoming an art house staple, something good for your rep, bad for your bank account. So he signed on for two projects with (he hoped) wider appeal: the Western two-hander *Zandy's Bride* and a fun little caprice: the rare opportunity to do broad comedy via an unbilled pop-up in Mel Brooks' *Young Frankenstein*.

Starting in the '50s, the films of Swedish writer-director Ingmar Bergman began to make their way to America. These Strindbergian tragedies of manners became staples of the art film circuit; as Bergman's reputation grew, his name became synonymous with that specialized form of exhibition. Other Swedish filmmakers, while lacking Bergman's psychological and philosophical depth, would ride his coattails—among them, Bo Widerberg and Jan Troell.

Troell had scored hits with the twin epics *The Emigrants* (1971) and *The New Land* (1972), a two-part chronicle of nineteenth-century Swedish peasantry transitioning to the U.S. Now he was making that journey himself, settling in Hollywood to again examine the human cost of deracination, this time within the venerable framework of the Western. As Zandy, the implacable Big Sur mountain man who

Gene Hackman in *The Conversation* (1974), perhaps his finest characterization of the 1970s (Paramount/Photofest).

gambles on a mail order bride, Hackman was paired with the premier female member of Bergman's stock company, Liv Ullmann.

This interesting film is unique in Hackman's canon, and not just because it was one of his early Westerns, a genre through which he'd regain respectability come the 1990s (he won a second Oscar as the sadistic lawman in Clint Eastwood's bleakly revisionist *Unforgiven*, 1992). It's also one of the few that extends his relationship with the opposite sex.

It's not love-hate but hate-love. The film's central relationship starts on an antagonistic note, settles into a controversial sexual arrangement, then semi-successfully aspires to egalitarianism. It's a feminist Western, devoted largely to Hackman-Zandy's politicization. Zandy is the prototypical American male: resilient, hard-working and direct. To him, women are a sexual and reproductive convenience and a personal and practical inconvenience. He is asked, in no uncertain terms, by his imported, unyielding wife, to adjust his brutish, chauvinistic disposition. In a long, climactic exchange between the two, the tug of war they have been staging throughout the film's laconic 88 minutes is replaced by the war being fought inside Zandy, as he strives to accept a new model of co-habitation.

Hackman is particularly good in that final scene, one of the few in the film demanding dimension over steadfastness. Strangely for a treatise on the struggle of women, Ullmann isn't afforded the same opportunity; she's just shy of symbolic. There's some masterful cinematography, and a colorful and authentic supporting cast, including Harry Dean Stanton and Susan Tyrrell. But it's no surprise that the picture didn't bowl anybody over. It's small, thin, and in its own low-key manner, deludedly self-important.

After all of that Swedish sobriety (and rancor: Hackman and Troell clashed repeatedly), Hackman longed to do something fun. Enter high-flying Mel Brooks, as far from the somber Troell as the Catskills are from the Scandinavian Mountains.

Brooks, the forever "on" comedy writer and cult personality, was rivaling Woody Allen at the time as America's leading comic auteur. He had parlayed his scattergun style into the big-screen expansion of the movie spoofs he had crafted for Sid Caesar's *Your Show of Shows* (1950–54), then *Caesar's Hour* (1954–57). At the behest of star–co-writer Gene Wilder, Brooks followed up his wildly successful Western send-up *Blazing Saddles* (1974) with a parody of Universal's *Frankenstein* franchise. In the end, while the cast of this reverent-irreverent homage was stocked with the top comic actors of the day, Hackman almost stole the show as a lonely blind man blithely attempting to befriend the visiting Monster.

It was a rare opportunity for Hackman, hitherto synonymous with grit and gravitas, to unleash his inner sketch comic. He demonstrates just the right touch in an all-too-brief turn that is perfectly in tune with Brooks' vaudevillian sensibility. Hackman's hope had probably been that he'd be offered more of these kinds of opportunities. While he'd remain primarily valued as a dramatic commodity, the chance to play comedy would always put stars in his eyes, for better (*Superman*) or for worse (*Lucky Lady*, 1975).

Unlike '74, '75 would be a year of quality. While no film in which Hackman appeared could claim a place in the exalted roster of American cinema produced in that remarkable annum—*One Flew Over the Cuckoo's Nest, Jaws, Dog Day Afternoon, Nashville*—they all constituted respectable work, generally appreciated by critics and reasonably successful at the box office. Interestingly, all three were exhibited over a two-month, late-spring period.

Before the aforementioned *Jaws* created the "big summer release" phenomenon, the big studios considered June-July-August a soft time for films. Audiences, went the thinking, didn't go to the theater (exception: the drive-in); they went to the mountains or the beach. Films deemed worthy of attention were released just before audiences packed up their pup tents and bathing suits, and again after everybody had returned home and prepped the kids for school.

Hackman started the year by re-affixing that ironic pork pie to his head, in the inevitable follow-up (yes, sequels were a thing now, thanks to *The Godfather Part II*) to the film that had made him a star.

French Connection II is set in Marseilles, where Popeye Doyle is imported to finish the job he has left undone in New York City. Little does he know that the French authorities, with whom ugly American Doyle clashes volubly, are using him as bait to lure criminal drug lord Charnier (Fernando Rey, remember?) out of hiding. When Charnier becomes aware of Doyle's presence, he subjects him to drug-induced torture. Once an obtrusive manhunt for the missing foreigner is put into motion, Charnier lets Doyle go. Doyle dries out, reteams with his French collaborators and finally takes down the bad guy.

Hackman is much more comfortable in Doyle's skin here than in the original. All barriers that had once made access to the character so difficult—Doyle's racism and fanaticism—are removed. This time around, Hackman positively revels in them. He spends the film in a single-minded fever, ragging on the French, assaulting suspects, even going so far as to set a hotel on fire.

And there's a virtuosic showpiece when Doyle, subjected to repeated doses of heroin at the hands of his oily captors, is forced to go cold turkey. In a series of long takes, Hackman puts on a veritable one-man show, a red-hot mix of woozy defeatism, existential anguish and explosive protest. Any doubts he had created about his status as an actor, that he was a sizable talent throwing it away on facile blockbusters and dead-end character pieces, were, with these small, impactful scenes, triumphantly expunged.

The film was a comeback too for the semi-forgotten John Frankenheimer, taking over from William Friedkin as director. Like his star, Frankenheimer saw the film as a way to remind audiences that he too remained a talent to be taken seriously. He knew what he had in his lead, having worked with Hackman on the underrated *The Gypsy Moths*, and so encouraged and unleashed him. Further, the veteran helmsman redemonstrated his chilling propensity for subjecting his heroes to resonant psycho-physical rigors (*The Manchurian Candidate*, 1962, *Seconds*, 1966, and later, *The Island of Dr. Moreau*, 1996), as well as his great technical facility for action (*The Train*, 1964, *Grand Prix*, 1966, and later, *Ronin*, 1998).

Hackman's next move: *Night Moves* (1975). Director Arthur Penn, with whom Hackman had worked in *Bonnie and Clyde*, had, in that film, shapeshifted that classic male archetype, the gangster. After that, he proceeded to update the others: the cowboy (*Little Big Man*) and, with *Night Moves*, the Bogart-esque P.I. By '73, when *Night*

Moves was in production, the detective had long been out of fashion as a persona to be taken seriously. His postwar heyday, aka film noir, had deteriorated in the '60s into a series of semi-cheeky homages such as *Harper* (1966). The wisecracking shamus had been replaced as America's premier righter of wrongs by rogue cops, including Popeye Doyle, *Dirty Harry* (1971) and *Serpico*. But that cynical, self-appointed do-gooder in the fedora and the trench coat was about to make a comeback.

In '73 alone, three films were being made that, together, would constitute a mini-movement that came to be known as "neo-noir": *The Long Goodbye*, *Chinatown* and *Night Moves*.

As '75 approached, director Penn was in a sorry state. He was deeply distressed, as was the entire country, over the failure of the topsy-turvy '60s to remake America into a kinder, gentler nation. Further, the Right had taken the wheel and had put a captain, Richard Nixon, in power. And Nixon was now linked to an unprecedented act of undemocratic chicanery. Everyone, Penn included, was asking: So, if not the solutions that had been so pushily essayed throughout the '60s, then what? In that, they were all detectives, on a lonely mission for answers that only brought obfuscation. Touching on *Night Moves*' mix of '30s nostalgia and '70s relevance, Matthew Asprey Gear wrote in *Moseby Confidential*, his molecular look at the production of the picture, "Gene Hackman's performance would expertly particularize an archetype fracturing before our eyes—the knightly private detective unable to solve his case, the macho American male desperate for certainty but lost at sea."[7]

Moseby is a former Oakland Raider heading his own investigation agency, Moseby Confidential. It's no coincidence that there's no image of an eye, as is the custom among P.I.s, on his business card; Moseby is blind to many things: his wife's infidelity, the emotional residue of his estranged relationship with his father (yes, that again!), the dead-end nature of his job, and the undercurrents of his latest assignment: to lure a Lolita-esque runaway from her stepfather in Key West and bring her back to her Nora Desmond–esque mother in Los Angeles. He also can't figure out why his country is in the state it's in, how he and his fellow citizens became the victims of a universe ruled by shadowy, unfathomable forces and how, with the assassinations of the Kennedys and the rise of their suspect successors, America became the most unsolvable case of all.

Night Moves, then, operates on myriad planes: as Bogart-esque homage (look for grace notes of *The Maltese Falcon*, 1941, *The Big Sleep*, 1946, and *Key Largo*, 1948), as midlife crisis and as socio-political allegory. It's sturdy as the first, worthy as the second, bowdlerizing as the third. Plus, it's topped by a slam-bang climax, guaranteed to elevate the most middling opinion of what preceded it.

As for Hackman, it's right up there, performance-wise, with *The Conversation*. His Moseby gets what he wants with distinctly Hackman-esque guile: sly chumminess, low-key straight talk, paternal docility and the odd flash of those steely-sad eyes. That's likely because the part, according to director Penn, held secret autobiographical overtones:

> There's a large dark streak in Hackman's personality, a despairing aspect to him that sometimes verges almost on the tragic. There are constant efforts on his part to find a way to live, and he doesn't succeed at it. He's a man very much damaged by life and who wears the damage. He doesn't deny this. You see it with the camera.[8]

This time, the petard by which Hackman's character is hoisted isn't his own scarred soul. It's circumstance, messing with him at every turn. It is this convention that allows Hackman to break type.

His Moseby is more akin, in fact, to the characters of Jack Nicholson, who compromise their intelligence to get by, only to pull out everything they've got when push inevitably comes to shove. With Moseby, there are even the same self-defeating consequences. Combine *Night Moves* with the two *French Connection*s and *The Conversation*, and you get a trio of conspiracy films with Hackman as that most Nicholsonian of things: the doomed shit-disturber. In Hackman's case, though, he's not a stand-in for the pissed-off Baby Boomer. He's the poster boy for the despondent middle American, trapped in something bigger than he is, a Damoclean betrayal of the American dream.

Solid as *Night Moves* is, it's easy to comprehend its lack of commercial appeal, even in the cynical era in which it was produced. *Chinatown* had set a very high bar for detective films; Alan Pakula's excellent *The Parallax View* had covered much of the same narrative and thematic ground; and the film is dark—not just figuratively, but literally. Bruce Surtees' metaphoric cinematography makes the films of Clint Eastwood (for whom Surtees had worked) look like a mid–July afternoon in a solarium. Over time, though, *Night Moves*' reputation has grown (how else could there be an entire book devoted to it?), setting many on another baffling investigation: Why Warner Bros.' opinion of the film was so low, it didn't release it until two years after it was made.

From Key West to the Old West: Undeterred by the disastrous *Zandy's Bride*, Hackman got back on the horse and headed the old-new *Bite the Bullet* (1975). Set in 1906, it dramatizes a grueling 700-mile cross-country horse race that becomes the talk of the West. While the participants competitively cross paths, half the country lays bets, leading to sabotage and subterfuge.

The film, written and directed by Studio Era holdover Richard Brooks, is clearly out to offer something old, something new, with the former overriding the latter. (The poster, in fact, lauded the film as being, "In the tradition of *Shane* and *High Noon*…") The old: the contenders, a cross-section of Western stereotypes: the old hand, the sharpie, the young buck, the dandy, the cowgirl. The plot: plenty of gambling, roughhousing, shooting and, of course, riding. The score: veteran Alex North's sweeping pastiche of the genre's greatest hits. The new: small nods to two contemporary developments, the animal rights movement and the rise of feminism.

Hackman plays the spokesperson for the first, with his constant concern for the health of the horses. Candice Bergen is the spokesperson for the second, out to prove that trying as the terrain may be, estrogen is as good as testosterone when it comes to treading trails. Then, there's the film's theme, clearly rooted in the dead end that had become Vietnam: the value of winning. "If you don't win, then you're not American," says Hackman. Coupled with his regard for the horses, he plays the film's Jiminy Cricket. But it's America's conscience, really, then struggling with the rattling reality that for the first time in its history, it would be losing a war.

In the end, though, *Bite the Bullet* can't reconcile with the idea. It converts to a buddy picture *à la Butch Cassidy* and has Hackman and film-long frenemy James

Coburn crossing the finish line together. The metaphoric message, then, is what? That Vietnam was a tie?

Brooks had left such philosophical hoofprints before, having long puzzled over the price of glory. His formative years as a sportswriter instilled it in him. The films that constituted his second career were stocked with broken heroes, often toiling for corrupt overseers and a prize not worth earning. The true reward of any task, Brooks always maintained, was professionalism (hence the title of his most respected film, *The Professionals*, 1966). In this, he was not alone among his directorial generation, which included such kindred thematic spirits as John Ford and Howard Hawks.

Despite its musings, *Bite the Bullet* is not to be included as part of the revisionist Western movement of the time, stretching from *The Wild Bunch* to *The Long Riders* (1980). Instead, it's an exercise in Studio Era nostalgia, a big thing with audiences at that "Give me the good ol' days!" time and a phenomenon that would dictate much of Hackman's career choices for the remainder of the decade. Still, it's a spirited and accomplished throwback—possibly the best of the many in which Hackman subsequently appeared. He's having a grand time in it too, showing off his riding skills, throwing himself into Fordian knockabout humor and, more characteristically, telling people what's what or quietly pondering the big picture.

After *French Connection II, Night Moves* and *Bite the Bullet*, Hackman suffered another spell of "big salary syndrome." Those modestly successful films might have re-established his reputation as one of the decade's best actors, but they had paled, box office–wise, against moneymaking machines like *Jaws*. A search for can't-miss material ensued, resulting, as the fickle fortunes of ambition would have it, in a succession of crowd-pleasers that crowds stayed away from. Each, though, was predicated on the aforementioned appetite for venerable genres: the adventure-romance *Lucky Lady*, the thriller *The Domino Principle*, the desert epic *March or Die* and the war film *A Bridge Too Far*.

Add *Superman* to the mix, and it's clear that Hackman was also indulging his inner child, appearing in the kinds of films he had grown up watching in the '30s and '40s. While he continued to play Alice in Wonderland (or Hollywood), the moviegoing generation to which he belonged was being eclipsed as the nation's leading consumers of cinematic product by a new demographic: the Baby Boomers. They did not go looking for Hackman's inner Cagney or Flynn but wonder instead where and why he had misplaced his Brando.

Lucky Lady was conceived by writers Willard Huyck and Gloria Katz, of *American Graffiti* (1973) fame, as a kooky, sassy relationship comedy interpolated with action. But Nervous Nellie producers re-prioritized the film: They took a high-living *ménage à trois* between seafaring rum runners in the '30s (Liza Minnelli, Burt Reynolds and Hackman) and screwed up Screwball.

Up-and-coming wunderkind Steven Spielberg was slated to direct, but he opted for another oceanic thrill ride, *Jaws*. Given *Lucky Lady*'s old-fashioned elements, thoughts ran to a Studio Era relic: Stanley Donen. But while Donen had built his reputation with a series of iconic musicals, his efforts to distinguish himself in other genres had been limited successes. Still, there are glimpses of what could have been. When the star trio is on land, their itchy relationship clicks: Minnelli is sexy,

Reynolds is goofy, Hackman is giddy. But when boats speed, bullets fly and the slapstick breaks out, different story. The film falls prey to bad stunts, bad editing and bad supporting acting. On a budget that bloated to $22 million, *Lucky Lady* recouped less than half. So, aside from the sizable salary he received, for Hackman, not so Lucky—except that, at least for a few stolen moments, he gets the girl, a convention traditionally denied him. A shame. Unlike his ambivalent or misogynistic contemporaries, Hackman, despite a ruffian's instinct, demonstrates a gentlemanly, almost fatherly regard for the opposite sex, even if it takes time (in the case of *Zandy's Bride*, a lot of time). Still, it wouldn't be enough to rescue him from roles operating foremost within the realm of men (De Niro would do same) whom he'd continue to call on the carpet and encourage to follow his example.

Reynolds, it should be said, operated in that world too, even if all he could gather around him were a bunch of high-livin' rag tags. His turf, more often than not, was the South. A proud Floridian, he, like Robert Duvall, set out to celebrate Southern culture on film, albeit in a less sober style. Like James Caan, Reynolds had been a failed collegiate athlete, cast in largely forgettable TV series and movies until his turn as a Hemingway-esque macho man in John Boorman's chilling *Deliverance* (1972). A subsequent nude spread in *Playgirl* magazine, feminism's answer to its male-oriented precursor, made Reynolds an instant sex symbol. It was an image he both embraced and reviled. Consequently, he would either trade on it or, in his more ambitious modes, attempt to transcend it. As the former, usually in tight jeans and a beige Stetson, he would play a downhome sharpie, the king of the yahoos. As the latter, as in *Lucky Lady* and that same year's *Nickelodeon*, sweet-tempered rubes just a step or two out of sync with the times.

Audiences, particularly his home crowd, appreciated him most as a modern-day cowboy, combining angst-age neurosis with countrified *bonhomie*. By decade's end, that admixture elevated Reynolds to the summit of the bankable commodities list, leaving (as his wily Bandit did that poor Smokey) the better actors in his dust.

Back to Hackman. After *Lucky Lady*, Hackman wasn't so lucky with his next slate of projects either, ultimately tarnishing the Big Brass Ring ethic on which he'd hitched his career.

The Domino Principle was one of the last gasps of the divisive Stanley Kramer, the proudly independent director-producer whose reputation rested on big-screen liberalism, including *Judgment at Nuremberg* (1962) and *Guess Who's Coming to Dinner?* (1968). Some called his *oeuvre* groundbreaking, important, even daring; others sensational, self-righteous and melodramatic. They were united, however, in their dissatisfaction with *The Domino Principle*.

True to his wont to capitalize on social relevance, Kramer turns his attention to the phenomenon of political assassination—specifically, America's frustration over lack of proper accountability, a national vexation rooted in the notoriously faulty Warren Report. Who are these mysterious murderers converting America to a high-profile shooting gallery, Kramer asks, and for whom are they *really* operating?

The answer, according to the screenplay, is ex-cons, including Hackman's Roy Tucker. A shady outfit springs Tucker from San Quentin to carry out a murder, a revelation that takes a looooong time. While Tucker waits for answers, he's reunited

Burt Reynolds (left) and Gene Hackman in the not-so-lucky *Lucky Lady* (1975) (20th Century–Fox/Photofest).

with his wife; it's a reunion-within-a-reunion, as Hackman is reteamed with Candice Bergen after their joint Westerns *The Hunting Party* and *Bite the Bullet*. Kramer suburbanizes her in an auburn wig, blue eyeshadow and lacy gowns, in hopes of making a real actor from this Swedish-American *objet d'art*. But Bergen is a microcosm of the film: novel at first, staid in the middle, then, unforgivably pushy. The picture's last act is especially galling. It tries to punch above its weight, only to flail into a state of semi-laughable ineffectiveness.

Hackman, who spends the film in states of icy inquisitiveness, teeth-gritting frustration and hangdog self-examination, confessed to walking away from this poor man's *Night Moves*, as critics and audiences did, baffled. But in a small way, he does break ground in it: Rather than giving the orders, he's the one who's put upon. The puppet master in this case is industry icon Richard Widmark, with whom Hackman, the movie buff, was delighted to work.

The next Old Schooler Hackman fell in with was writer-director Dick Richards. After his seriocomic road movie *Rafferty and the Gold Dust Twins* (1975) failed to win a following, Richards turned to the surer bet of genres. Unlike his contemporaries, however, he was not out to modernize them or camp them up. His was a decidedly reverent approach, which he had pulled off admirably with his well-respected 1975 adaptation of Raymond Chandler's *Farewell My Lovely*.

Next, Richards tried his hand at recreating the adventure epics of the '30s. Nineteen thirty-nine alone gave audiences *Beau Geste*, *Gunga Din* and *The Four Feathers*.

Collaborating with David Zelag Goodman (Sam Peckinpah's co-scenarist on *Straw Dogs*), Richards fashioned *March or Die*, the tale of an American war hero in the French Foreign Legion, whose platoon is assigned to protect an archaeological dig from a pack of politically put-out Bedouins.

Underwritten by the great British showman Lew Grade, the Hackman-starring production featured an international cast: Catherine Deneuve, Terence Stamp, Max von Sydow. Hackman was there to guarantee American distribution, of course, but the film only got picked up in America because Columbia wanted Grade's other sober-faced throwback, *The Eagle Has Landed* (1976).

To its credit, *March or Die* delivers all that's expected of it. There's much trudging through desert sands, oohing and aahing over the deified Deneuve, carbon-dated dialogue and, as its poster promised, a climactic battle scene. And while the film also remains faithful to Studio Era stereotyping—its Arabs are exotic savages, whose battle cries, presented in sour close-ups, go so far as to trigger Hackman's PTSD (!)—it cursorily investigates questions of cultural appropriation. In the main, though, it's classy corn, kowtowing to the genre as dutifully as the Legionnaires (with the exception of twinkly-eyed upstart Stamp) kowtow to taskmaster Hackman.

Hackman's appearance in this unapologetic homage befuddled both fans and critics, who accused him once again of either slumming or subscribing to idiosyncratic or outdated taste. While both contentions are likely true, there was more to the mix, as any dedicated follower of his career can detect. You can argue, in fact, that his mid-sized contribution to the film predictably personifies the '70s Hackman: an authority figure slightly colorized by personal afflictions, who goes self-deflatingly rogue; a father figure at war with a "son" (Stamp), with whom he enjoys a prolonged game of one-upmanship; an unconventional Romeo who falls into a dangerous, diplomatic dalliance with the leading lady.

Next for the incurable nostalgist: a World War II film, albeit an atypical one. So, another big film, another big letdown. While Hackman's role in the all-star war epic *A Bridge Too Far* was limited, he classified it as one of the biggest challenges of his career. And indeed, as real-life Major General Stanislaw Sosabowski, Hackman looks uncharacteristically uncomfortable. The Polish accent is notably challenging (Hackman is a distinctly American personality) and, surrounded by sex symbols like James Caan, Ryan O'Neal, Robert Redford and Sean Connery, his common looks are exacerbated to the brink of invisibility. The film's a bummer, too—one of the rare American World War II films devoted to a disastrous campaign: a notoriously failed Allied operation to seize a series of critical byways in the heart of the Netherlands. Soon, American film would be casting its eye on another war, Vietnam, just as unnecessarily messy but more dramatically dimensional.

If World War II heroes wouldn't do, America, hungry for new, post–Vietnam role models that would personify the country's recovering spirit, would turn to other relics. True, the anti-hero, the confused, slovenly Brando-spawned archetype that had dethroned the square-jawed white knight, still ruled the roost. Now, though, he was about to have company: a careful, slightly campier reincarnation of his predecessor. It started with the surprise success of the low-budget *Rocky* (1976), its eponymous pugilist a perfect split of the aforementioned Brando and the simpler protagonists of the years preceding the upset (yes, Sylvester Stallone was once equated with the world's greatest actor!), then, progress to another sleeper, *Superman*.

Curiously for a big-budget production, *Superman* went with unknowns in the leads and stars in the supporting roles. That's an even bigger gamble when you consider how desperately the film had to succeed: Producers Ilya and Alexander Salkind had bought the rights to the title character for 25 years. If the first film flopped ... this, then, was the *real* Domino Principle. To hedge their bets, the first two films were shot simultaneously, with Hackman's arch-villain, Lex Luthor, appearing in both.

In *Superman*, Hackman found himself second-billed after Brando. What a thrill it must have been for him to see their names hyperbolically featured in the same opening credit roll (which, btw, takes forever). That, though, would be the closest that hero and worshipper would get; the two have no scenes together. Brando, as Superman's father Jor-El, sets up the action. Hackman, meanwhile, *is* the action: Lex Luthor, the criminal mastermind whose grand evil scheme is to set off the San Andreas fault with a pair of hijacked nuclear warheads.

From his first off-screen sarcasm about his lumpy sidekick Ned Beatty ("It's amazing that brain can generate enough power to keep those legs moving"), we're laughing. Hackman's Lex Luthor is full of small side remarks, delivered with unabashed relish. Hackman's enjoying himself here, discernibly thrilled to once again be awarded another rare opportunity (after *Young Frankenstein*) to play broad comedy.

It's a welcome contrast to Brando, who, for once, takes the whole film too seriously, and to star Christopher Reeve, who plays the Man of Steel in a minor, if winning, key. It's Hackman, then, who makes the whole thing fun. He camps up his hair and wardrobe, adding allusions to an evil clown, and is clearly as fond of his bits of business as his barbs. Hammy? Yes, but just. He's too smart an actor to overdo it (why weren't you watching, Jack Nicholson?), unlike the rest of the film which, while likable in parts, tries a little too hard.

Critics classified it as minor work, but the public loved this new, ham-fisted Hackman, who thrilled them by appearing, with just as much enthusiasm, in the sequel and later (1987) in the forgettable fourth installment.

After the *Superman* films, Hackman proved less than a superman. He was nearing 50, and the rigors of big-budget productions—the logistics, the stunts, the delays—had worn him out. Completely. And the character films, if subject to some critical appreciation, hadn't helped him out much either. He lost the desire to appear in films at all. The route his career had taken had turned out to be a cautionary tale: On the whole, he had cast too many pearls (his talents) before swine (his films). So, on the brink of '79, Hackman took his money, went home and told the press he was retiring. Hackman's sabbatical lasted, incredibly, close to three full years—a sizable risk for an artist at the height of his fame.

Then the acting bug, an extremely invasive species, resurfaced. No longer, however, would Hackman necessarily play the star. Been there, done that, collected the paycheck. The plan was to combine the best parts of the two worlds of which he had been a citizen, setting him off on a search for character studies with popular appeal. He'd be exercising his Midwestern taste, appearing in dependable middlebrow material, what the simple folk call "a good yarn." Pauline Kael talked about this phenomenon, a common syndrome shared by aging actors:

> When actors are young, they're eager for great roles, but when they become stars, they generally become fearful that the public won't accept them in something different. They look for roles that seem a little more worthwhile than the general run.[9]

Hackman now worked almost exclusively for proven, mid-rung directors (Roger Spottiswoode, Ted Kotcheff, Bud Yorkin, etc.) with just enough hits on their CVs to upstage their misses. But it was good timing. America, transitioning to the new conservatism of the '80s, had developed an appetite for the familiar, the uncomplicated and the sentimental. Hackman vehicles exceeded studio expectations: the war film *Uncommon Valor* (1983), the melodrama *Twice in a Lifetime* (1985) and especially the sports story *Hoosiers*, a simple-minded valentine to the American heartland. They reshaped Hackman as a proverbial "ol' reliable," his churlish naturalism and shy wit guaranteeing a pleasant, none-too-taxing afternoon at the theater or evening in front of the VCR.

In the ensuing decade, Hackman was reinvented yet again, after near-stealing the aforementioned *Unforgiven*. He'd spend much of the rest of his career playing baddies, permitting critic David Thomson to note in the 2010 edition of *The New Biographical Dictionary of Film,* "All too often, [Hackman] is asked to deliver little more than a standard version of gruff decency. So, it's no surprise if he's more interesting when nasty."[10]

From "a sorry son of a bitch," then, to a mean one.

Jack Nicholson
The Rebel King

"He's the one who will last," a playwright friend of mine once prophesized, as we discussed the ensemble of male film actors that had dominated our generation. "You know how in the '70s college kids had posters of Bogart on the walls of their dorms? In the future, that'll be Nicholson."

Time will tell, but it sounds like a sure bet to me—prompting the question: What is it about Nicholson that so resonates?

First, America loves a bad boy. Let's face it: Historically, America *was* a bad boy, bombastically breaking off from superpower Britain to go its own way. That narrative, the little guy triumphing over the big guy, has been American film's leading plotline since the medium's infancy. Even the odd times the industry has had a hit conceding to defeatism—say, shadowy Paul Muni in *I Am a Fugitive from a Chain Gang* (1932), those poor, dust-covered Joads in *The Grapes of Wrath* (1940), or the bruised and bloodied Brando in *On the Waterfront*—they went out of their way to end the picture on the qualification "Yeah, but I'm still standing." If you can't have large-scale usurpation, then small personal victories will make for a credible stand-in.

Through a variety of popular genres, America's male film heroes have, historically, foiled the villain, rescued the girl, conquered the West, defeated foreign adversaries, sanitized the streets, restored our institutions, and died for our beliefs. In the '30s, they played the proverbial little man who showed the big world that it wasn't so big; in the '40s, they were war heroes or detectives determined to uphold devaluated lawfulness; in the '50s, they donned helmets and plumes and helped bring down empires; in the '60s and '70s, they became working-class nobodies who suffered or died to keep the spirit of outlier vs. oppressor alive. There you have it: a century-long (almost) parade of symbols for the spirit of the American Revolution, a War of Independence being fought on-screen today by ubiquitous Marvel heroes or via the equally unending Jedi-Empire conflict.

For the Baby Boomers, Brando was the first such upstart. Nothing about him fit the cultural cloth of the anal retentive '50s: the physique was supersized, sweat-stained and sexualized, the voice slurred, understated and prone to other oratorial sins, the behavior crass, offhand and completely un–self-conscious. He should have come across as some kind of coarse, sour joke—but an authentic brutality exuded from it all, a primal genuineness that got under your skin, gave you goosebumps, and left no doubt that this sashaying philistine could kick the proper world's air-tight behind. Elvis Presley, and rock'n'roll itself, created the same effect musically, as did, on the literary circuit, Jack Kerouac. Nicholson, coming of age just as these artists were making waves, had felt a pull to become popular culture's next great muckraker. As he put it in Marc Elliott's *Nicholson*, "Everybody in my age bracket [were] Marlon Brando fans."[1]

But if Brando came to rattling society's cage by accident, if Dustin Hoffman was preoccupied with the effects of that behavior on the individual, if Al Pacino was consumed by making it feel like it was happening in real time, if Gene Hackman got his pleasure just from playing with it, if Robert Duvall always did it in the service of an establishmentarian cause, and if Robert De Niro resorted to it because the repressed are always destined to explode, then Nicholson did it because the world wouldn't leave him to his natural, self-serving, protective introversion. Bobby Dupea in *Five Easy Pieces* just wants to live life according to his own rhythms; the last thing Billy "Bad Ass" Buddusky wants to do in *The Last Detail* is to go chasing after some dumb kid; J.J. Gittes in *Chinatown* is happy to draw his own conclusions, which the grander scheme keeps insisting on upsetting; R.P. McMurphy of *One Flew Over the Cuckoo's Nest* just wants to have fun; Jack Torrance in *The Shining* longs to be left to write ... need we go on? Nicholson, then, hybridizes Brando and Brando's anti-hero predecessor, Bogart. His wont is to amble along to his own proud code like the latter, but he keeps getting forced into ugly, volatile, soul-searching confrontations like the former. Here's Donald Spoto on that phenomenon, from his *Camerado: Hollywood and the American Man*:

> Nicholson stands for the intelligent man who's deliberately let his mind go to smash. He's seen through the basic ennui of modern life, and he defends others' right to break down in the face of it, which is why he can accept a verdict of madness for himself, and fight for the right to it.... Nicholson is not a romantic hero, nor is he a man who seems to take romance very seriously; in this regard, he seems to have inherited some of Bogart's mantle, and updated it.[2]

Back to the Nicholsonian appeal: Before he came onto the scene, on-screen spokespeople for the emotional state of his generation, while noticeably rattled, still subscribed to a squeaky, sanitized quality from earlier, more innocent times. Yes, Benjamin Braddock disrupted respectable middle-class society, but it was strictly an innocent's errand. (Said director Mike Nichols of Hoffman's *Graduate*, "He had a kind of pole-axed quality with life."[3]) With the arrival of Nicholson via *Easy Rider*, the archetypical Baby Boomer hero alchemizes innocuousness into ire.

In that singular performance, Nicholson unveiled the other qualities of that generation which feature films had purposefully repressed: their audacity (veteran director Billy Wilder attributed Nicholson's appeal to the prospect that his characters might say "Go fuck yourself!" at a moment's notice to anyone with whom they shared the screen[4]), their hedonism and their transience. After he proved in *Five Easy Pieces* that indeed, these dimensions could combine to constitute a lasting persona, Nicholson usurped Hoffman as America's counterculture poster boy. And as his disciples aged, they stuck with him.

Next: He's a great actor in great films. Pardon my lack of analytic due diligence here, but frankly, it's as simple as that. From '69 to '83, he starred in *Five Easy Pieces*, *The Last Detail*, *Chinatown*, *One Flew Over the Cuckoo's Nest*, *The Shining*, *Reds* (1982) and *Terms of Endearment* (1983). Aside from Brando's introductory whammies—*A Streetcar Named Desire*, *Viva Zapata!*, *The Wild One* and *On the Waterfront*—name another period in which so many films that could be deemed classics, all starring the same actor, share such a concentrated timeline. Hoffman and Pacino, over that same period, come close until, near the end of the '70s, they fell into industry disfavor and cockeyed personal vehicles. Not that Nicholson didn't have his self-indulgent missteps, but they were few, forgivable and, today, forgotten. Otherwise, he alone provided the manly electricity introduced *en masse* by his brethren throughout American cinema's most intelligent, impactful and appreciated period.

Last: star factor. Unlike his contemporaries, working-class heroes who had stardom improbably thrust upon them while they were looking for the next job, Nicholson had always set his sights high. And such was his talent that, even at an early stage, friends expected it of him, with struggling screenwriter Robert Towne, who'd write both *The Last Detail* and *Chinatown* for him, leading the pack. Swagger, then, had always been part of Nicholson's game—a stark contrast to his peers, who, to a person, eschewed or embarrassed themselves in front of the press. You'll find a few books on Hoffman, Hackman and Pacino, even fewer on De Niro (one, by Andrew Dougan, is even called *Untouchable*), and almost nothing on Duvall—but when it comes to works about Nicholson, bring a steamer trunk. Comparatively, the man offered interviews almost as readily as flashes of his iconic killer's smile, if mostly to hip-chic publications (*Playboy*, *Rolling Stone*, *Vanity Fair*, etc.). According to those closest to him, he was prone to pontification from his earliest years, about acting, sex, therapy, you name it. A born storyteller, then, whether on camera or off, a capacity forged in his formative years talking Kerouac and Camus in cappuccino-happy coffeehouses.

As his reputation grew, this showman's instinct would take over more and more of his act. His characters became larger than life. He'd take to mugging and preening, until the myth virtually replaced the man. The tipping point, he once confessed, had been *The Shining*, in which he'd been encouraged, by director Stanley Kubrick, to worry less about making his actions believable and more about making them entertaining. The result was a new, more image-conscious Nicholson, more Barnum than badass, perpetually choosing the pleasing over the personal. Audiences loved him anyway. By that time, American cinema had become, like Nicholson's McMurphy, lobotomized. The butcher responsible had not been Nurse Ratched but Ronald Reagan, with his simpleton's politics and avuncular grin. Society wanted the easy, the immediate, the camp. All you have to do for proof is to compare *The Godfather* to *Prizzi's Honor* (1985).

So Nicholson, like the Boomers for whom he had always played adjutant, "sold out." Again, he was in perfect sync with his audience. The others—Hoffman, Hackman, Pacino, Duvall, De Niro—stuck to their guns and enjoyed hit-and-miss careers. Nicholson switched tack and enjoyed uninterrupted adulation.

His slumming years began in Neptune City, New Jersey. It was an offbeat childhood, in which he was raised by a mother-sister combo that turned out to be a grandmother-mother combo—a revelation not made plain to him until he was starring in 1975's *The Fortune*. (Biographers love to conveniently posit it during the making of *Chinatown*, wherein Nicholson has that famous "mother-sister" interrogation with Faye Dunaway.) Is it a coincidence, then, that Nicholson's characters perpetually duel with two-faced women, from humble housewives full of hidden heat (*The Postman Always Rings Twice*, 1982) to lovers secretly plotting to kill him (*Prizzi's Honor*)? When he can't equalize things with his cock, *à la* the equally frustrated Brando, he's mired in soul-wrenching separation anxiety, a love-hate trap with partners including Karen Black in *Five Easy Pieces*, Candice Bergen and Ann-Margret in *Carnal Knowledge* (1971) and the aforementioned Faye Dunaway in *Chinatown*, to name but a few.

Further, they often go on to betray him, like Jessica Lange in *Postman*, Kathleen Turner in *Prizzi's Honor*, and every female on the planet in *The Witches of Eastwick* (1987). An early subject of Reichian therapy, Nicholson, both off- and on-screen, never lost his taste for the examination of sexually based spiritual discomfort. If Brando's babes brought out the best in him, Nicholson's brought out the worst. Remarkably, though, he'd dodge outright accusations of misogyny. His style grew broader just as they were being flung at him, rendering him a feminist ally: He became a laugh-out-loud parody of the hipster cockswain. As such, he was deemed a member of the proper political side. Irony saves the day and, sometimes, a career.

Relocating to California, Nicholson finagled a Joe job as an office boy at MGM while taking classes with blacklisted character actor Jeff Corey. Then, like a lot of promising young talent at that time, he fell in with exploitation king Roger Corman. As part of that low-budget factory system, Nicholson made close to 20 pictures—horror films, cult Westerns, "dopers" and motorcycle movies—until a few other Corman graduates broke off to make the first (maybe only) *real* motorcycle movie: *Easy Rider*.

Rider was first pitched to Corman, who dragged his feet over the financing. You snooze, you lose, Roger. Nicholson, acting as no more than a kindly production liaison, brought the property to Raybert Productions. Ray- was Bob Rafelson, -Bert was Bert Schneider—the duo that had produced TV's hit cash-in on the Beatles, *The Monkees* (1966–68), and that band's psychedelic abortion of a feature, *Head* (1968), on which Nicholson had worked in a below-the-line capacity.

Told that cult novelist-screenwriter Terry Southern would be involved in the project, Raybert's boys gave Nicholson's boys, Peter Fonda and Dennis Hopper, the green light. Off Fonda-Hopper roared, on gleaming, stars'n'stripes–embossed choppers emblematic of their drug-dealing drifters' quest for a redemptively uncorrupted America.

As plot goes, that's pretty much it. Captain America (Fonda) and Billy (Hopper, who directed) cruise the highways and byways of the Western and Southern parts of the country, sharing the beauty of the geography (cinematographer Laszlo Kovacs' Monument Valley at twilight is a lavender-ocher masterwork), introducing us to Native-influenced fringe elements living off the land, and espousing an anti-urban way of life from which anybody over 30, including some very vocal rednecks who dress our heroes down in a roadside diner, is stubbornly excluded.

At the time, this combination Kerouac-ian travelogue and counterculture battle cry was embraced as a relevant sociological representation of the aspirational hippie lifestyle. Today, it's an invaluable timepiece, the best cinematic record of the spirit and style of the late '60s that mainstream American cinema ever produced. (The most profitable, too: $60 million on a $400,000 budget!) The ethic and energy of the era come off the screen like a blast of exhaust from the sparkling tailpipe of Fonda's hallowed hog. Just watch Fonda and Hopper rev up to Steppenwolf's anthemic "Born to Be Wild" and try not to get goosebumps. You'll fare about as well as they do in the film's explosive, defeatist climax, which serves as a tragic pronouncement on the hopelessness of society's conversion to a freer model for living.

Along their wandering way from L.A. to New Orleans, Captain America and Billy endure a jail stint in small-town Texas. Enter Nicholson as George Hanson, the village yahoo, recovering from yet another bender. He's halfway to hippiedom himself. He looks the establishmentarian, but it's a mask affixed with loose strings. Like his newfound compadres, all Hanson's looking for is a little undisturbed self-indulgence. Right now, it's the bottle, which makes him flap his right arm like a one-winged chicken after every swig (a mannerism Nicholson picked up from a member of the film crew). Soon it'll be marijuana, which will make him go on and on about the ideal society that they have on Venus, where a kind of cosmic socialism is at work. Hanson is the square—well, really, semi-square—that the Captain and Billy osmotically convert. He's a Terry Southern creation (by way of literary influence William Faulkner, the screenwriter later admitted), there to precisely verbalize what the other characters are only capable of living.

Hanson is the template for the Nicholson-to-be. He's a guy too hip for the room (in this case, the town); he maintains a professional reputation, but just; and he's one good push from take-no-prisoners intemperance. He's sly, sardonic and sexually obsessed. He'll scheme his way out of reprimand, wisecrack his way into friendships, and leer at any woman in his purview, regardless of age, looks or temperament. A small circle of sycophants adore him; the wider world holds a decidedly different opinion, particularly the aforementioned rednecks. In the end, he comes to tragedy, martyred, like the heroes of Nicholson's idol Brando, for his fundamental restlessness.

For those of us who watched Nicholson over the gamut of his career, that's very familiar stuff; in '69, it wasn't. The freshness of his persona—a new kind of supporting player—gut-punched audiences. Nicholson, who had taken the part for peanuts (and, okay, all of the dope he could ingest) after Rip Torn had clashed with batshit crazy Hopper, became an instant star. Dig: "The irony is inescapable: in a movie steeped in counterculture idioms, the most conventional character has the greatest impact."[5] Whether that impact could be sustained was a matter of whether or not American cinema would keep producing the kinds of pictures that would permit its newest bad boy to make good on his potential.

The immediate answer was yes. After taking on a thankless assignment—a bit in the lesser Barbra Streisand musical *On a Clear Day You Can See Forever* (1970), in which Nicholson looks visibly uncomfortable—Raybert, now restructured and renamed BBS, this time came to Nicholson. Another of the actor's ol' buds was Carole Eastman, whom he had befriended back in Jeff Corey's acting class; under the pseudonym Adrien Joyce, she had written a searing contemporary character study specifically for him. For a more detailed description of Eastman-Joyce's story, here's historian David Brinkley, quoted in Marc Eliot's *Nicholson*: "It's Kerouac's wanderlust intermingled with a Bergman-esque rondo of adult sexual relationships, topped with a dose of Chaplin-esque expressionism."[6] That clear? No? Okay. Let's elucidate:

In *Five Easy Pieces*, Bobby Dupea is a creature of two worlds (shades of Dustin Hoffman's signature duality), at once working-class hero and blue-blooded black sheep. We meet him getting dirty in the Texas oil fields, where he spends his leisure hours in the company of a kittenish country girl. He cleans up and reassumes his original identity, going home to the isolated mansion keeping his brainy, well-to-do family, who play classical music (himself included), entertain pseudo-intellectuals, and look after the ailing paterfamilias. Their erudite company includes a tense, leggy interloper, who has a difficult dalliance with our prodigal hero. Bobby, though, fits neither milieu, neither woman. He's consumed with a more sophisticated version of Brando's discomfort and an edgier edition of Benjamin Braddock's ennui. In the end, he sneaks out on both circumstances to find something freer, something that won't force him to suppress or devalue his talents and emotions.

When Nicholson took that journey as George Hanson in *Easy Rider*, he paid the ultimate price. As Bobby Dupea, there's still a chance that a small slice of the world might accommodate him. Bobby's the seeker, a new cinematic archetype that had blossomed in the late '60s. But by '70, the seeker, Nicholson's performance affirmed, has become a different man. He's grown frustrated, hair-trigger. He's given up the game or is at least trying to. Left with nothing but himself, he settles for easy pleasures—but even those come with admonishment. What to do? For Bobby, it's like trying to talk to his father, who's gone incommunicado from a series of debilitating strokes. You can't do anything in this world, and you can't talk to anybody about the fact that you can't do anything either, Bobby stews. You're left to have hissy fits in roadside restaurants (the famous "chicken salad" scene, in which a hungry Nicholson explodes at an uncooperative waitress), in cars and, occasionally, in the company of the ones you could learn to love if you hadn't been brought to discounting your capacity to do so.

With the deeply divided Bobby, Nicholson announced that, as an actor, he was here to stay. This was everyone's first full dose of him, his slyness, his lasciviousness, his combustibility. In putting it before modern audiences, the counterculture had found a new representative. Forget about Hoffman's Graduate—that had been three long, eventful years ago. We were long past naïve now, long past wide-eyed wondering about the future. We were mad: mad at the world, at ourselves, at the heavens. We wanted, *needed* somebody to act up for us—and not some crazy, lovestruck innocent either. An adult, in the good-bad sense of the word, with full, mature firepower.

So Jack it would be. Next came—after a few interesting blips—*The Last Detail*, *Chinatown* and *One Flew Over the Cuckoo's Nest*, solidifying his position as the personification of our primal scream. From *Five Easy Pieces* on, Jack, at all times, would be both actor and symbol, flesh and blood as well as deity. The more his canny, compromised characters prostituted themselves, the higher the man himself was hoisted upon popular culture's pedestal.

There's a lot of the real Nicholson in Bobby Dupea. Eastman, the writer and personal confidante, had seen to that—and Nicholson had seen to it too, relying even more than the script had asked on his natural character. It's an unabashedly self-revelatory performance, like idol Brando in the later *Last Tango in Paris*. Nicholson doesn't have to worry about putting on a show here, as he does in later films. He's fully cognizant of the inherent showmanship of his emotional make-up. He even gives us his rarely seen sensitive side, in the climactic confrontation with his ghostly father. Note the tears, something we will not get from him again until *The King of Marvin Gardens* (1972), then, many years later, in *About Schmidt* (2002).

Nicholson's layered, bravura performance in this darkly sensitive film created a sensation. Not only had a new, relevant persona officially arrived, but so had an interesting and accomplished actor. On *Five Easy Pieces*' fiftieth anniversary, a sharp reassessment of Nicholson's performance printed in *The Guardian* put it this way:

> In the hands of a lesser actor—or even a very good actor—Bobby could come off as a sour, abusive drip, unworthy of our interest, much less our sympathy. But Nicholson plays the audience like Bobby doing Prelude in E Minor, utterly confident that he'll seduce us into caring about a man who's incapable of returning the love he attracts so effortlessly.[7]

Unfortunately, Nicholson's next film would take Bobby and reduce him in size, restricting him to his less sympathetic characteristics.

After the smash that had been *The Graduate*, Mike Nichols spent three years making *Catch-22* (1970), the much-anticipated film adaptation of Joseph Heller's darkly comic best-seller. Heller's picaresque comic epic was a satire of the labyrinthine nature of military bureaucracy; Nichols' messy movie was a more universal commentary on the elusive nature of the American dream. An immigrant, with alopecia to boot, Nichols was well-versed in the frustrations of the new American. Like *The Graduate*'s Benjamin Braddock, Nichols might have been casting a cold eye on WASP culture but was looking, all the same, for comfort in his own right. He wanted the girl, the career, the home—the big prizes guarded by the proper Protestant populace.

As a student at the University of Chicago in the conservative '50s, Nichols had suffered the added indignity of the times. Postwar America left little room for personal pleasure other than the most innocent types of indulgences. Commodities like sex, a Nichols leitmotif, were restricted by implacable notions of social protocol.

Cartoonist Jules Feiffer, then revolutionizing the daily comic strip with adult explorations of our existential mood swings, was a kindred spirit. Though a born-and-bred New Yorker, Feiffer had come of age in synchronicity with Nichols. As such, he had squirmed inside the same social straitjacket. Come the overdue sexual revolution of the '60s, male artists like Nichols, Feiffer, Philip Roth and John Updike, to name but a few, felt free to investigate their sexual identities in unabashed form. Roth had been first out of the gate with his crass comic classic *Portnoy's Complaint*. The cultural shock wave brought on by that riffy, angst-ridden confessional was still being felt by the time Feiffer crafted his screenplay for *Carnal Knowledge*.

The film is anchored on contrasting personalities; it's a buddy film then, if of the urban, sexualized variety. Art Garfunkel is Dr. Jekyll, the proverbial "nice Jewish

Jack Nicholson and Karen Black in *Five Easy Pieces* (1970), an early manifestation of his onscreen struggles with women (Columbia/Photofest).

boy" with illusions of domesticity. Nicholson is Mr. Hyde, the libidinous libertarian with a deep-seated fear of commitment. Together, they constitute the two major facets of the male personality. Throughout their 20-year friendship, from postwar Puritanism to contemporary promiscuity, they try every mode of relationship there is. In the end, Garfunkel settles for hippie-style self-examination, while Nicholson sticks to his chauvinistic guns.

Neither solution offers a pleasing, plausible alternative to the film's vision of men as horny idiots. That interpretation could have been played up as black comedy. Instead, it's offered as legitimate food for thought, in the film's cool, intellectual style. Times were changing and men were scared—so scared that they were circling their wagons, clinging to dated notions of women as sexual objects and marriage as the cul-de-sac on the road to prurient adventure. That said, the film falls shy of an unapologetically anti-feminist treaty. Its women, sensitively and memorably portrayed by Candice Bergen and Ann-Margret (giving, arguably, career performances), are sympathetic, faceted characters. Their suffering at the hands of their male counterparts may not be the film's primary focus (as perhaps, it should have been), but it's what gives the picture its emotional impact. And it's responsible for the film's best, and most sustained, scene: a protracted squabble between Nicholson and Ann-Margret over the legitimization of their union, in which the former spews blood and thunder while the latter plays pained, protesting audience.

The monogamy-polygamy debate was a hot topic at the time. While Nichols' generation was proudly upholding the institution of marriage, the succeeding one had serious reservations about the rigid arrangement that had made their parents so resignedly miserable. Hence, Garfunkel and Nicholson, as romantic explorers, weren't doing anything particularly shocking—save for the language by which they were expressing it. *Carnal Knowledge* was the cinematic coming-out party for the liberal use of "tits," "ass" and "fuck." As such, it burdened the film with a controversial reputation. Theaters were shut down, court battles were fought. An ad campaign was devised to cash in on it all. In the end, it was determined that all the film did was break national dialogue, another step on America's path to cultural maturation.

With *Five Easy Pieces* and *Carnal Knowledge*, Nicholson, while making great strides as an actor, was being typecast as a hip, horny hedonist with a temper. After helping out Henry Jaglom (whom he had befriended as the cult-filmmaker-to-be edited *Easy Rider*) with his first feature *A Safe Place* (1971), Nicholson went on to address his own image. He would upset audience expectations, more or less, with a pair of explorations of strictly male relationships: *The King of Marvin Gardens* and *The Last Detail*.

Marvin Gardens was another case of Rafelson to the rescue. (There'd be three more Nicholson-Rafelson collaborations: the semi-successful *The Postman Always Rings Twice*, the forgettable *Man Trouble*, 1992, and the underrated *Blood and Wine*, 1996.) The title refers to a primo Monopoly property, the household name board game modeled on the film's setting, Atlantic City. Once one of America's premier dens of glitzy inequity, that coastal resort was, by the early '70s, in its death throes. (For a cinematic look at its resurgence, see Louis Malle's *Atlantic City*, 1980.)

In the film, the decay of the terrain and its hollow rituals of yore, like an improvised, Fellini-esque beauty pageant, stand in for the decay of the entrepreneurial spirit, the sorry, dead-end state of contemporary capitalism. This milieu-based vision of a fallen paradise serves to make long-faced Bruce Dern, as a checkered real estate huckster, a tragically comic figure. Dern self-deludedly tries to breathe life into this geographic corpse, all the while fantasizing about setting up shop in faraway Hawaii as a means of unhooking himself from agents of corruption—namely, the gangster syndicate lording over his affairs. Then, there's the added burden of his hysterical harpy girlfriend and her toothy stepdaughter, making up another of Rafelson's sticky, eccentric families. Nicholson completes the set as Dern's passive brother, an overnight talk-jock offering long, writerly self-reflections between snippets of classical music. He leaves his lonely life in Philadelphia to participate in his brother's pipe dream, only to have to police the man's professional and personal politics.

Rafelson, like contemporary Nichols, is obsessed with the fundamental elusiveness of the American dream. His heroes, including fast-talking quick-buck artist Dern, remain convinced that that form of professional-personal validation is well within their grasp; all they have to do is sweet-talk enough and the prize is theirs, as poor, perpetually put-out Bobby had assumed in *Five Easy Pieces*. But they have to learn and re-learn that there's no free lunch—further, that there's no free *any*thing. Freedom is just a respite from the next fatalistic pursuit, the next sandcastle you and your brother will build on the Jersey shore before it's inevitably washed away.

The film's central dynamic harkens back to (what else?) Kazan-Brando's *On the Waterfront*, with its clash between a brother mixed up with criminals and another serving as interloping conscience. But Nicholson here is no Brando. Far from it. In a bit of stunt casting, Dern plays the part originally intended for Nicholson and vice versa. An interesting notion for the marketing team, a dramatic challenge for the actors, and a disappointment for the audience. You want to see a muffled Nicholson as much as you want to see an anesthetized Brando. Why load a cannon with spitballs? Nicholson does a yeoman's job, diminishing his stature with horn rims, a neutral-colored raincoat and a colorless monotone, but nondescript is not in his repertoire. You long throughout for more of his midnight monologues, the only true showpieces the film awards him. No matter. Like Clark Kent transitioning to Superman, Nicholson will soon lose the glasses to emerge as a force to be reckoned with.

Up to this point, Nicholson had evolved from B-movie obscurity and established himself as an interesting, at times explosive actor. Over the next three years, he'd go hyperspace, officially joining Hoffman, Hackman and Pacino to form American male screen acting's Mount Rushmore. Jack, in his purest, most potent form, was about to take America. He alone, cinematically, would keep the waning spirit of rebellion alive, would act to remind his generation that yes, the system has taken a lot of us down and may yet take the rest of us down; until then, though, let's all continue to rage, rage against the dying of the '60s.

"No *#@!!* Navy's going to give some poor *!!@ kid eight years in the #@!* brig without me taking him out for the time of his *#@!!* life." So declares Billy "Badass" Buddusky, the scowling, shirtless, cigar-smoking sailor played by Nicholson, as he stares out icily from the poster for Hal Ashby's *The Last Detail*. That quote, full of *Mad* magazine–inspired grawlixes, not only revealed the film's premise, it warned about the salty extremism of its language; *Detail* was out to make *Carnal Knowledge* sound like dinner table conversation. These were sailors, after all, about to be portrayed in a new, bullshit-free fashion (no singing and dancing alongside Gene Kelly). Studios, in fact, were competing to do so: Columbia had *Last Detail* and Fox had *Cinderella Liberty*, both released in December '73, and both based on the work of Darryl Ponicsan, an ex-sailor–cum–novelist.

Robert Towne, the celebrated screenwriter who served as one-time roomie Nicholson's on-off muse from the '70s to the '90s, borrowed a page from Carole Eastman and adapted Ponicsan's source material to better reflect his BFF's personality. Buddusky, a posturing, paternal signalman, and fellow Navy lifer "Mule" Mulholland are assigned to escort gawky klepto Larry Meadows to an eight-year stint in the brig, Towne distilled Nicholson to his essence: Buddusky becomes a brassy Bobby

Dupea, a bawdy bon vivant at war with the world and, more than he realizes, himself. As he's confined to military culture, however, there are no hippies to befriend as in *Easy Rider*, no holier-than-thou family members with which to do battle as in *Five Easy Pieces*, no complicated women to negotiate with as in *Carnal Knowledge*— nothing to smooth, dull or trim the Nicholsonian edges. Buddusky-Nicholson's immediate company constitutes lesser personalities, the low-key, professional "Mule" and the Li'l Abner–esque Meadows. His only real challenge is the unchallenged core of his own personality.

Traditionally, that's generational unrest, the same itching powder that had affected Hoffman's Benjamin Braddock but had manifested itself, in Nicholson, in a seething, occasionally volcanic contempt. But Towne adds new notes to that tune, preserving the Nicholson we've come to know while affording him fresher aspects.

In deciding to show the doughy, dull-witted Meadows as good a time as can be had on their shared trek across the diners, bus stations and pinball parlors of Washington, New York and Boston, Buddusky-Nicholson develops an embryotic paternalism. Hitherto, Nicholson's characters, while happy (relatively) to be in the company of others, single-mindedly prioritized their own needs and desires. Stick a flat hat on Nicholson's head, though, and suddenly he's capable, even occasionally insists, on putting others above himself. No doubt it helped that by that time, Nicholson had become part of a tight personal brotherhood that had included himself, Towne, Warren Beatty and playboy producer Robert Evans. He and Towne were well-steeped in the "bros before hos" mentality, long before that expression had been minted.

Towne, through Buddusky, also converts Nicholson to that grass roots '60s folk hero, the defender of the people. Towne had committed this kind of elevation before when, ghostwriting on *Bonnie and Clyde*, he added a scene in which those Depression-era degenerates lent their pistol to a hard-luck farmer and his black farmhand, inviting them to fire vengeful shots at the property the bank had taken away from them. With that one, early moment in the film, Bonnie and Clyde switched from figures of dubious morality to symbols of the empathetic left. For the rest of the picture, while they robbed, killed, and robbed and killed again, we forgave them their trespasses and, in the end, felt the full tragedy of their Peckinpah-esque perforation.

That same quality manifests itself in Buddusky-Nicholson when he insists that the kindly, pathetic Meadows show anger over his shitty circumstance. In so prompting, Buddusky-Nicholson was asking all of America to rage, to rise and scream at the indignity inflicted by "the man," that proverbial overlord who won't tolerate our complete natures. As the '70s progressed, there'd be more of these frustrated, inspirational figures, culminating in Peter Finch and his demands that we synchronize shouts of "I'm as mad as hell and I'm not gonna *take* this any more!" in *Network* (1976).

Nicholson is even a different man physically. While he might be too small for the part (does the U.S. Navy have a height requirement?), he's beefed himself up, grown a mustache and developed a thing for phallic cigars. The outer Nicholson finally resembles the inner. We have no problem accepting him as the Alpha, especially as his Betas, the whatever-happened-to Otis Young as "Mule" (a part originally assigned to a then unknown John Travolta) and the don't-know-shit-from-shinola Meadows (Randy Quaid, who was almost disqualified for the part due to his unwieldy physicality), are no matches for his raw insistence. Together, they make for a welcome variation on the buddy film, indulging in semi-improvised *bonhomie* framed by director Hal Ashby's considerate, almost anonymous camera. Like the cult classic with which Ashby had made his name, *Harold and Maude* (1971), and the film that marked the climax of his all-too-brief career, *Being There* (1979), this is the semi-rambling tale of an innocent (Meadows) who falls in with quirky, kindly mentors or superiors, the semi-silent spiritual exchange between them, and the climactic, cautionary criticism of society that is the symbolic weight of their association.

Nicholson took home the Best Actor prize from Cannes for his performance while garnering another Oscar nomination. He was in Trophyland now. It was just a matter of time before that bafflingly elusive Oscar was his, just a matter of the next good script, maybe two, until it would end up in his hands.

He got his next shot at it with *Chinatown*, another Towne script (so, *China-Towne*?), this time an original the writer had been working on for eons. Fascinated by his hometown's sketchy, dirty history, Towne brought a quietly shady episode of Los Angeles' past to the venerable film noir.

Water is essential to a desert community, and here, in the hardscrabble '30s, the powers behind Water & Power secretly divert it to perpetuate a drought that will force farmers to sell their land. Once purchased, irrigation would be restored, driving up asking prices and making wealthy men of the conniving untouchables behind this classic example of grandiose American chicanery.

That's pretty big stuff for a small-time operator like J.J. Gittes, the P.I. played by Nicholson, to get embroiled in, even if he fancies himself a pomaded dandy able to hold his own with a higher class of people than the lowlifes whose wives and husbands he catches *in flagrante*.

One day, though, a new breed of client enters his surprisingly sunny offices (don't look for the traditional low lighting of the genre, save for the odd shadows cast by blinds): the sonorously named Evelyn Mulwray, played by the striking and accomplished Faye Dunaway. La Mulwray looks like Joan Crawford in *Mildred Pierce* (1945) and acts like Mary Astor in *The Maltese Falcon* (1941). She's cool on the outside, addressing Gittes in a bloodless, measured tone, and nervous on the inside, bristling at every mention of her father, the sly old coot behind the waterworks scheme (played by John Huston, father of Nicholson's then-girlfriend Angelica). Gittes doesn't know about that scheme yet. True to the plot conventions of the genre, he starts off trying to appease a small request—to keep the friction between Evelyn and her husband, her father's business partner, out of the papers—then finds that it's just one thread in a trampoline-sized spider web. Determined to disentangle it, Gittes gets his nose cut, his gut punched, and his romantic inclinations—for the bony beauty who's as bad at cover-ups as her father is good—tragically thwarted.

Such narrative templates—civic corruption rooted in the closet history of dysfunctional families—have long been staples of the genre, from the works of Dashiell Hammett to the *oeuvre* of Raymond Chandler. It was Hammett who gave us the twentieth-century detective (no more Holmesian deerstalkers) and Chandler who perfected the archetype. The cynical, solitary, smart-mouthed heroes created by these cynical, solitary, smart-mouthed writers operated in a world gone melodramatically mad, in which the Spades and the Marlowes quietly held themselves up as self-appointed keepers of an eroding morality.

These characters called what they did a thankless job, or, at best, a tough way to make a living. (In *Chinatown*, Gittes defends himself to an uppity audience in a barber shop.) But that working-class hero talk was as see-through as the lying dames who liked to drop by their chiaroscurist offices. Problem was, while somebody had to clean the world's dirty laundry, it was a true test of character not to get caught up in the easy avails that came with the corruption.

The lives of these characters spoke of the all-too-erasable line between the professional and the personal, a theme imported from the pages of the pulp paperback and B-movie grist mill to the upper echelons of on-screen gangsterism via Francis Ford Coppola. *The Godfather Part II*, in fact, was *Chinatown*'s big rival for critical and audience appreciation in '74, two distinct examinations of the same central theme.

In Hollywood, you don't make a living as a male actor without playing a P.I., a cop, a soldier and/or a cowboy. Throughout his long career, Nicholson tried his hand at all of the above. He fared best as the detective. It's a professional persona that suits him like a well-fitted fedora. Consider its defining adjectives: aloof, cynical, combative. If you can't equate that with Nicholson, you don't know Jack. Again, Towne knew the man intimately and knew where, in his tight, much-revered script, to place and exaggerate his signature qualities.

That said, in *Chinatown*, Towne also dresses Nicholson down (as opposed to up; that was the responsibility of Anthea Sylbert, whose suits and hats prove that Jack can clean up good). In previous roles, we watched Nicholson the same way we watched a volcano: Every gesture, every line was a small wisp of tell-tale smoke. Any second now, he was going to blow. Gittes, too, is carefully contained but our admiration for him is different. It's the perpetuation of his cool on which were buoyed. How long can he hold it all in, we ask ourselves? How long before Faye Dunaway becomes Ann-Margret in *Carnal Knowledge*, before the scheme he gets involved in becomes the chicken sandwich in *Five Easy Pieces*? It happens, but late, and in very small measure. Again, as in *The Last Detail*, Towne is honoring Nicholson's trademark bents while giving him something new to play. This is Jack the class act, the downplayer, the voyeur, the guy who knows the value of keeping your feet firmly on the sidelines. He's still the archetypical Baby Boomer hero: defender of the common man, the guy who can be driven to take on that corrosive, elusive entity known colloquially as "the man" (or in this case, "the Huston"). But Gittes doesn't stick that straight-razored neck of his out due to sentimentality, as Buddusky of *The Last Detail* does; out of filial obligation, like Nicholson's guilt-ridden nerd in *The King of Marvin Gardens* does; or out of anything else that's familiar. With Gittes, the Nicholsonian persona has found professionalism, the pilot light of characters played by contemporaries Hackman and Duvall. In the end, the job's the thing, even if it costs you your nose (almost), your sexual plaything and your ideals.

Nicholson as J.J. Gittes in *Chinatown* (1974). Screenwriter-friend Robert Towne drew regularly on Nicholson's natural personality to create personages like Gittes (Paramount/Photofest).

As the years passed, the reputation afforded Towne's sharp, intricate screenplay grew. In its time, it won the Oscar. By the '80s, when screenplay-writing had become the middle-class hobby *du jour*, it had been positively gilded, thanks to guru Syd Field's best-selling handbooks. And indeed, for all that *Chinatown* has going for it, Towne is its shiniest star. In importing conspiracy theory–era suspicion, born of the Kennedy assassinations and the Watergate scandal, to film noir, Towne brought new relevancy and edge to a tired genre. Others were also playing that revisionist game, but Towne's script was the only one that had set out, and succeeded, as equal parts act of reverence and truly contemporary drama.

The film was directed by the soon-to-be-notorious Roman Polanski, the diminutive Polish wunderkind who established himself with tales of victimized innocents, often female, at the hands of a pop-up horror. Polanski knew whereof he spoke: His parents had been murdered by the Nazis and his wife by the Manson gang. Polanski was a deeply scarred survivor. Consequently, so were his heroes, from *Chinatown*'s Gittes to the eponymous protagonist in *The Pianist* (2002). But Polanski couldn't survive a rape scandal, which took place in 1977, after he had embedded himself with the high-flying party types that were Nicholson and his coterie, most of whom he had met planning *Chinatown*. Like Gittes keeping a cool distance from his clients, Nicholson kept his association with the Polanski affair constructively at bay.

Looking to mix things up, Nicholson started '75 with a leap from the low-key to the over-the-top. His career-long association with Mike Nichols ultimately produced four films of varying quality. Their second, *The Fortune*, re-teamed Nicholson with writer Carole Eastman aka Adrien Joyce of *Five Easy Pieces*. But this would be no *Pieces* or *Carnal Knowledge*. Coming off of two flops (*Catch-22* and the unjustly maligned *The Day of the Dolphin*, 1973), Nichols hedged his bets and cashed in on the '20s-'30s craze put into motion by the box office bonanza of *The Sting* (1973). (That appetite had also helped *Chinatown* get the green light.)

In *The Fortune* as in *The Sting*, two con men are at large, but less Newman-Redford and more Laurel-Hardy: Dapper Dan Warren Beatty and baggy pants comic Nicholson. They're a pair of know-nothing fortune hunters, out to molest and murder a kooky heiress (the sexily androgynous Stockard Channing, in her film debut). Nicholson, predictably, proves the greater comedian. His performance foreshadows the broader strokes he'd apply as his career progressed into the big-scale '80s. He leers, mugs and performs feats of slapstick with unashamed relish. Fast becoming typecast as a frustrated smartie, here he gets to play the happy idiot.

Beatty, as the straight man, counters Nicholson with shaky self-righteousness. Beatty too specialized in personalities out to cut their own easy path through life, only to find themselves up against a world bigger and badder than they'd estimated. Foiled by this realization, Nicholson's characters raged; Beatty's took on a little-boy-lost quality. The quintessential Beatty role came out the same year as *The Fortune*: *Shampoo*, a New Age sex farce directed by Hal Ashby (and co-written by Beatty and Nicholson's good friend Robert Towne). Beatty's a Beverly Hills hairdresser who has his pick, sexually, of clients. In the end, though, this blow-dried

Arthur Penn (left) directs Warren Beatty, last of the original Method men (Photofest).

bohemian is exposed for what he fundamentally *is*: a shallow hangover from the waning '60s, left out from the switch to less indulgent times. So again, a guy who thought that his looks, his savvy and his moxie would always be enough, only to discover that they buy him very little.

Beatty, too, had been a student of the Method, coming to the fore just as actors bearing that pedigree were falling out of fashion. By the early '60s, the Actors Studio was in the throes of dissolution. A decision to mount full-scale theatrical productions had proven a disaster. Plus, the facility's star pupils—James Dean, Marilyn Monroe, Montgomery Clift and Marlon Brando—had all become tragic figures. So, left to Beatty, the last of that dying breed, was the opportunity to validate its work. He was far from the best actor that place had produced, but he had absorbed enough to get by on more than just his looks, creating complex characters from simplistic templates in such films as *Bonnie and Clyde*. Further, the fresh-faced, mid–Atlantic Beatty embodied a new spirit at large in America with the election of John F. Kennedy. Like JFK, Beatty was a handsome, ambitious young Alpha with steely ideals, a healthy sexual appetite and a less-than-firm hand on the political wheel by which he could crash or emerge simply scratched.

One of the industry's many successful actor-producer hyphenates (later adding writer and director), Beatty selectively appeared throughout the '70s, balancing his own projects with service work. He spent most of his time in the public eye on the cover of tabloids, his reputation as a cocksman usurping his professional predispositions.

Given the Beatty-Nicholson-Nichols pairing in *The Fortune*, critics expected a lot more than what they got, especially as, by the third act, the film turns into a Gatsby-era *Weekend at Bernie's* (1989).

In communist Czechoslovakia, director Milos Forman had dared to make dark comedies about idiosyncratic proletariat victimized by corrupt bureaucracies. That said, his hero was not the proverbial "good man" but an interesting variation: the good madman, the kid with the crazy audacity to scream that the emperor, the *bad* madman, had no clothes. After immigrating to America, Forman continued to spotlight such figures, including Andy Kaufmann and Larry Flynt. But his greatest spokesperson may well have been Randall P. McMurphy, the shit-disturber's shit-disturber who, posing as emotionally unbalanced to exchange a stint in jail for a stay in a mental health facility, not only wreaks havoc but takes bets on just how successfully he can do it, in *One Flew Over the Cuckoo's Nest*.

The Oregon–based operation McMurphy weasels his way into is policed by the no-nonsense Nurse Ratched, whose icy professionalism grows icier with every challenge to the workaday ways of her ward. It's the hip vs. square battle that was now, in '75, going into its umpteenth round; now added to the mix were questions about the new powers being afforded women. The ward is, metaphorically, society, and McMurphy the new premium on loose living out to triumph over the emphatically controlled. When his efforts, popular as they are among his fellow patients, result in a dramatic comeuppance—martyred, *à la* Brando, for the cause—it's a clear signal from Forman that the great age of permissiveness, i.e., the '60s and early '70s, was over. Put your wide-leg jeans in mothballs, the film's ending warned its original audience; we're going back to a straight-legged era.

Forman goes so far as to footnote the generational divide that had been the point of the novel, smartly considering the aging nature of that battle. He downplays its symbolic value, opting for increased realism. In so doing, he creates a central conflict that is personal, a fairer, baser fight between equally dimensional opponents. The perpetual deadpan of Louise Fletcher, as Ratched, is a veritable dam of emotions, struggling to maintain resiliency against every crack. Nicholson, as sparring partner McMurphy, is no simple savior but a man ultimately set to question the validity of his mission. Typical Nicholson doppelgangers had always been able to triumph, at least enough of the time, using guile, charm, sex, anger or all of the above—then, almost always walk away, frustrated maybe but still their own man.

Now, though, the Nicholson persona finds himself up against his first truly worthy opponent. Fletcher-Ratched is no Karen Black you can abandon at a filling station, no Ann-Margret you can drive to suicide, no Faye Dunaway you can slap into confessional submission. As such, Nicholson's McMurphy spends a lot more time than Ken Kesey had afforded him scratching the thinning hair atop his head.

Pauline Kael, catty contessa of the critical cognoscenti, positively exploded with encomiums for both performances. Of Nicholson, she wrote,

> [Nicholson] doesn't keep a piece of himself out of the character, guarding it and making the audience aware that he's got his control center and can turn on the juice. He actually looks relaxed at times, punchy, almost helpless—you can forget it's Nicholson. McMurphy is a tired, baffled man, and with his character more unresolved, he gains depth ... it's Nicholson's best performance.[8]

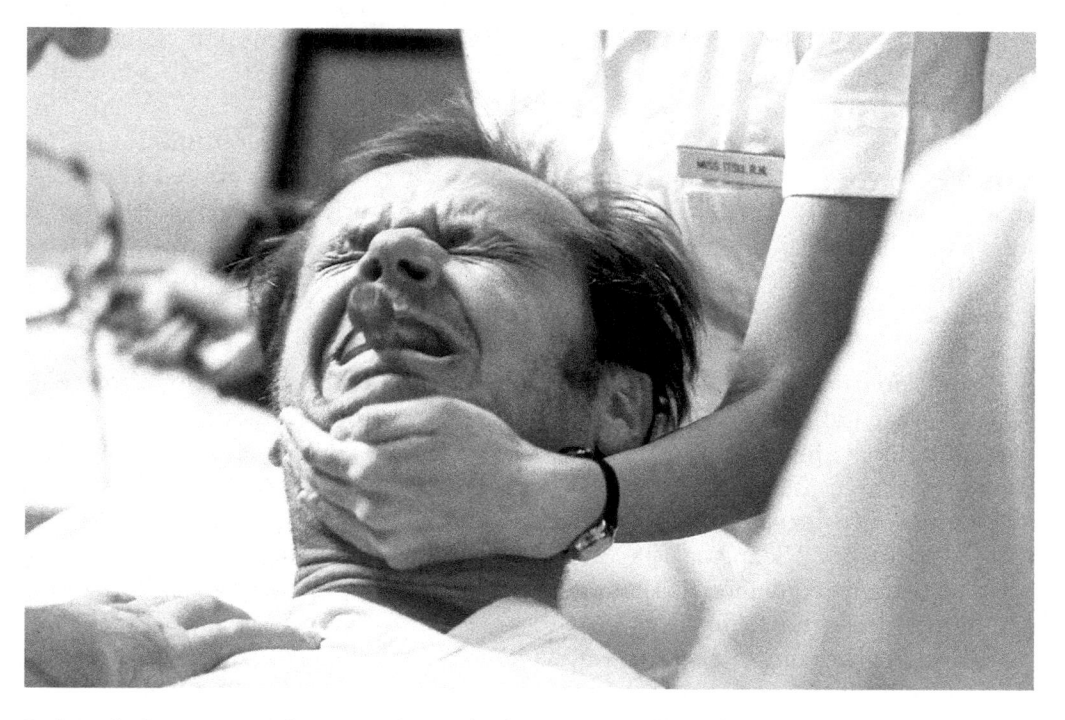

Jack Nicholson in *One Flew Over the Cuckoo's Nest* (1975), being martyred Brando-style (UA/Photofest).

The world concurred. For all of the personal investment of Carole Eastman and Robert Towne, it's Forman, along with screenwriters Lawrence Hauben and Bo Goldman, who ended up devising Nicholson's top showcase, one that gilded the identity and style he had developed to that point and permitted him to expand his range without conventions that could have led to showy shortcuts or other alienating self-indulgences.

Nicholson finally bagged his first Oscar for it, part of an above-the-line sweep those awards hadn't seen since Frank Capra's *It Happened One Night* (1934). The sentiment was that Nicholson, while certainly not done, had probably peaked. Whatever followed would be anticlimactic ... then, hopefully, there'd be a return to form.

Subscribers to that assumption were proven veritably psychic. Nicholson's next appearances offered but sample sizes of his potential. For the rest of the decade, he was a diminished presence. It speaks, in part, to the fading relevance of his persona. Forman had been right: America was mellowing. There was no further need for anti-establishmentarian hotheads. Plus, Nicholson admittedly feared overexposure. His succeeding films constituted a musical caprice, followed by an auteur piece that made middling use of him. Then he worked in idol Brando's sizable shadow, did a stint in Brando mentor Elia Kazan's last, tired effort, and foolishly risked his reputation by running shamelessly amok in a self-directed Western comedy. That was it, until his return as a powerhouse in Stanley Kubrick's operatic horror-comedy *The Shining*.

The first of the two walk-ons was in Ken Russell's pop fantasia *Tommy* (1975), the bombastically expressionistic film adaptation of The Who's groundbreaking rock opera. As a flirtatious doctor, Nicholson again gets his mitts on Ann-Margret, singing-talking his way into the boudoir of the disabled hero's mother. It's an "anything goes" kind of film, and still you find yourself asking, "What the hell is *he* doing there?"

That same busy year, Nicholson agreed to front Michelangelo Antonioni's *The Passenger*. Actors of Nicholson's generation longed to service the exalted European auteurs, whose work had profoundly influenced the American cinema of which they were a part. That kind of marriage rarely worked. In such a world, the director is the star. The actor becomes footnoted, often reduced to a symbol, an ideal, or an image. It was a safe bet that even a personality as dynamic as Nicholson's would be reduced to size.

Antonioni framed his actors in long, painterly takes, making them minuscule, almost incidental figures. He liked to catch the expository, the confessional or the confrontational almost imperceptibly, his laconically restless camera acting as if at the mercy of an uninterested D.O.P. Further, he often reduced his actors to vessels of an all-consuming existential apathy, his scripts offering their characters but a modicum of backstory. Nicholson's participation, then, constituted a rare act of *noblesse oblige*, a committed deference that declawed his instinctive showmanship. He was gambling with his box office clout.

Foreign film came to America via the Italian neo-realist tradition. Films such as *Rome, Open City* (1945), *Shoeshine* (1946) and *The Bicycle Thief* (1948), deeply humanist allegories offering slices of life during and after the Nazi occupation, made their way to North America as a new kind of newsreel, a mix of dramatic and documentary styles revealing the imprint of Italy's wartime experiences on ordinary citizens. Antonioni, a foot soldier in that movement, broke away from it in the affluent '50s in favor of melodramatic examinations of the new middle class. By the early '60s, he had determined that its members had become subscribers of a chic spiritual malaise, a fundamental soullessness at war with the prosperity they had procured. Antonioni's first full declaration of this contention, *L'Avventura* (1960), was an international sensation. His imploding civilizations, dwarfed by oppressively impassive geography and slow, arcane camera movement, constituted a new cinematic mood: a sterility the art-house set found, ironically, invigorating. In '66, he demonstrated that this disease of the soul had spread to other parts of Europe, including the most spirited place going, Swinging London. His first English-language film, *Blow-Up* (1966), captured the mod tenor of the times while holding up its foundational emptiness to ridicule. This New Age murder mystery, with its controversially playful sex scenes and ambiguous dramatic climax, was hailed as an iconoclastic classic. Further, it greatly influenced the filmmakers of Nicholson's generation (see Coppola's *The Conversation* and Brian De Palma's *Blow-Out*, 1981). Nine hit-and-miss years later, Antonioni cannibalized some of its elements to create another enigmatic thriller, *The Passenger*.

Nicholson, in a part that could have been played by almost anybody, is David Locke, an investigative TV reporter saddled with procuring proximity to a group of rebels fighting in Africa. He befriends a mysterious arms dealer who suffers a heart attack; Locke, looking to adjust his lot in life, assumes the man's identity. As such, Locke becomes entitled to the privileges of the man's lifestyle. For a while, this affords Locke a cooler, quieter version of the mercifully solitary existence sought by previous Nicholson characters. Just like the members of that rogues' gallery, however, Locke discovers that there's no transcending life's stultifying bullshit, not even in the arms of a pouty young beauty. The target of a series of manhunts, Locke ultimately finds freedom in the only convention that can truly provide it: death.

If you're noting parallels to *Last Tango in Paris*—middle-aged, despondent American abroad canoodles with a nubile free spirit in a doomed search for spiritual relief—move to the front of the Film Studies class. You can even go so far as to call this Antonioni's response to Bertolucci, complete with the still toothsome Maria Schneider as the film's sex interest. But Nicholson is never afforded the depth that had been awarded Brando. His dialogue is largely execrable, his sex scenes suggested rather than demonstrated, his angst more sigh than cry. And as a reporter, a profession dependent upon the suppression of one's individuality for the sake of the story, he's hard to swallow. He's so naturally self-centered that that capacity comes across even in the few inquisitions he's given.

Needless to add, Nicholson's fanbase was seriously disappointed, failing to appreciate that after a bravura, nay, iconic performance in *Cuckoo's Nest*, the actor was looking, like any performer worth their mettle, to change tack. Same lesson for Nicholson as for Locke, then, another victim of identity switch: While exchanging personalities can be fun, it can also be fatal.

Nicholson's emasculation didn't prevent the highbrows from unharnessing the huzzahs, some for him, most for Antonioni. Vincent Canby of *The New York Times* veritably gushed about the film, while David Thomson went so far as to call it "one of the great films of the seventies."[9] All hyperbole aside, *The Passenger* is an interesting and worthy work. It's not good Nicholson but it is good, though certainly not great, Antonioni.

Nicholson, too, liked the film. Further, his admiration for its director never waned. In '94, Nicholson proudly bestowed an honorary Oscar upon the ailing filmmaker, who struggled mightily, post-stroke, to express his appreciation. (Antonioni died in 2007, on the same day as an even bigger art house divinity, Ingmar Bergman.) And when *The Passenger* was released on DVD in 2006, Nicholson contributed to the commentary.

If *The Passenger* failed to reaffirm the prodigiousness of Nicholson's talent, he nevertheless remained, thanks to the fresh memory of *Cuckoo's Nest*, the world's biggest male movie star. So why would he let himself be dwarfed a second time? Answer: for a chance to work with his idol, Marlon Brando.

Anticipation ran high about the pairing of the two, especially as it would be in a script by esteemed novelist Tom McGuane and under the direction of Arthur Penn. But *The Missouri Breaks*, though it has its merits, failed to provide the sparks audiences and critics were looking for. Brando, as a gunfighter hired by a land baron to eliminate grungy rustler Nicholson, spends too much of the film entertaining himself, with crazy costumes, varying accents and episodes of masochistic relish. And Nicholson, in an act of reverence one supposes, stays largely on the sidelines.

It's not that it's non-role or a non-film. Big Jack—well, Small Jack here—does indeed have a handful of good moments, including an obliquely flirty romance with a sexually independent spirit (Kathleen Lloyd). But on the whole, he's happy, it appears, to let Brando act while he in turn *reacts*. What should have been a Jack Nicholson film becomes, despite his co-star having a lot less screen time, a Marlon Brando film. Like *Last Tango*, the movie becomes *about* Brando. His idiosyncratic choices dictate its rhythms and resonance.

What Nicholson needed after *Breaks* was a break, a return to his rightful spotlight. He had the pull now to do whatever he wanted, to branch out, to remind the world on the largest scale yet afforded him that he had begun as a cinematic multi-talent: actor, writer, director. Before that, though, he'd grab a quick chance to work with Elia Kazan, the directorial God of his generation, in *The Last Tycoon* (1976), based on F. Scott Fitzgerald's unfinished fictionalization of the lonely life of MGM overlord Irving Thalberg. And Nicholson's scenes would pit him *mano a mano* against the rising young actor aspiring to take his place as America's go-to anti-hero: Robert De Niro. Funny. Less than a year earlier, Nicholson had been the cock of the walk; already, he was the Grand Old Man of the game, feeling the hot breath of the coming generation against his neck.

Nicholson and De Niro's scenes play on that very notion. There's a palpably personal friction to their battles, as Nicholson's Communist agitator is coerced into taking on the proudly capitalist studio head, played by De Niro, in a game of emotionally charged ping pong. These precious, better-late-than-never moments, coming in at the film's 98-minute mark, provide the only true sparks in what is otherwise a disappointingly staid adaptation. Still, Nicholson got to work with Kazan while sizing up the new kid in town.

No more high-profile pairings. After failing to create the anticipated chemistry with both the old, Brando, and the new, De Niro, Nicholson set out to hog the screen for himself.

And hog it he did. In the self-directed *Goin' South* (1978), Nicholson was looking to again unleash his inner clown, a facet of his personality he'd been keeping in a box since *The Fortune*. Now it was released under the wide Texas sky, as he wrangled his way out of the grip of a posse looking to hang him for horse thievery. A post–Civil War loophole releases him into the arms of a wan, loopy widow—one so sexually starchy, however, that she nearly makes him second-guess his bureaucratic good fortune.

If that dynamic sounds familiar, it's borrowed from John Huston, who likely influenced Nicholson as his pseudo-father-in-law in life and co-star in *Chinatown*. Many a critic pointed out the ruffian vs. virgin schtick from Huston hits like *The African Queen* (1951) and *Heaven Knows, Mr. Allison* (1957). But Nicholson, directorially, is no Huston. Even though he had directed before—*Drive He Said* (1971)—he shows a wonky facility for cinematic storytelling. He'd try his luck and fail again with *The Two Jakes* (1990), his ill-fated follow-up to *Chinatown*.

Goin' South, then, despite romcom aspirations, is one long comeuppance. For every loutish offense Nicholson's hero commits, there's a circumstantial admonishment. Female lead Mary Steenburgen, with the healthy hand of Providence, is the amalgamation of previous Nicholson heroines (Karen Black, Candice Bergen, Ann-Margret, Louise Fletcher, etc.) finally triumphing over the man who has made their lives a tortuous affair. Steenburgen accomplishes the impossible and tames him, forcing him to work her land, cut ties with his grubby gang, and trade rape for romance. By subscribing to such submission, Jack the public figure—the high-livin' misogynist who keeps company with suspect types like Roman Polanski—subversively atones for his sins, addressing the ire afforded him by the less merciful critics for his crass on-screen cocksmanship.

As for Nicholson's acting, you find yourself scratching your head like McMurphy and asking, "Well ... is it?" His shameless display of mugs, leers and other facial contortions sets you to entertain definitions of his actions from "Grand Guignol" to "shameless self-parody." In the end, you decide that it isn't acting at all, or even overacting—it's acting up, an infantile variation. Maybe Nicholson was too eager to please. Maybe he remained uncertain about the funniness of the script. Maybe he was too determined to reestablish himself as a bona fide star after so long a time in the woods. Whatever the case, it's a baffling dismantling of the reputation for integrity and dependability he had worked so hard to establish.

Further, this broader style helped pave a new path, one he'd set out on for good in his next film—his *real* comeback picture.

After putting other actors through their paces, it was time for Nicholson to be put through his again—and then some. He'd be working for Film Studies demiurge Stanley Kubrick, making his first film since his visually stunning, dramatically bereft *Barry Lyndon* (1975). Kubrick was known as an aloof intellectual, a brilliant cinematic technician, and an actor's nightmare; a William Wyler–esque 75 takes (or more) per scene was not out of the question. So Jack had his work cut out for him in

The Shining. Plus, there was the role: a novelist and family man who, snowbound in a haunted hotel, converts to homicidal maniac and goes after the wife and kid.

Before *Goin' South*, Nicholson had been prized as a naturalistic actor with, yes, a propensity for a violating garishness. *The Shining* affirmed that the latter capacity, which he had chancily demonstrated in that self-directed Western, had not been a caprice but a conversion. A leap had been irrevocably made, from portraiture to caricature. Taking the Kazan-Brando ethic a step further, Nicholson wasn't just out to surprise any more. He was out to shock, to stun, to smother. He had decided to go big, not home. Hence the new nickname he'd acquire, reflecting not only his larger-than-life roles but the extravagant lifestyle that went with them: Big Jack.

In *Terms of Endearment* (1983), he plays an ex-astronaut whose naughtier habits—his sarcasm, his lasciviousness, his contempt for social protocol—don't detract from his popularity but instead enhance it. Nicholson drew not from his own emotional experiences but from his rep. Pauline Kael, reflecting on the transition from actor to icon in her famous essay on Cary Grant, was also foreshadowing the fate of Nicholson: "It was his one creation, and it had become the only role for him to play—the only role, finally, he *could* play."[10] Nicholson would still be cast to act, yes, but primarily to afford properties "that Jack Nicholson feeling." So Big Jack's characters became just that: big. Film by film, they grew larger and more buffoonish. He was the Devil (*The Witches of Eastwick*), the Joker (*Batman*, 1989), Jimmy Hoffa (*Hoffa*, 1992) and other larger-than-life figures. Of this, he offered, "I love to put myself somewhere where they can say, 'Jeez, he's overacting again!' Which I am, but damn, that's why I'm good!"[11]

This mythomania culminated in *The Bucket List* (2007), a part so modeled on his own personality and image—in the new way, not the *Five Easy Pieces* way—that Jack the actor, like his character's final trek into the geographic beyond, disappears.

Al Pacino

Forever Wired

The moment the audience gets to know Al Pacino, his characters are finished; no longer will we accept them on their own terms. We'll see the guide wire on the flying man, the milky white wrist of the puppeteer, the spirit gum holding the mustache to the face. We won't see Michael Corleone or Frank Serpico but Al Pacino as Michael Corleone or Frank Serpico—a bifurcation that is the intensely immersive Pacino's worst nightmare.

But this, the palimpsest, the awareness of the manipulator behind the mask, is inevitable. Even the world's greatest actors have limitations: signature looks, voices, gestures and other tell-tale traits that cannot be entirely subsumed—not to mention a propensity for picking parts reflecting autobiographical themes. So, sorry, Al, try as you might—and God knows you do, by both your dedication to disguise and your distance from the press—you are not entirely overwhelmed bank robber Sonny Wortzik or romantic race car driver Bobby Deerfield (you should thank God for that one). You're Bronx-born, coarse-voiced, fiery-tempered Al Pacino.

Plus, you have those eyes, those famously large, dark eyes…

"Al Pacino tries to suit his looks to the characters," director Sidney Lumet wrote in *Making Movies*, "but somehow, it's the way his eyes express an enormous rage, even in tender moments, that enthralls me and everyone else."[1]

The windows of the soul, people call them. In your case, Al, a soul that is perpetually on fire, reflecting a burning rage against circumstance's continual tests of your precarious sanity. It's there in *The Godfather* when you improbably plot your first kill, and in its sequel when your wife tips you over the edge by confessing the fate of your baby. It's there in *Dog Day Afternoon* when the heist you pull goes ridiculously awry and you find yourself the nervous, unwitting star of the world's first Reality TV show. It's there in *…And Justice for All* when you rabidly spout those catchphrases at top volume in the climactic courtroom contretemps.

You're a powder keg—an Italian American version of your equally Brando-influenced contemporary Jack Nicholson. When Brando got all worked up, he called it "lightning states"; when Nicholson did it, he called it "overacting"; when you do it, you call it "life on the wire." The definition is the only differential.

"A life on the wire." You once explained that phrase to the one interviewer you've ever taken a shine to, Lawrence Grobel: "You know the [trapeze artists]

Flying Wallendas? The accident they had?" (an eight-person high-wire stunt engineered by Papa Carl Wallenda, which ended in a tragic fall). "He was up there, and they said, 'How can you go up there again after that tragedy?' And he said, 'Life's on the wire. The rest is just waiting.' That's where life is for me. That's where it happens."[2]

As for *how* you make it happen, that explication was appropriated by Andrew Yule: In his unauthorized biography, you're quoted as saying, "I like to get caught up in a world and make it imaginative and alive. I *need* to do it!"[3]

If that sounds like an only child having to amuse himself, Dear Reader, you're right. That's what Pacino was, in the Bronx in the '40s, a life made even lonelier by the early departure of his father (yes, the father-son thing again). As a result, Pacino sought out substitute dads, including two seminal figures: actor Charles Laughton (not *that* Charles Laughton) and Lee Strasberg. Strasberg, after having rejected Pacino for the famous Actors Studio four times, finally set him straight: "There is a freshness and spontaneity in you," he admitted to the struggling performer, "but now, they need to serve a greater aliveness."[4]

As Pacino was short, alcoholic and unfocused, the Studio remained uncertain that they could slap the harness of dedication on him. So poor, put-out Pacino toiled at a series of thankless day jobs. Finally, he was admitted to Strasbergland in 1967, the same year as another what-the-hell-do-we-do-with-this-guy type, Dustin Hoffman.

Within the year, Hoffman, through the movies, became a household name. Pacino, conversely, distinguished himself first off-, then on, Broadway. The reviews would land him, too, in the movies. Even as an unproven cinematic commodity, though, when it came to roles, he would insist on playing the chooser, not the beggar.

Inexperienced as Pacino was in front of the camera, he came to the movies with a mission: to bring the immediacy of the stage to the more passive medium of film. A tall order, but the times were right for it. Hollywood had offered staid, overblown, unadventurous fare for so long, it left the door open for European, independent and even exploitative work to reinvent the form. Part of that reform was the introduction of social realism. It had had a few practitioners—foremost, Elia Kazan—but now, the times being what they were, it became *de rigueur* to sucker punch audiences with an unsavory authenticity reflecting the highly dysfunctional zeitgeist. Big-budget artifice was out, low-budget rawness was in. Square-jawed heroes who saved the day could eat *Easy Rider*'s dust. Fallible anti-heroes who couldn't save themselves could take their exalted place among the lonesome losers of *Midnight Cowboy*.

Midnight Cowboy initiated the "New York film," a subgenre concentrating on those dramatically marginalized by the urban decay of that once proud metropolis. The protagonists of those films were prostitutes, junkies, vigilantes and the hard-nosed cops forced to deal with them. Together, they suffered the abasement of urban life, each a failed idealist looking to hold his or her head high under the weighty oppressiveness of daily, discounted existence. It made for films marked by grit, tragedy and volatility—the very qualities Pacino was looking to impart to the screen. In time, he became the New York film's crown prince, the embodiment of the confrontational survivor's spirit in a dispirited place and time.

Serpico (1973) helped to make Al Pacino synonymous with the "New York film" (Paramount/Photofest).

Pacino's first overture to this identity was *The Panic in Needle Park*, directed by ex–still photographer Jerry Schatzberg, who worked with Pacino again on *Scarecrow*. There's little doubt, watching *Panic*, of the debt the film owes to *Midnight Cowboy*. Both feature the dirty underside of New York City, the loose vagrants calling its noisy streets their home, and the central relationship between two good-hearted losers who fall into a love-hate arrangement as they attempt to look out for one another.

Pacino, making his first on-screen impression, even looks and sounds like a slight variation on Hoffman's Ratso Rizzo. He scrounges and clowns his way around "Needle Park" (a notorious heroin addict hangout at 72nd and Broadway), staking claim to what he unabashedly calls, in his nasal Bronx accent, his turf. Through an artist friend (a young Raul Julia), Pacino's Bobby (so named for the bob in his step when he's high?) meets Helen, a sweetly sad import from Indiana (played by the underrated Kitty Winn, who took home the Best Actress prize at Cannes for her performance). Much of the rest of the first act is a Cook's tour as she—and vicariously, we—are introduced to Bobby's world, as well as the leitmotifs that will run throughout the career of Bobby's puppet master Pacino.

First, there's the complicated father-son, or sometimes big brother-little brother, bent. This time, it's Bobby's criminal relative; later, as Michael Corleone, it will be James Caan's Sonny. Then there's the stance on women. In Pacino pictures, women are creatures of greater purity than himself; he must keep them away from the dangerous environment he inhabits. This is Helen in *Panic*, Kay in the *Godfather* films, Serpico's flirty female neighbor, and Sonny Wortzik's same-sex lover in *Dog Day Afternoon*. And note the central character's hollow vow to clean up his act, only to fall deeper into the mire. It'll come up again as Michael wrestles with the mob,

Serpico fights for justice, and poor, trapped Sonny attempts to negotiate his way to safety.

We are also introduced to the noticeable influence of Pacino's idol, Brando. These tells include Pacino's fundamental restlessness, the offhanded delivery of his lines (many likely ad-libbed) and his propensity for monkeyshines—and also the unleashing of his magnified pique. When Pacino lets out his ire, mostly at poor, scared Kitty as she prostitutes herself to support their mutual drug dependency, we are stunned that a fit of anger of such magnitude can come out of such a small physical presence. Brando had the body for this kind of thing, but watching the diminutive Pacino unleash it is like witnessing a lion's roar come out of a chihuahua.

By film's end, there was no doubt in the minds of those who bothered to originally see it that amid this oppressively realistic examination of the everyday indignities of drug addiction, there was an exciting new talent at work. Here was a fresh, electric presence with the capabilities to give full, resonant voice to contemporary discontent. When Brando provided this service back in the '50s, it was in movies that had made a very big splash. *Panic*, despite the buzz at Cannes, did little more than cut American film's ties with facile, overblown examinations of the phenomenon of addiction. That said, one figure of importance did see the film—an up-and-coming filmmaker transitioning from DIY maverick to studio-backed wunderkind: Francis Ford Coppola.

Though *Panic* earned respectable reviews and developed a cult following, when Coppola cast Pacino in *The Godfather*, the actor was still largely unknown. He had to audition for the role of good son Michael Corleone several times, in fact, after repeatedly acting indifferent and making up much of the dialogue. He wanted the part and he didn't. Sidney Lumet, in his literary portrait of the actor, went on to call him an instinctive animal but one who makes slow decisions. In life as in art, it appeared. And hey, in both cases, doesn't that kind of behavior sound like Brando?

But from Coppola, who had a sound reputation for working with actors, this wild young buck learned much. Pacino's performance in the film is no less than a master class in the art of acting for the screen. In contrast to *Panic*, it's a rendering of great, redolent interiority. For a volatile type whose mission was to bring the abrasive quality of live theater to the movies, Pacino demonstrates a brilliantly studied facility for conspiring with the camera. He uses his small stature, stooped posture and vivid, busy eyes (of course) to do most of the talking. Even in *Panic*, we saw a stage actor. Here, he's a film actor.

From the opening scene, in which white-sheep-of-the-black-family Michael tests his WASPy fiancée's (Diane Keaton) tolerance for the Corleones' crime-ridden lineage, there is always something visibly at work in Michael. Michael assures her that he is not cut from the familial cloth but it's obvious that already, he's unsure of the assertion. We see, with nothing more than expert body language, the prospective tragedy of his conversion.

It's a transmutation rooted in a simple sentiment: a son's pure love for his father. After the Don is cut down in a mounting rivalry with other families, Michael finds himself at the old man's bedside. There, he whispers to his bullet-ridden father, "I'm with you." This is not a declaration of political affiliation. There is none of that yet. Michael is speaking strictly as a caregiver. It's an important decision on Pacino's part. In so emphasizing, the Corleones become not a "family" but a family, any family. As such, we automatically forgive them their trespasses. Suddenly, they are us and we are them. We'll even end up rooting for them, as brutal as their actions will become, when their war with their enemies escalates.

It's this uncorrupted affection, in fact, that sparks good-son-goes-bad Michael's rise to the head of the family. Discovering in that same scene that his father's bodyguards have been dangerously evacuated from the hospital in which he's housed, Michael's protestation is met with a dramatic punch in the mouth from a corrupt cop (the perfectly cast Sterling Hayden). Thus, the tipping point is set into motion: Michael begins to plot his murderous revenge, triggering the criminal education that will alchemize father-son affection into Machiavellian ambition.

From there, a quiet sureness begins to visibly mount within Pacino's Michael, loaded with elliptical pauses borrowed from Brando's Don to better suggest Michael's succession within the family (the dust-up he suffers at the hands of the cop helps, giving him the same jutting jaw and muffled speech as Brando's Don Corleone). He remains an introspective creature, but the introspection grows weighty, creating a subworld within a subworld. The head is heavy even before the crown has been fit. This Damoclean pensiveness provides a clever, fitting and effective contrast to everybody else, who are all so verbal (even the low-key Robert Duvall).

The revelation is that Pacino is a smart, studied actor who's very careful with what he makes big and what he makes small; simply put, an artist who makes consistently good decisions. The suspense inherent in the actions of the character is, as a result, positively Hitchcockian. It carries the post–Brando section of the film. And all of this with little more than hooded eyes set deep in an emphatic deadpan. Pacino goes over the top but once, when his now-wife (Keaton), at film's end, chancily inquires about the nature of her now all-powerful husband's professional actions.

In that moment, the film returns to one of its major thematic investigations: the weightiness of manhood. Michael, on less than sure feet, is determined to break the family mold, only to be fitted, in the end, for his father's shoes. In the film's impactful last shot, Michael's office door closes, literally, on his wife, sealing him in his new identity.

Needless to add, after Brando, Pacino collected the bulk of the critical kudos. It was clear that with sympathetic but stern direction, the qualities unveiled in *Panic in Needle Park* could be expertly applied to suit a variety of characters and narratives. For the next few years, the famously selective Pacino would ensure that the roles, stories and directors he chose made good on that assumption.

One of the ways he achieved this was by remaining in New York. Unlike others who might have made the pilgrimage to Hollywood after such a success, Pacino stood fast to his stage actor's belief that being at the heart of the film industry might corrupt his instincts, making him something less than a commanding presence. Plus, the place was dullsville. New York remained the place to be. He continued to devote himself to the promotion of "the New York film," bold, location-shot dramas about the confused characters in the crannies of that eroding metropolis.

Before that, though, a diversion: the aforementioned *Scarecrow*, a road movie co-starring Gene Hackman, helmed by Jerry Schatzberg.

Since the exploratory '60s, the drifter had become a quintessential American character. Folk songs were populated with good-time ramblers who, after a meal, a chance fuck or a hand-out, were "bound for movin' on." They were searching, in their own penniless, locus-eating fashion, for the proverbial "real America," a genuinely democratic spirit that capitalism, monogamy, racism and other '60s bugaboos had sent into hiding. Kids across the country were leaving their stodgy suburban homes for wide open spaces, even if all that geography offered was not much more than the catch-as-catch-can rewards of belonging to the loosely knit counterculture (the heroes of *Easy Rider* constituting the black-leather version of it).

In *Scarecrow*, Pacino's "Lion" (short for Lionel) is cut from such a cloth. Adrift in California, he meets up with Max, a like spirit who plays big brother and lets him in on his dream: the establishment of a car wash in Pittsburgh. Max is Hackman. Director Schatzberg let the two actors loose within the film's thin, ultimately sentimental narrative, in hopes of creating a sociological study of society's lost element akin to the realism he had brought to *Panic in Needle Park*. What he got, at least from Pacino, was the full liberation of the actor's inner Brando—and not Brando on his best behavior either. There's a lot of restlessness, a lot of buffoonery, a lot of fiddling with props, a lot of obtuse wit. After a while, you wonder whether there's a characterization going on at all. When not indulging himself, Pacino sits at Hackman's feet and, as in *The Godfather*, lets himself be shaped by an older, wiser figure.

It's interesting to contrast Schatzberg's looseness with Coppola's control. Both, it's obvious, were dedicated admirers of Pacino's talents. This infatuation, and the *cinema verité* bent he was looking to pursue, led the former to simply stay out of the actor's way. Conversely, Coppola's appreciation prompted him to strictly discipline Pacino lest he violate the director's script-based classicism.

Classify *Scarecrow*, then, for Pacino, a breather, before his return to more focused, worthier work.

Aside from Woody Allen, nobody made films that exuded the spirit of contemporary New York more than Sidney Lumet. Unlike his comic counterpart, Lumet was not interested in the sexual politics or existential angst of the city's cultural elite. He was a product of the streets. That point of pride would become more pronounced as he turned to filmmaking.

Though he was hardly a Baby Boomer, having come of age during the Great Depression, Lumet was the perfect director to uphold the tenets of the younger generation. He had championed the anti-hero long before that archetype had been affixed a label, and the martyr long before dying for the world's sins had become the ultimate act of personal rebellion and social critique. Lumet's heroes were whistle-blowers, respectable enough on the outside but dangerously intuitive on the in-. Each is nudged until set into influential motion: Henry Fonda as the dissenting minority in *Twelve Angry Men* (1959), George Segal as the sensitive intellectual in *Bye, Bye Braverman* (1968), Albert Finney in *j'accuse* mode in *Murder on the Orient Express* (1974), to name but a few. Rogue cop Frank Serpico, then, is the ultimate Lumet hero, obsessed, as Lumet was, with justice, and destined to suffer the sting of guilt and the ignominy of righteousness.

The real-life Serpico's saga was first conveyed in biographical form, via journalist Peter Maas. Maas had a thing for informants, having previously told the story of Joe Valachi, the first Mafia insider to play government witness (adapted for the screen as the Charles Bronson *Godfather* cash-in *The Valachi Papers*, 1972). It was a fascination shared by the man who turned Maas' book into a screenplay, Waldo Salt (of *Midnight Cowboy*). Salt, outed as a Communist at the 1951 round of HUAC hearings, had been on the receiving end of the practice; *Serpico* even directly equates police corruption with McCarthyism.

The film's other writer was Norman Wexler, a complex character with a feel for the cultural tenor of modern-day New York, having written the generational tug-of-war satire *Joe* (1970) and a few short years away from expanding a *New York* magazine article into the iconic *Saturday Night Fever* (1977). Together, Salt and Wexler cobbled an accusatory exposé of the modern metropolitan police force, whose members make an ancillary living off the avails of criminals.

Like *On the Waterfront*, *Serpico* makes no bones about the Christ-like nature of its protagonist. The hirsute Serpico is a fallen figure as soon as the picture opens, fighting for his life in the back of a squad car. The first words in the film, in fact, are "Jesus Christ!," spoken by a police colleague at the news of Serpico's impending death. Cue two hours (plus) of sequential flashbacks, tracing Serpico's rise from taciturn patrolman to vocal detective, refusing all the while to be cut in on the proliferation of side money being distributed throughout the force (in Serpico's precinct alone, $250,000). Serpico discovers a mass cover-up that, in Watergate style, goes all the way to the top. It's a slippery slope—small wonder our holier-than-thou hero suffers a dramatic descent into mortality.

The multi-faceted Serpico is an amalgam of heroes portrayed by Pacino's contemporaries. He's an innocent brought to resignation, like the characters of Dustin Hoffman; a rebel working within an institution, like the characters of Gene Hackman; a bohemian hothead, like the characters of Jack Nicholson; a stickler for protocol, like the characters of Robert Duvall; and a man of small triumphs, like the characters of Robert De Niro. Interestingly, he's also filmdom's only hippie for the establishment. Throughout his travails, Serpico's respect for the American policeman holds firm. He may look the part of a counterculture spokesperson, but he does not classify the boys in blue as "pigs" or "fuzz." What he's advocating for is neo-traditionalism: A return to the principles on which law enforcement was founded. This unusual stance affirms a Pacino precedent set forth in *The Godfather*: his characters are not anarchists but nostalgists, putting their necks on the line for such old-fashioned values as institutional integrity and operational efficiency.

Despite its main character's pro-police stance, *Serpico* nevertheless resonated with the youth audience. The protagonist's struggles still managed to parallel their all-consuming battles for social justice and the deeply discombobulating effect of those melees on their personal lives.

Serpico was Pacino's first bona fide starring role (he is in almost every scene, and there are plenty: the film boasts over 150 locations). There's no sharing the screen with anybody else, other than a plethora of contrasting character actors: older, taller and predominantly Irish. Serpico, on the other hand, is young, short and

Italian. He lives in the Village, where he experiments with facial hair, listens to opera and picks up free-spirited blondes on his motorcycle. He's newfangled on the outside, old-fashioned on the inside; his thrift store wardrobe suggests the peace-love generation, his incorruptible morality classic Hollywood heroes. Unlike his work in *The Godfather*, and in a bit of a return to *The Panic in Needle Park*, Pacino delivers an unabashedly extroverted performance. He spends the first third of the film humanizing the character, lest audiences go on to write Serpico off as a mere symbol. And so out comes the *Panic* Pacino, the loose, playful man of the streets, the peppy "paisan." He lets kids hose him down with a fire hydrant, clowns for prospective girlfriends, and plays up his bohemian image for his stuffier colleagues back at the precinct. Later, as Serpico's *Lenny*-like fight for justice goes into its final rounds, a hangdog pensiveness sets in, interpolated with well-placed explosions of pent-up exasperation. And there's a moving climax, revisiting Pacino's pet theme of father-son relationships when Serpico's mentor, Chief Sidney Green (played by John Randolph, another HUAC victim), visits him in the hospital after his young charge suffers the face-piercing gun wound that opened the film.

Director Lumet, trained in the formative days of television, understood the value of blocking, rehearsing and turning things around at lightning speed. His films, like dialogue-happy, CU-centric and generally melodramatic '50s TV, implacably placed the premium on the actor. As a result, try finding one who had a bad word to say about him. Lumet instinctively understood the innate strengths of his chosen performers, as well as their behavioral pitfalls. In Pacino, he no doubt recognized, as Coppola had before him, an animal in search of a cage. With constructive control, Lumet does one better than Coppola, and certainly Schatzberg: He frees Pacino from the exacerbated interiority of *The Godfather* while tempering the self-indulgence that had muddled *Scarecrow*. The result is an impressively varied performance, at once studied and spontaneous. For the first time, audiences were made aware of Pacino's full range. So privileged, they became aware that he could carry the ball by himself. Hitherto, Pacino had been classified a character actor. Now, he was a star.

What better form of attestation of this newfound status than a return to the role that had put him on the map? Intrigued by a slim middle backstory in the thick of Mario Puzo's pulpy (and occasionally absurd) best-seller, Coppola contacted his former collaborator and suggested a second *Godfather*. This one would serve as both prequel and sequel, tracing the roots of the infamous Corleone family while checking in on the state of the regime under the watch of its new capo, Michael. As proof that great minds think alike, Puzo had been at work on a follow-up of his own, picking up the saga where it had left off. Wine was imbibed, ideas were exchanged, financing was secured. Reassembly of the original cast proved another matter.

Coppola and Puzo had incorporated a flashback involving Don Corleone and hotheaded successor Number One, Sonny. While both Brando and James Caan had agreed to appear, both ultimately balked, though Caan eventually acquiesced. Richard Castellano, aka "Fat" Clemenza, passed on appearing in the film altogether, necessitating the creation of a role for coarse-voiced actor-playwright Michael V. Gazzo. Pacino was also trouble. Unhappy with the direction in which Coppola and Puzo had taken Michael, he insisted on a rewrite. Finally, he, too, signed on.

With *The Godfather Part II*, Coppola set out to make two films in one, an interwoven double-feature. He would make a modern American gangster picture as well as a foreign film, the first in the manner of the original *Godfather*, the second in the manner of the Italian auteurs then at large: Fellini, Visconti, Bertolucci, Antonioni, etc.

The introductory story picked up the saga of Michael Corleone as he struggles to maintain and expand the crime empire established by his father, no easy feat when dealing with double-crossing business partners and an executive investigation. *Part II* chronicled the original Don's rise from Sicilian orphan to immigrant despot, after his relocation to New York City (a replication of the expatriate experience that is a glowing testament to the collective talents of Coppola's production team).

Even after the film, rendered on an epic scale, was assembled (in a remarkably short period, to accommodate a Christmas Day release), Coppola was repeatedly reprimanded for its twin narratives. The contention was that he had created not a whole cloth, but pieces too loosely stitched together. Ironically, today, it's the comprehensive quality of the film that is its biggest distinction. Its diptych-like structure serves to historically contextualize Michael's burden, as he investigates an assassination attempt on himself and his family while ironing out the tricky business of international expansion in a more complex and scrutinous age. Meanwhile, the film periodically reflects on how that empire was established, through young Vito Corleone's rise from humble newcomer to defender of his people against the notorious Black Hand. By giving us both stories, Coppola is able to show the historical sacrifices made in the name of the Corleones' sacred virtue, family and its climactic erosion under the struggling Michael.

Michael, the last stop in this long parade of murders and other forms of corruption, is a figure haunted by the specter of death. His sunken body, tired eyes (yes, those eyes again) and reflective melancholy attest to it. The sins of the family have physically reshaped him. As for his manner, this is not a man who can mentally rest. Not for a second. Pacino's conveyance of the high-stakes chess game that is continuously being played in Michael's mind affirms the actor's remarkable facility with demonstrable subtext. By Michael's face alone, we become acutely aware of a professional exhaustion and post-traumatic sadness he cannot afford to wear on the outside. In the same way that Michael controls a frail fiefdom with deep intuition and despotic taciturnity, Pacino controls Michael with a darkly hypnotic minimalism.

It's Pacino's first fully mature performance as a fully mature character. Hitherto, his heroes had always started from a place of naivete, making their way to resignation—including his original Michael. But this Michael is tragically formed from the film's first frames. He's long been trapped in the persona he assumed at the conclusion of the first movie. There is no going back to innocence, despite his poor, suffering wife's pleas to make good on his promise to go clean. Nor can he go forward: The crime syndicate of which he is a part is already "bigger than U.S. Steel," a jacquerie is threatening his stake in Bautista's Cuba, and bullets keep coming at him like the barrage that took down his brother Sonny.

Brotherhood, a healthy component of the Corleone family dynamic, plays a major part in the film. Small surprise, as Pacino films have probed this dynamic before. The tension between Michael and Fredo, the sickly elder brother who is always looking to restore the family pecking order, reminds us yet again, like so many films made by Coppola, Martin Scorsese and the rest of Pacino's generation, of the influential *On the Waterfront* and the complicated relationship between Marlon Brando and Rod Steiger. Here, though, it's the Steiger figure who triumphs, as Michael is forced to eradicate Fredo. By committing fratricide, Michael turns his back on the fundamental principle that has fueled all of his actions, as well as those of his father.

Father-son relations, another Pacino pursuit, run deep here too. We see Vito repeatedly bestow affection upon his boys, and Michael do the same. When Michael's wife Kay "loses" a baby boy, the former is brought to outright ire. Then there's the father-son relationship between Michael and business partner Hyman Roth (played at Pacino's insistence by one of his own father figures, acting mentor Strasberg). All of this to reinforce one of the film's major preponderances: the price of filial affection.

Part of paying that price includes a climactic witch hunt akin to the one that concluded the original film. At the time of the film's release, 1974, it paralleled the paranoia then at large in the Nixon White House, as that corrupt president conspired to put down all threats to his influence. (There's a nod to the Kennedy years in the film, too, with the Jack Ruby–style assassination of the Strasberg character.) So, while the film might comprise two period pieces—one set early in the twentieth century, the other at the midpoint—what Coppola and Puzo had fashioned was a contemporary commentary.

While *The Godfather Part II* didn't make the money or garner the instant accolades that the first film did, it nevertheless caused a sensation. Coppola & Co. swept the Oscars, though Pacino was passed over for Art Carney in Paul Mazursky's picaresque road movie *Harry and Tonto* (1974). Worthily nuanced as Carney's performance was, the gesture, along with the co-snub of Jack Nicholson in *Chinatown*, was proof that the Motion Picture Academy was not yet ready to embrace the work of the emergent class of male movie stars. (Curiously, their female counterparts were being heartily accepted, with wins for Jane Fonda in *Klute*, 1971, and Ellen Burstyn in *Alice Doesn't Live Here Anymore*, 1974.)

Sold on working for directors with an innate sense of how to control him, Pacino next put himself in another pair of trusted hands.

On a sweltering day in 1972, a trio of first-time thieves entered the Chase Manhattan Bank in the heart of Brooklyn. Finding themselves the victim of faulty information (the bank's reserves had been hauled away earlier that morning), one of them fled while the other two, hellbent on money, took the employees hostage for an ad hoc ransom. Ringleader Sonny Wojtowicz (renamed, less than cleverly, Wotzik in the movie) was desperate to finance a sex change operation for his same-sex lover. The four-hour stand-off which ensued turned into one of America's first media circuses.

Brooklyn, heat, madness ... sounds like a New York movie to me. In fact, alongside *Taxi Driver*, *Dog Day Afternoon* (originally named *The Boys in the Bank*) is considered *the* New York movie. Who better to direct than Lumet, one of the architects of the subgenre?

Al Pacino's search for father figures, off- and on-screen, was exhibited by his relationship with mentor Lee Strasberg (left) in *The Godfather Part II* (1974) (Paramount/Photofest).

Borrowing from his pedigree in the formative days of television, and the success of the courtroom drama *Twelve Angry Men* (his first film), Lumet designed a bank with movable walls. Further, he put his camera crew on roller skates, helping to create visual fluency within an otherwise restrictive environment. While some aspects of the film remain play-like, Lumet's pushes, pulls, tracking shots and zooms bring a distinctly cinematic fluidity to the proceedings.

For the exterior scenes—a replication of the rowdy real-life crowds that gathered to jeer the cops and cheer the criminals—Lumet went with a newsreel feel. His purpose was twofold: to remind the audience of the event's roots in actuality, and to have satiric fun with the increasingly savage nature of television (something Lumet would pick up again in his next film, *Network*).

As for the cast, Lumet was almost forced to go with Dustin Hoffman, who, still making a career out of investigating sexual differences, had no problems with playing the bisexual lead. Pacino, though, was less convinced that America was ready for such a sexually conflicted leading man. While the sexual revolution had come and gone, the gay liberation movement remained in its infancy. Lumet agreed to tone down certain aspects of the character, going so far as to concede to Pacino in other ways: He let him (and the rest of the cast) ad-lib generously and took Pacino's advice on the supporting cast.

Dog Day Afternoon is the film that comes the closest to Pacino's dream of making the movies seem like live theater. David Thomson in his *Have you Seen…?* calls it "very close to that sense of burning street theater that was so self-conscious in New York in the 1970s."[5] It's as immersive an experience as the medium can provide. In watching Sonny and Sal, aka Pacino and John Cazale, you take your place among the sweaty, cranky, curious New Yorkers who crowd the otherwise nondescript street as personal cheerleading squad for angst comedy's newest vessels.

Previously, that style of neuroses-based humor could be found on Broadway—largely in the work of Neil Simon—and in cult film comedies starring existential hysterics like Alan Arkin and Gene Wilder. Even Woody Allen, the form's primary practitioner, wasn't fully at it yet; he was still stringing together jokes both lowbrow and high in search of a cohesive, relevant narrative. So Lumet, Pacino & Co. were the style's first big cinematic splash. (The film's basis in angst comedy would never abate. Comedy writer Rick Kaulbars, to whom this book is dedicated, posits *Dog Day*'s premise as, "What if Seinfeld robbed a bank?")

Pacino's Sonny is cut from the same cloth as the classic comic archetype, the kind played for years by klutzy, nervous cowards like Bob Hope and Danny Kaye. Undersized and unsure, Sonny's both physically and spiritually unfit for a role demanding bodily intimidation and internal fortitude. Pacino establishes this from the get-go with—surprise!—those tell-tale eyes of his. They seem rounder and glassier this time, snow globes in which little worlds of fear can be seen. He ambles with foolish determination into the bank, then affirms his unfit status with the struggle to liberate his archaic weapon from its guise, a florist's delivery box. No sooner has he made his criminal intentions clear to the bank's staff—who, comically, will begin to criticize his technique as it continues to falter—than the first of his accomplices turns tail, leaving only Sonny and deadpan partner Sal to carry out the robbery. We're still laughing by the time Mishap #2 takes place: the revelation that the money is missing and that Sonny and Sal are the victims of a bad tip.

By this time, it is the bank robbers, and not the hostages, who have our full sympathy—the first of the film's many bait 'n' switches. And our pity for them grows. As events progress, poor, overwhelmed Sonny finds himself forced to look after the needy, prickly hostages, negotiate with the equally underqualified and overwhelmed cops and their icy FBI counterparts, and—the film's comic topper—deal with his own loopy, loose-knit family, from his blowsy wife and his secret same-sex lover to his overprotective Jewish mother.

Sonny is a comic Michael Corleone. He's the self-appointed mastermind, never entirely certain that he's up to the task. He's the half-crazed caretaker of the world, whose last resort is the necessity of violence. Sonny even enjoys a father-son relationship akin to that of Michael and Vito Corleone, when his back-and-forth with the small-time police chief (a never-better Charles Durning) reveals itself to be a respectful but tricky back-and-forth between a young loose cannon and a dangerous figurehead with paternal instincts.

Like Michael, Sonny has a million things to think about at once and is just as visibly brought to the brink. Unlike Michael, there's no cool-headedness or strategic savvy. Sonny has no time to retreat into a darkly lit den and internalize. He can only bang his head against the door of the empty bank vault crying, "I gotta think … gotta think…." When he yells to the hostages, to the cops, to the crowd to spur this anti-hero-in-the-making on, it is not from the force of righteousness but from the sheer adrenaline of nervousness.

His only overture to confidence occurs serendipitously, when TV newscasts begin to make him, and those surrounding him, stars. In Lumet's wry commentary on the shapeshifting nature of public attention, Sonny eats it up and begins to delight in his status as a midday news commodity. So grandstanding, he begins to equate his situation with the famous Attica prison riots, reminding his growing fanbase of the suspect character of those who enforce the law. (Cops, in the wake of incidents like Kent State and Attica, were high on society's shit list at the time.)

But by the third act, it all becomes too much for Sonny: the tyrannous summer day, the constant clamoring of the media, the additional albatross of his cloying family. After an emotional phone call with his lover (the underrated Chris Sarandon), for whom Sonny staged the robbery in the first place, he finds himself spurned and crying. Seamlessly, the film shifts from dark comedy to a more somber, personal tone, as Sonny dictates his last will and testament, transitioning from crown clown to fatalistic figure.

Great as the film is—a small-scale thrill ride with expertly built laughs—it is not without its shortcomings, particularly skewed through the lens of social progress. The punchline-of-all-punchlines is the revelation of Sonny's bisexuality and his cranky-old-couple conversation with his mentally disturbed male lover. The ultimate example of New York madness at the time, a sour, sorry misstep in our pluralist

Pacino is a one-man show in *Dog Day Afternoon* (1975); it's perhaps the best single film performance by a member of his generation (Warner Bros./Photofest).

age. Otherwise, *Dog Day Afternoon* remains as funny and impactful as it was back in the day. How spoiled we were in 1975 to have robust tragicomedies the caliber of *Dog Day Afternoon* and *Cuckoo's Nest* released over the same period (and, in a different but equally enervating manner, *Jaws*). More than one revisionist has convincingly argued that that year constituted the apex of American filmmaking.

It was certainly an apex for Pacino, whose work waned as the decade progressed. Then again, how to top this performance? Despite its large, colorful cast, *Dog Day Afternoon* is essentially a one-man show. Over its kinetic two-plus hours, we watch Pacino run the gamut and then some. By film's end, he's been everything: broad joke, deluded lunatic, public spectacle, proletariat spokesperson, sensitive lover ... and finally, a full, fallible human being, exhausted by our basest instincts and inherent follies. It may well be the greatest performance of his career: indefatigably energetic, devotedly varied, masterfully regulated. It would have been easy to play the part in a simpler, more direct fashion and to let Frank Pierson's solidly constructed screenplay (peppered generously with spontaneous dialogue, to simulate naturalism) carry the Dog Day. Great as Dustin Hoffman can be, that's exactly what might have happened had he been cast, with Sonny becoming another of his clued-out personas out to extricate himself from a mess via his own hubristic intentions. Instead, Pacino helps the film be both a broad, black comedy and a tragic commentary anchored on the slippery status of our rationality, our foolish capacity for love, and our insurmountable fallibility.

Speaking of fallibility, let's segue from the exalted year of 1975 to the cinematic anticlimax of 1976. What the hell was in the water that year? Almost the entire class of Hollywood's top actors had their careers seriously sidelined: Dustin Hoffman settled for a co-star role in *All the President's Men* and fronted the critically polarizing *Marathon Man*; Gene Hackman was in *Lucky Lady*, a big-budget fiasco launched in late '75; Jack Nicholson was in a foreign film that made scant use of him, and did a handful of forgettable cameos; Robert De Niro had *Taxi Driver*, yes, but also played the eponymous hero in the disappointingly staid *The Last Tycoon*; and Pacino went on hiatus, convinced, despite what he had achieved in *Dog Day Afternoon*, that his films were failing to rise to the caliber of his performances on the stage. Only Robert Duvall was spared the mass ignominy of that bafflingly askew annum, appearing in no less three critical and financial successes: *Network, The Eagle Has Landed* and *The Seven-Per-Cent Solution*.

Pacino got his share of the misfortune the following year. With *Bobby Deerfield* (1977), the actor was truly out of his element—figuratively and literally. This dyed-in-the-wool, working-class, motormouthed New Yorker was imported to beatific Europe, to play a romantic figure no less: an internationally renowned race car driver. Rattled by the death of a colleague on the Formula One circuit, the eponymous Deerfield falls for a disturbed beauty, only to discover that she, too, is stamped for death (clue #1: hair loss). It sounds like poetic Eurocentric twaddle, heavily influenced by "la-la-la-la-la" work like Claude Lelouch's *A Man and a Woman* (1966). Sydney Pollack, who was making a name for himself as a director of conservative, autumnal romances, was hoping to convert it to poetic American twaddle, an artsy-fartsy version of his mega-hit *The Way We Were* (1973).

For Pacino, the choice of a love story is a significant one. Hitherto, his films, *Panic in Needle Park* excepted, had operated largely within the world of men (a major commonality with many of his contemporaries). As such, he had grown very popular with that demographic. And though he had become something of a sex symbol, he had yet to play up that part of his game (it went against his instincts as a purist). It was time he got the girl—and not a dysfunctional one as in *Panic,* an acquiescing one as in the *Godfather* films, or a woman-to-be as in *Dog Day Afternoon.*

He was also looking to break from the image he had created. Ever afraid of typecasting, he was looking to stretch—not just to try his hand at a different mode of acting but to appear in a different kind of film, with adjustments in location, characters, energy, sensibility and ideology.

European cinema was riding high at the time. Auteurs, including Fellini, Bergman and Truffaut, had become Old Masters, each making their last great successes. Many an American filmmaker, trapped within studio dictates, longed to unleash their reflective, intellectual sides, to throw over brash social relevance for poetic meditation, to wax verbally and visually on larger, loftier matters such as death, love and fate, complete with arcane framing, gauzy cinematography, and lush bucolic backgrounds and/or expressionistic art direction.

And so Pollack, long a fan of foreign film, tried his hand at it. The result is a poseur's picture, borrowing from the Europeans but unable to bring anything organic or newfangled to their conventions. It's like watching the work of a bad impressionist—and indeed, there *is* one in the film: In a flat comic scene, Pacino attempts to cheer up his doomed, troubled lover by imitating Mae West. (He also tries his hand at both singing and dancing, with the same execrable results.) While the film might have been rescued by the offbeat synergy of the central relationship, Pacino and co-star Marthe Keller offer nary a spark. She simply talks ad infinitum—her intellectual verbosity is supposed to pass for some kind of mental health issue—while he sits back and plays straight man. Who wants to see Al Pacino play straight man?

Finally, somewhere in the midpoint, Pacino is given a little backstory—but even that fails to animate either him or the film. He remains a placid figure, and the metaphorical romance—a man in a dangerous occupation who falls in love with the personification of death—an unvaried flatline. (Trivia: While they showed no on-screen compatibility, Pacino and Keller went on to enjoy a real-life romance.)

Pauline Kael, in her vitriolic inventory of the film, posited Pacino's performance by speculating, "If Al Pacino had sent forth his agent to search the world for the role that would call attention to all his weaknesses, the agent could not have come up with an unholier Grail than *Bobby Deerfield.*"[6] As for his quintessentially '70s Euro-boy look—feathered hair, aviator sunglasses, leather jackets—and implacably doleful coolness, she describes the effect as "a Polo Lounge pimp playing Hamlet."[7] Harsh, but hard to argue.

The movies found out that if you take these New York actors and sanitize or glamorize them, something essential is lost. Tame their animal appeal instead of harnessing it Coppola- or Lumet-style and they become soulless and uninteresting. The fire has been put out, whether it be smothered by a shiny tuxedo, period clothing or Ralph Lauren casuals. Hadn't these wrongheaded producers and directors seen Brando as the foppish Fletcher Christian in *Mutiny on the Bounty* (1962) or as the bridled ambassador in *A Countess from Hong Kong* (1967)? Disguise is okay, these actors have all done it and had fun (see Pacino in *Dick Tracy*, 1990) but cleaning and preening are completely out of the question.

After the shocking upset of Pacino's win streak that had been *Bobby Deerfield*, the actor again retreated to the woods. The kind of film with which he had become synonymous—New York–based character studies marked by urbanity, confrontation and the fight for fairness, even if in idiosyncratic form—was disappearing. Times were in transition. America was going into a period of much-needed recovery. The burden of the late '60s and early '70s was lifting, making way for a little breathing room. Citizens of the counterculture, after a decade's worth of groupthink, were trading solidarity for self-indulgence. In time, they'd be labeled "the Me generation," with their love of self-help, easy sex, cocaine, disco dancing and other forms of purely personal pleasure. The volatile martyrs they couldn't get enough of a few short years ago were now just a pile of dead bodies to them. They'd boogie past them on their way to simpler heroes in simpler films, ones that reflected their new, fun-loving personality. Burt Reynolds, playing on his Southern roots, was one of the first to catch the wave, transforming into a new male archetype: the "good ol' boy." He'd don tight jeans and a cowboy hat and speed his way across state lines for kicks in plotless, feel-good fare like *Smokey and the Bandit* (1977). In so doing, he'd shoot to #1 at the box office for six consecutive years, leaving Pacino and the rest of his Method-Brando generation in the exhaust of his Pontiac Trans Am LE.

Southern fried as his signature persona might have purported, the truth was that Reynolds had been born and raised in suburban Michigan. He didn't become a Floridian until his teens. He blossomed in that state, though, first as a collegiate football star, then as an aspiring stage actor. His physical and facial resemblance to the then-popular Brando prompted fellow thespians and instructors alike to reorient him from the South to the West. In Hollywood, Reynolds struggled for almost a decade to achieve recognition, until a three-season stint on TV's *Gunsmoke* (from 1962 to '65). When a pair of detective TV series proved short-lived, Reynolds took to humorizing his failures on the TV talk show circuit. Ironically, it was these small acts of unabashed self-deprecation, a new commodity for beefcake, that made him a star. Going forward, he'd interpolate straight-faced drama with lighter vehicles designed to bring out his cornpone composure and common, confessional wit. As a whole, he was forward but fallible, implacable but infantile, sexy but silly.

Unlike Reynolds, who continued to connect with mainstream audiences throughout the '70s, Pacino needed, after the disastrous *Bobby Deerfield*, to make amends to them. As providence would have it, along came one of the best screenplays of the decade, by husband-wife team Barry Levinson and Valerie Curtin, offering Pacino everything he had become known for in lighter, more digestible form.

...And Justice for All is an agile admixture of kooky characterizations, sharp dialogue and subtextual depth. Pacino plays Arthur Kirkland (the least Pacino-esque

name for one of his characters ever), a temperamental lawyer who, after attacking an unscrupulous judge, is blackmailed into defending him. As its elliptical title suggests, the film questions the human cost of a maladjusted judicial system. It also boasts great set pieces for Pacino.

While *Dog Day Afternoon* had had its share of laughs, the initial buzz about *...And Justice for All* was, "Uhhh ... okayyyy.... Al Pacino in a *comedy*?" (In 1999, a similar sentiment set in with Robert De Niro's appearance in *Analyze This*.) But it ended up being one of the actor's all-time best performances. Pacino smartly settles for quiet, flip sincerity, until he's driven to a now famous "lightning state" in the oft-quoted conclusion ("*You're* out of order! The whole trial is out of order!"). He's also aided by a great supporting cast, from Jack Warden and John Forsythe to Christine Lahti and Jeffrey Tambor, in what should have been a career-making turn as Pacino's patsy of a partner. Collectively, they're a testament to director Norman Jewison, the master of light comedy with a social message (and sometimes, films that have it the other way around). Yes, there are some sorry-assed production values (a badly assembled centerpiece of helicopter slapstick, a pseudo–Kenny G score, and a closing CU that's a veritable embarrassment). But on the whole, it's unabashedly commercial entertainment with just the right amount of brains.

That climactic court scene, and that catchphrase-loaded speech, both ingratiated Pacino to audiences and, ultimately, alienated him from them. It set him on a path marked by soapboxes; in time, what would a Pacino picture be without a closing pronouncement screaming (literally), "Author's message!!!"? He was, tragically, on the road to reduction. Not that he was going to stop trying; Pacino remains a restless soul, forever looking to push the envelope. But he had fallen into a preference, a pattern, a self-important violation of the spontaneity he had vowed to bring to the screen.

That said, a fundamental fire would continue to burn within him, one impossible to extinguish. A man who never lost his abiding love for the theater despite many movies, Pacino, throughout his long, prolific career, has continued to honor the spirit of live performance within the confines of film. From the get-go, he wanted movie audiences to forget the cameras, the cutting and everything else, converting, through performance, the studio sound stage into a Broadway (or really, off–Broadway) proscenium. He wanted them to feel a raw, unnerving, dimensional quality that the flatness and passivity of film cannot convey. As he once told Lawrence Grobel about his formative experiences attending the theater,

> There was an explosion of emotion from the audience.... It was frightening. You didn't want to be there. I felt, *Something's going to happen to me here; this is going to turn into a riot*.... It was like this enormous dynamite keg that they were maneuvering, and I knew that it came from a lifetime of devotion to this kind of thing. It registered. I never forgot it. It's motivated me throughout my life.[8]

As Dilys Powell wrote of the actor, "It is Pacino's astonishing ease which strikes one, the fluidity of his movements, the absolute freedom, or so it seems, from the conventions of acting. He doesn't look as if he's giving a performance. It looks *real*."[9] In time, this quality becomes forced, even cloying, incongruous, parodic and tired (see the overrated *Scarface*, 1983). But throughout Pacino's '70s heyday, it constituted a new, incendiary quality in American film acting. Thanks to the example of Brando, they were all capable of it, Hoffman, Hackman, Nicholson, Duvall and De Niro; but Pacino proceeded with the least amount of caution. He was the most brazen member of the high-wire act.

Robert Duvall
A Good Soldier

He came from naval stock. His father had risen to admiral; Duvall shocked him by going into the army. So, a rebel but not a rebel: Tom Hagen, working for the mob but still a perfectly respectable lawyer; Frank Hackett, working for a money-hungry TV network but just playing the good bureaucrat; Colonel Max Radl, working for the Nazis but as an exemplary officer. Duvall specialized in such roles: the professional, often on the sidelines, doggedly doing his duty, even if said duty was for a suspect source. More often than not, he was the key insider, the proverbial "boy in the back room," the parlor politician.

Sometimes he'd be front and center (*Tomorrow*, 1972, *The Outfit*, 1973, *The Great Santini*, 1979, *Tender Mercies*, 1983, *The Apostle*, 1997). But Hollywood preferred him

In the first two *Godfather* movies, Robert Duvall (left, with Al Pacino) played Tom Hagen, the no-nonsense "boy in the back room" working for a suspect cause (Paramount/Photofest).

in medium-sized doses. Select critics, too, preferred his small brush strokes to his broad swaths.

It was as if Duvall had understood, from the get-go, that a life in show business would mean a life as a second banana. Part of that realization, no doubt, was the subservience ingrained by coming of age in both a military milieu and as the product of devout Christian Scientists. Another part of it was probably his looks, not exactly those of a traditional leading man, or even a leading man in a more forgiving era. And yet Duvall distinguished himself, rising above the busy pack of '60s-70s character actors and occasionally being awarded a marquee vehicle. It was his emphatic integrity that did the trick, his electric doggedness.

Duvall did what he did, played characters who did what they had to do, with a more operatic investment than audiences had hitherto witnessed. Most characters in '70s cinema achieved this by bending the rules, anywhere from a little to a lot: Popeye Doyle beat criminals until his partner had to restrain him; Dirty Harry was kicked off the force for brandishing his magnum a little too liberally; the Bandit wreaked Road Runner–worthy highway havoc on poor, frustrated Smokey. But Duvall's characters individualized themselves by simply carrying out their assignments, by always, *always* coloring within the lines. Keep your head low, do your job, and remind the next guy, in no uncertain terms, of the importance of doing same, regardless of how ridiculous the circumstance—like the woozily surreal Vietnam in *Apocalypse Now*.

In a time when it was cool to embody neurosis, uncertainty, and anti-establishmentarian anger, to promote confused, transitioning identities, to wisecrack, play the fool or assume the stance of the cynical sybarite, Duvall's characters reminded audiences that there was still value in solidity, professionalism and kowtowing. It didn't warp your politics, make you a square, or cause people to call you a sell-out. You could be a hard-working stiff doing what the world expected of you and still be accepted, nay, respected, by your peers.

Occasionally, yes, there'd be a price to pay—usually watching loved ones get hurt. But in army-navy parlance, those are called "casualties," and they happen all the time. You get gut-punched, then you dutifully fulfill your orders. So you watch your adopted family take their licks (*The Godfather*), your girl get killed (*The Outfit*), or you remain estranged from your daughter (*Tender Mercies*). Ouch, sure, but hey, that's life.

Take Duvall's upbringing. A steady home would have been nice. Instead, the Duvalls were nomads, settling down wherever the patriarch's career path took them. But Robert, or "Bodge" as he was nicknamed, made the best of it. He played the class clown wherever they went, predicated on an innate gift for mimicry—something a bit hard to accept, given the sobriety of his eventual film roles. (Throughout the shooting of *The Godfather*, he would parrot Brando.)

When Duvall hit college, he was encouraged to major in drama. His rise as an actor was interrupted by his stint in the army; later, on the G.I. Bill, he hightailed it for New York where he found odd jobs, TV work, summer stock and Sandford Meisner. Meisner, like the other Stanislavski scions at work at that time, enforced a bold break with the long-standing representational school. The emphasis was on the natural, the sensorial, the personal—dictates that defined the busy sincerity of Duvall and his two best friends, Gene Hackman and Dustin Hoffman.

While Hackman and Hoffman stayed in New York, Duvall vacillated between the Big Apple and LaLaLand. He made his film debut as a shadow. Even then, unobtrusive as it was supposed to be, that silhouette suggested something grander. It belonged to Boo Radley, the mysterious, mythologized source of communal shame in playwright Horton Foote's adaptation of *To Kill a Mockingbird* (1962), the seismic Hollywood hit of the Civil Rights era. As the developmentally delayed Radley, Duvall, without so much as a line (he had one but it was chopped in post), introduced us to the abstruse silence he'd continue to put to good use, alternating it, when a role demanded, with score-settling straight talk. In either mode, whether he was ostracized for his isolationism or his obtrusiveness, we sympathized. An innate humanity resonated, no matter how narrow or broad the vessel it had been afforded.

Mockingbird served as a resonant sample size of Duvall personas to come. Though his screen time is limited (largely to the film's climax), it's all there: the minimalism (that haunting face), the duality (monster-mensch), the familial milieu (the Finches), the enforcer of the rules (in this case, by way of self-made justice)—elements, as faithful fans, we would be exposed to serially.

For the remainder of the decade, Duvall fell into bit parts as those two classic male archetypes, the cowboy and the cop. Back east, he made a splash on Broadway as the metamorphosing lead criminal in the thriller *Wait Until Dark*, a part assumed in the 1967 film adaptation by the equally versatile Alan Arkin, much to Duvall's chagrin.

Finally, Duvall was adopted by Zoetrope Studios, Francis Ford Coppola's self-financed San Francisco–based fiefdom. The struggling Zoetrope was an ambitious attempt at artistic autonomy, producing TV ads for Rice-A-Roni to finance small, sober-faced art films hoping to impress major distributors. The first in which Duvall appeared was writer-director Coppola's *The Rain People*.

The Rain People was a road movie—literally. Coppola set up an eight-caravan movie studio on wheels, which he took from New York to Denver. Along the way, he made periodic stops in small towns, in which much of the drama takes place. Most of it involves Shirley Knight as a troubled, pregnant housewife who, in a nod to the feminist movement, blindly bolts from her abusive husband. She undergoes a less than sentimental education, falling in with James Caan as a brain-injured college football star and Duvall as a flirty, fiery motorcycle cop recovering from the ugly death of two-thirds of his family. Unlike the heroes in other films of the time, Coppola's are not members of the counterculture, off to look, *à la Easy Rider*, for a freer version of America. They're citizens of the middle classes and working classes, searching for connection and purpose in their collapsed universes.

It's a tragic, moody miniature, also serving as a precursor to the *Godfather* films: There's the Coppola-Caan-Duvall team-up, a celebratory wedding sequence, and a frail marriage complicated by that Catholic bargaining chip, abortion (shades of Kay and Michael in *The Godfather Part II*). And while the film is designed to belong to Knight, it is subtly stolen by Caan.

That said, Duvall's contribution to *The Rain People* is also important. His lonely,

James Caan: A James Cagney for more nervous times (Paramount/Photofest).

tricky good-bad cop contains the identities and themes the actor pursued throughout the '70s: the steely side figure tied to a deeply fractured family whose thoughts and desires find themselves frustratingly thwarted, often with explosive consequences.

George Lucas was on set, making a mini-documentary about the shoot. While there, he recruited Duvall to appear in an extension of another of his shorts, a sci-fi exercise he called *THX 1138*. Before that, though, Duvall played the establishmentarian stooge in a New Age service comedy that took the industry by storm: director Robert Altman's *MASH*.

Altman had been a typically anonymous TV director for the bulk of his career. In middle age, he became the last, desperate choice to helm a slightly sexualized, run-of-the-mill service comedy. Going for broke, he unleashed his inner hipster and became the first American director to successfully apply European filmmaking techniques to a mainstream American property.

Critics framed the sensorial comedy *MASH* as a brazen anti–Vietnam commentary, but it served even more as a coming-out party for the new generational mores: explicit sex, drugs, long hair and disrespect for authority. Its only plot, in fact, is a string of prankish assaults on its two tight-asses: Major Burns, played by Duvall, and his no-nonsense mistress Major Houlihan, played by Sally Kellerman.

Wisely, Duvall recognized that the more gravitas he exuded in the role, the more the wild and woolly comedy would play, and the more Altman's pro-hippie battle cry would sound. He plays the buttoned-down Burns with such unyielding sobriety, you remember him just as much as his comic oppressors.

And again, Duvall's idiosyncratic relationship with women, established in *The Rain People*, holds. Burns and Houlihan enjoy a clandestine relationship, subject to *coitus interruptus* on a public scale (the famous "microphone under the bed" sequence). If Duvall's buddy Hoffman had to work to get the girl, and his buddy Hackman could only get her now and again, Duvall's gentlemanly gravitas never failed to draw her near—he just couldn't seem to keep her. Even the one with whom he truly connects, Karen Black in *The Outfit*, dies.

MASH proved a veritable sensation. It was a key film in the establishment of the American auteur movement, affording, for better or worse, a long leash to a new, self-indulgent generation of directors. One of them was the aforementioned Lucas, an up-and-comer fresh out of film school. By decade's end, he had unwittingly revolutionized on-screen science fiction, and film itself, with his giddy pastiche of Flash Gordon and Buck Rogers serials, *Star Wars* (1977). Before that famous-infamous infantilization of the genre, however, he joined the more earnest sci-fi renaissance that bloomed in the wake of Stanley Kubrick's *2001: A Space Odyssey* (1968). That movement included *The Omega Man* (1971), *Silent Running* (1972), *Soylent Green* (1973), *Zardoz* (1974) and *Logan's Run* (1976).

Each film is set in a dystopian society, rebuilt after the collapse of civilization by mysterious, cultish overlords, often using technological and pharmaceutical advancement to dehumanize the population. Trapped therein is either a lonely, frustrated rebel or a pair of put-out lovers. Typical plotlines have them railing against the system by committing acts of subversion aimed at restoring the pre-fascist order or engineering some improbable form of escape. Even Woody Allen tried his neurotic hand at it with *Sleeper* (1973).

Many of those films were responsible for the renewed relevance (and box office clout) of Charlton Heston. Heston had preceded Brando as part of a postwar generation of male actors that had included Burt Lancaster, Robert Mitchum and Kirk Douglas. They maintained the moralism of patriotic mouthpieces like James Stewart and the physical forthrightness of action stars like John Wayne. But the toll of these responsibilities, thanks to the emotional aftershock of World War II, was showing. This generation's shared persona, the authority figure brought to consider his deep-seated shortcomings and un–American cynicism in the pursuit of a greater mission, represented a tug of war: the unsteady middle ground between the white-hatted heroes of the past and the psychologically scarred figures of the future. American Eagles with ruffled feathers.

The movies' new audience, the Baby Boomers, had grown up on sci-fi via paperbacks, popular science publications, and pennyante horror pictures. The twin threats of nuclear annihilation and widespread Communism over the pristine suburban skies of their formative years, the '50s, created a voracious appetite for metaphoric movie monsters, aliens and other invaders of godless, unknown origin with grand, despotic intentions, almost always victimizing decent American communities. When the '60s came along, bringing the space race, accessible hallucinogens and alternatives to Dick-and-Jane domesticity, interests in new worlds, new technologies and new customs flourished.

As the proverbial "last man standing" in regimes ruled by talking apes, black-caped cultists and over-industrializing overlords, Heston, trying to hold America's faded postwar glory, represented something even larger than a frayed, challenging society: mankind's End of Days. This evolution into symbolism ended up ingratiating him to the box office's warring demographics: his own generation, who recognized their mass cultural resignation in his actions, and the succeeding one, for whom Heston served as affirmation of their decade-long warnings to their elders about their military-industrial ways. Throughout the early '70s, it made the limited Heston a big draw, something he was able to sustain when the disaster genre eclipsed sci-fi in the second half of the decade. That switch in preferred genres made him, once again, America's all-saving hero, even helping him win nubile New Hollywood heroines like Karen Black.

While Heston didn't front *THX 1138*, shades of his classic sci-fi persona are visible in the spirit of the central character. There are shades of Coppola therein, too, whose ideological influence can clearly be seen on writer-director Lucas. The film shares the same theme that will distinguish *The Godfather*: the conflict between business and personal. Duvall, as the eponymous THX, is an undistinguished laborer, a cog in the mass production of the robotic police that keep the sterile society of which he's a member in line. But he's subversively influenced to shirk his duties and investigate the possibilities of self-fulfillment, including sexual relations with a co-worker. After that union is ignominiously broken up (an echo of the brutally severed Knight-Duvall relationship in *The Rain People*), THX hops a futuristic vehicle and makes his way from the oppressive ivory underground in which he toils to the sun-dappled promise of the surface.

Like many a Lucasian protagonist, the eponymous THX struggles with the notion of escape. It's the same discomfort Curt (Richard Dreyfuss) experiences in *American Graffiti* (1973) upon leaving his hermetic hometown for college; the same discomfort that *Star Wars*' Luke Skywalker undergoes in his quest to trade the family farm for a life of interstellar adventure. It's a sensibility rooted in Lucas' Baby Boomer adolescence, with its Brando-influenced yearning to break free from the straitjacket of conventional society.

In the 1970s, the science fiction and disaster genres kept Charlton Heston (seen here in 1971's *The Omega Man*) a viable on-screen commodity (Warner Bros./Photofest).

THX 1138 displays the imprint of the '50s in other

ways too: foremost, its Cold War vision of a godless industrial juggernaut servicing the state ... sounds like a Communist scare–spawned vision of Russia or China to me. Then there's the infatuation with cars, robots and other technological fetishes, right out of *Popular Mechanics*.

As for Duvall, THX is almost a designer role. Lucas must have recognized in the actor the key qualities required for the character while observing him on set in *The Rain People*. Duvall's inherent invisibility perfectly suits the part; a recognizable star would have overstated the film's message. Duvall's assignment, in the main, is to leak humanity through placid conformity. Only an actor with a tremendous grasp of nuance can pull this off. Duvall the minimalist, as he first proved as Boo Radley, does it with aplomb. He's a master of connotative silence. He spends much of the time in a state of pensive discomfort, using his deep-set, sorrowful eyes— brought out by his shaved head—to convey both the weight of conformity and that of individuality. That said, you long to feel for him more than both actor and director will allow. It would have made the film less conceptual and more relatable. But it's important to remember that Duvall's THX is only incidentally humanized. His run to freedom is less an act of political rebellion than it is of personal investigation.

Lucas' mentor, meanwhile, was busy priming to direct the film version of the 1969 best-seller *The Godfather*, on a promise to bring cultural authenticity and an operatic sense of narrative to it. The hope was that this sensibility would elevate the book's pulpy intentions and help the film negotiate the sand traps of gangster genre cliché. For this task, Coppola brought along a lot of his *Rain People* co-workers, including Caan and Duvall. While Caan enjoyed the privilege of auditioning for the major subordinate roles, Duvall, based on his pale, blond looks, contemplative demeanor, and yes-sir ethic, was handpicked for the role of the central family's adopted Irish-German consigliere, Tom Hagen.

Hagen is Duvall incarnate. Even more than in *The Rain People*, Duvall's character establishes the template for the screen persona that will last him (with interesting grace notes but few major violations) for the bulk of his career. As Pauline Kael noted in her *Godfather* review, "[A]s the bland, despicably loyal Tom Hagen ... Robert Duvall, a powerful recessive actor, is practically a genius at keeping himself in the background."[1] Mull that for a minute: "a genius at keeping himself in the background"—think of how hard that is. It's just a notch above "he may be the greatest extra of all time."

Then there's Robert Osborne, from the 1973 edition of his *Academy Awards Oscar Annual*: "More than any other character in this massive saga, [Duvall] expressed the film's concept of the Mafia as a corporate business run methodically and matter-of-factly, as if it were dealing in daily matters such as stocks and bonds rather than gunnings and cold-blooded murders."[2]

Or try Robert Slawson, in one of the few Duvall biographies: "[He] played Hagen low-key, loyal, an eye always on business, efficiently carrying out his duties with a minimum of waves; it was a powerful performance that added immeasurably to the film."[3] How often does one get raves as the third, make that fourth, man in, and in the least colorful role in the picture?

Apparently, nobody had ever told Duvall that expository dialogue was just a necessary evil. The traditional practice is to assign that thankless task to the least interesting actor. Have him give us the narrative skinny, then quickly get out of the stars' way and let the Big Boys emote. Much to his credit, Duvall decidedly broke with precedent, embracing these small acts of editorial responsibility not as unrewarded tasks but as scenes as big as those afforded the people that audiences came to see. Watch Duvall go nose to nose with Caan's hotheaded Sonny, the family's hair-trigger son, explaining the risks of the Corleones striking back against the families who put a hit on their figurehead. Duvall matches the seething, nervy Caan with elemental force, almost out–Caaning him. To almost any other actor, it's a small scene; to Duvall, it was one of the biggest and most important in the picture.

"This is business. Not personal!" he screams, making clear the film's central message: the intractability of professional obligation and emotional involvement. Duvall's Hagen is the film's moral mouthpiece, the zealous voice of reason, the outsider policing the insiders. Had the Corleones listened to him and gotten into drugs like the surrounding families had suggested, the refutation that triggered the hit on the Don would have been averted. No implosion, no Michael deciding to go from angel to devil. But though this is eventually pointed out, Duvall's Hagen never seethes nor gloats. Instead, he obediently retreats, with but a sign of tired resignation. After all, his very first line in the film is, "I have to go back to work"—a self-directive that pretty much says it all, for both Hagen the character and, in perpetuity, Duvall the actor.

There's high-octane discipline, when necessary, then there's low-key servility. We respect him for the former but feel for him for the latter. When Hagen-Duvall uses it for his biggest elucidatory task, informing the bedridden Don that good son Michael was the one responsible for the cold-blooded hit that avenged the senior Corleone's brush with death, we feel the enormity and pain of humble, hard-working Hagen's burden in his miniaturist's nod of the head and thoughtful whisper.

You do what you have to: the Hagen-Duvall motto. When, near film's end, kindly-faced Salvatore Tessio (Abe Vigoda) appeals to Hagen's better nature after Tessio's quiet condemnation as a co-conspirator in the industry-wide squeeze on the Corleones ("Can you let me off the hook for old time's sake?"), the only violation of Hagen-Duvall's stalwart character poor Tessio gets is a nostalgic, almost bemused smirk, then a friendly but firm, "Can't do it, Sally."

It's a soft, human moment previewing aspects of the character that will be inflated in *The Godfather Part II*. In that epic, cross-cutting Michael's increasingly slippery grip on both the business and the family with his father's rise from orphaned immigrant to figure of suspect respect, we get Tom Hagen in toto. He's still the consigliere, steering the unmoored Michael as best he can, but now, he's forced to assume a greater role. He's been tipped over the sidelines by Michael's insistence that he be directly accountable for what remains of the family after its endless external and internal battles. For the first time, Hagen feels the weight of direct responsibility. This humanizes Hagen, who begins to subscribe to a see-through vulnerability. After all, he's the last line of defense against the total annihilation of the Corleones—and already, he has seen and suffered much. An elegiac fatigue, bordering on sentimentality, sets in. Ah, for the easy, halcyon days of playing consort, his every breath suggests.

Who knows what dimension the character would next take on. Duvall bowed out of *The Godfather Part III* (1990), citing issues with the script and the paltry salary. In so doing, he unwittingly set himself up as the scapegoat for the film's failure. It's a ridiculous contention, given that final installment's more glaring shortcomings.

While the *Godfather* films helped to raise Duvall's profile, it did not set him on the path of choosiness that his brethren took. Cognizant that he was not New Hollywood star material like Hoffman, Nicholson and Pacino, and doubting that he might luck into top-billing like Hackman, he contented himself with remaining a working actor.

He fronted the film version of a teleplay by his favorite playwright, Horton Foote, the kindred spirit who had landed him the role of Boo Radley in *To Kill a Mockingbird*. *Tomorrow*, a two-hander (mostly) co-starring the compatible Olga Bellin (a stage actor in her only film role) so captured the vibe of William Faulkner, on whose short story the drama was based, the two-time Pulitzer Prize winner awarded Foote half the dramatic rights. In this hermetic black-and-white production, a hulking Duvall portrays, with a thick Mississippian accent ("Some other time" becomes "Some other tiiii…"), a lone wolf of a cotton farmer who builds incidental ties with a pregnant runaway. Their loaded friendships converts to a complicated romance, culminating in tragedy.

For all of its value as a heartfelt Southern miniature, Foote's work is, like Faulkner's, an acquired taste. It's spare stuff, loaded with laconic musings to which Duvall plays pensive sounding board. But if Duvall had a slogan, it would be "Simplicity R Us." As the many close-ups awarded him in the film attest, he suspends I.Q. points better than any other actor. He can innately reduce someone to their essential intelligence and primary instincts. It's not that anything more complex is beyond them; it's simply that, according to the character, those qualities are not of public use. Instead, they're grist for the mills of their souls, conveyed through hooded eyes, heavy heads and misty, gnawing gazes.

That said, Duvall's characterizations know that it's folly to be sealed. Connection is also important. Redemptive as it is from life's general gloom, however, it's small and precious. His characters have just enough time to bask, at least a little, in the much-appreciated respite before the next storm. It's especially true with women. His affection for them is genuine but always tinged with a sense of impending tragedy. Love does not sustain. It makes a cameo, then leaves one to hard self-examination. Families, too, suffer from this same vulnerability, including the one that develops here, in the *Godfather* films, and in *The Great Santini*. Coming from a perpetually disrupted home no doubt forged ties between Duvall and these kinds of properties.

Vanity projects like *Tomorrow* aside, Duvall, over this period, mostly took parts in middling films whose primary purpose was to keep him in front of the cameras. The *Godfather*s, for example, are linked by a flatline of forgotten titles disrupted by odd spikes of moderate success.

Those films, role-wise, represent a split between two classic American male archetypes: the cop and the cowboy. The first draws on Duvall's reputation as a figure of duty, the second on his pedigree as a product of the West and South (his California-Texas-Virginia stock).

Joe Kidd offered Duvall the opportunity to interact with Clint Eastwood. Duvall later appeared alongside another star synonymous with action, Charles Bronson. While Duvall and his generation were collecting the critical raves, the more traditional personalities, Eastwood and Bronson, were monopolizing the box office.

The lanky, taciturn Eastwood had made his career in Sergio Leone's "spaghetti Westerns," with their rhapsodic take on the tropes of John Ford, Howard Hawks and other practitioners of Hollywood's cowboy tradition. Now, in the '70s, Eastwood was alternating the personality he had developed for those films, the famous Man with No Name, with its urban equivalent: Dirty Harry, the magnum-wielding rogue cop with the unstoppable hate-on for San Francisco's dodgier hippie element. Bronson, too, was making a name as a vigilante, a persona that had elevated him from a stone-faced character actor in mostly forgettable films to a household name in bloodthirsty revenge fantasies such as *Death Wish* (1974). Despite the dimension that Duvall and his generation brought to the male hero, it was evident that America had never lost its taste for the model those actors were attempting to usurp. The spirit of John Wayne was alive and well (as was Wayne himself, until 1979) in the pro-gun stances of the more accessible Eastwood and Bronson.

Helming *Joe Kidd* was the venerable John Sturges, whose more popular successes had not only brought a sense of novelty to the Western and war genres but had helped groom the screen's first hip action heroes, including Steve McQueen and James Coburn. Sturges didn't put them through paces that were markedly different from those of their predecessors, giving them about as much dialogue as you'd afford Gary Cooper and enough gun-slinging to rival Wayne. In so doing, however, he made certain that their contemporary coolness came through. Sturges was a great fit, then, for Eastwood, the big screen's latest old-new hero.

As an actor, Eastwood was an acquired taste. But as action speaks louder than words, all he had to do was brandish a gun or a fist enough times. Eastwood's role model had been Gary Cooper, from whom he'd borrow the body type and taciturnity but replace the leaky humanity with a steely weirdness. In so doing, Eastwood made sure that those on-screen stalwarts, the cowboy, the cop and the soldier, remained relevant in topsy-turvy times. Eventually, he assumed greater control over his image and career, expanding into producing and directing. Improbably, he became a critically respected auteur, grinding out shadowy epics and whimsical (if still dark) curios into his 90s.

Long before Eastwood, and before him Leone, spawned the revisionist Western, there was Sturges. In pictures such as *The Magnificent Seven*, he proudly displayed pluralist politics wherein his heroes were coerced into the defense of downtrodden minorities. In *Joe Kidd*, like *The Magnificent Seven*, that culture is a micro demography of agrarian Mexicans. Here, they're looking to have their land claims validated. White resistance isn't the only complication in their lives. There's also the offbeat nature of their leader, a kind of anti–Zapata (played, in that politically incorrect era, by the Caucasian John Saxon) who, like his gringo adversaries, advocates a style of justice beyond the law.

A mustachioed Duvall plays Frank Harlan, a disgruntled landowner who intends to take back the disputed territory by force. Eastwood, as in many of his

In the '70s, the vigilante genre flourished, popularizing heroes like man of action Clint Eastwood (Warner Bros./Photofest).

Westerns bookending *Joe Kidd*, plays the middleman. In his idiosyncratic fashion, his eponymous hero attempts to bring each side to justice, only to be pushed to extremism. In the end, the referee becomes the heavyweight champ.

As *Joe Kidd* demonstrates, such films are a golden opportunity for Duvall to play his signature persona—the most informed guy in the room, the guy who sets and upholds the rules—not in a sideline capacity *à la* Tom Hagen but as an authority figure in his own right. Eastwood's Kidd takes issue with this, of course, leading to a climactic gun fight. When Eastwood sets the sights of his pistol on dead duck Duvall, there's a genuine fear of death in the latter's eyes. For a few precious seconds, *Joe Kidd* is not a tight, teasy game of cowboys and Indians. Something genuine has been imposed, alluding to a dramatic depth neither Eastwood nor Sturges nor writer Elmore Leonard was willing to investigate.

Duvall was allowed to import even more dimension to the genre when he was given license to flesh out one of Western lore's most iconic characters, Jesse James. The film was *The Great Northfield Minnesota Raid* (1972), an account of the notorious James gang's most daring and debilitating robbery, written and directed by Philip Kaufman.

Kaufman, a history teacher, came to the movies with an agenda to replace romanticization with reality. Unlike John Ford's famous advice in his *The Man Who Shot Liberty Valance* (1962)—"When the legend becomes fact, print the legend"—Kaufman's motto was, "When the legend becomes fact, stick with the facts." That said, he was not beyond a schoolboy admiration for traditional American manhood, best exhibited in his valentine to the Mercury Seven astronauts *The Right Stuff* (1982).

A world traveler, Kaufman also kept an outside eye on his homeland, periodically picking up on its love of cockeyed cultural indulgence and self-celebratory simplicity. In this, he was a kind of Michael Ritchie, though a more forgiving version.

True to his pedagogical pedigree, Kaufman presents *Northfield Minnesota* as a sort of lecture, his smooth-toned narrator contextualizing the big event—the James gang's failed attempt to rob the largest bank west of the Mississippi, with plans to buy back a corruptly thwarted amnesty using the spoils—in factual terms. Authenticity continues to carry the day, as Kaufman holds our hand through a muddy, buggy post–Civil War West, where shaggy versions of Cole Younger (the traditionally sober Cliff Robertson, in a surprisingly likable performance) and cousin Jesse James (Duvall) prey on a corrupt social structure to assist the poor. They're a hillbilly Robin Hood and Little John. Meanwhile, there's pressure from all sides: a posse is threatening their lives, mechanization is threatening their way of life, and interpersonal fireworks are threatening the plan that will secure their legend, grant them their freedom and allow them to spend more time at their favorite Scandinavian whorehouse.

Even though Kaufman's hirsute hayseeds are clearly stand-ins for the then-burgeoning counterculture, he cheers for his uppity anti-heroes both for their "sticking it to the man" ethic and for retaining the kind of old-fashioned manliness associated with the generation against which they're rebelling. For a purported exercise in demythologization, Kaufman equates Younger and James with the noble heroes of Sir Walter Scott, calling their climactic fool's errand "a knightly crusade or a noble quest."

Bringing his own twist to this already twisted bent is Duvall. On the one hand, his Jesse James is the gentlemanly figure of yore Kaufman maintains: a decent-hearted man of the people, forging mother-son bonds with lonely old widows and enforcing the code that will protect the precious fellowship of which he is a member. Every now and again, though, his thoroughly convincing Missourian accent will break out into a visionary fervor learned at the hands of country preachers (something Duvall will borrow again for *The Apostle*) and his trigger finger will go into psychotic repeat motion.

It's one of the more obvious examples of Duvall's affinity for contradiction—and one of his most successful. Despite the size of his character's legendary reputation, it's a minor role—the picture belongs to Kaufman's deep immersion into the milieu and to the happily loosened Robertson. But Duvall manages to stand out. It was one of the few opportunities the actor had at that still-forming stage in his career to have fun, to bring something broader and chancier to the mix, to flirt with abstraction.

So much for Duvall the cowboy. There's also Duvall the cop, who pops up just as frequently throughout the '70s.

A representative exemplification is *Lady Ice* (1973), a cool, classy crime caper (well, that was the idea) directed by Tom Gries. Gries was a product of male-oriented TV series (most notably, the popular series *The Rat Patrol*, 1966–68). As a creature of that culture, calling him an auteur is like calling an In-N-Out burger filet mignon. And yet Duvall, who could have restricted himself to a better class of helmsmen, worked with Gries no fewer than three times. A foot soldier–type himself, the actor no doubt considered the get-the-job-done Gries a kindred spirit.

The star of *Lady Ice* is another stalwart of the '70s, Donald Sutherland, with whom Duvall had worked (a little) in *M*A*S*H* and would work with again, along with Sturges, in *The Eagle Has Landed* (1976). In the pantheon of male actors of that era, Sutherland is a curious case. As rebels went, the Canadian-born Sutherland specialized in the offbeat variety; he was even a little weird to the weirdos. That precedent was established with the broad facial commentary he offered in *The Dirty Dozen* (1967).

From that ingratiating act of adolescent anti-establishmentarianism forward, Sutherland, subscribing to his own quiet, quirky subversiveness, committed on-screen subterfuge not through grand gestures or scenery-chewing verbosity but by less ostentatious acts of kooky or spooky pranksterism. His characters didn't want to change the world, nor did they want to strip it for personal purposes. They just wanted to test themselves against it now and again, for little more than kicks. Whenever it proved too resistant, they retreated into dark, reflective spaces, regrouped and came at it again.

As for women, Sutherland's characters, like those of his contemporaries, tended to fall in with strong, sexy neurotics, whom he bested or bedded or both but on occasion. More often than not, the two ended up settling for a diplomatic understanding.

The love interest here is Jennifer O'Neill, a flat-voiced '70s TV makeup pitch person who was a kind of glamorized girl-next-door (she made her splash in film as an idealized beauty in the sentimental *Summer of '42*, 1971). But like the film itself, the tension between her and Sutherland comes up shy of aspirations as a hip, stylish

Donald Sutherland, one of the 1970s' more offbeat heroes (UA/Photofest).

throwback. They're a TV-worthy Steve McQueen–Faye Dunaway in a TV-worthy *The Thomas Crowne Affair* (1968).

Duvall, in heavy horn rims, shows up as a justice official forced to work with loopy insurance agent Sutherland as they mutually attempt to break up a criminal operation. Duvall's stint is representative of the thankless roles the actor had been asked to fulfill before his coming-out party in *The Godfather*, and for a few years afterward. As is his habit in these kinds of commercial exercises, he adds a soupçon of verisimilitude to the proceedings, a capacity so instinctual it cannot be suppressed in the service of genre.

Occasionally, the dual cowboy-cop monopoly was broken up by the addition of the gangster. Even there, Duvall proved that while asked to slip on the hardened skin of a cigar-smoking archetype, he could capably maintain his cool humanity.

The Outfit was written and directed by the underrated John Flynn, who was later responsible for the cult *Taxi Driver* cash-in *Rolling Thunder* (1977). Both *The Outfit* and *Rolling Thunder* are entries in the then-popular urban avenger genre, allowing Duvall to revel in one of his other signature personas, the man hard-done-by. As an actor lacking traditional star quality, and a product of often overlooked parts of the United States, characters awarded the short shrift were ones with which he could identify. Here it's a small-time bank robber who, along with his brother, accidentally hits up a mob-run financial institution. He goes to jail, his brother is killed, and the syndicate responsible for it all goes on his shit list. He puts together a small working unit and stages a series of surprise attacks, taking down each poker-playing, gun-wielding mobster assembly line style.

The Outfit was Duvall's first wide-release starring role (let's excuse the little-seen *Tomorrow*, interesting as that film is). As such, he's awarded all of the conventions to which a leading man is entitled. He's the mastermind, the man of action, even the guy who gets the girl (the kookily sexy Karen Black). Too bad it's a B movie … or rather, an homage to B movies. The pulpy purposefulness positively pulsates, until the film flatlines in the middle when it flirts with trading truth for trope. Otherwise, the spirit of such B practitioners as Raoul Walsh, Mark Hellinger and Don Siegel is alive and well. And if that doesn't tip you off, consider the cast, Hollywood footnotes old and new: Marie Windsor (once known as "the Queen of the Bs"), Elisha Cook, Jr., and Archie Moore, plus Joe Don Baker, Sheree North and, splitting the A-B difference, Robert Ryan.

Duvall's Earl (his name reminds us of Mad Dog Roy Earle, the hero of Walsh's *High Sierra*, 1941) is a man who's cut himself off from his feelings in favor of professional passivity. Now and again, something cracks his earthen exterior, and a wisp of volcanic smoke shoots forth. Earl is simultaneously cool and hot—Tom Hagen unleashing his inner Sonny Corleone. For Duvall, this was a rare opportunity to play a man in the trenches of warfare instead of a strategist behind a desk. Too wise an actor to give us the stripped-down urban Galahad of most of these exercises, *à la* Bronson or Eastwood, Duvall joins their company while adding an inviolable depth, bringing Method to their madness.

The Outfit was admired, slightly, at the time of its release (mostly drive-ins) for punching above its weight. The film went on to enjoy an inflated reputation years later, when Gen X divinity Quentin Tarantino lauded it to his followers.

Looking to balance fluff with substance, Duvall returned to the *Godfather* franchise in '74, before reuniting with Tom Gries for *Breakout* (1975).

Throughout the '70s, Charles Bronson seemed to appear in some vehicle or other every week. After years as a middling talent for hire (often playing, in orangey body makeup, Indian warriors), Bronson was coerced into copying the template to stardom fashioned by contemporary man-of-action Eastwood. Bronson began to appear in European Westerns and action films in which, fittingly, he was more icon than actor. While this made him a huge international celebrity, his home country continued to afford him short shrift. It took a significant spike in the American urban crime rate to award Bronson on-screen relevancy.

Bronson began to appear in a string of box office hits in which he played the two-fisted, bullet-happy defender of the people, taking the law into his own hands as answer to urban decay, police corruption and institutional indifference. By the time he starred in the ultimate manifestation of these DIY revenge fantasies, the career-making *Death Wish*, he was a well-creased 52. A domestic commodity at last, with worldwide clout to boot, Bronson could now control his destiny.

Bronson immediately set about making himself a brand, churning out small-scale Western, detective and action pictures in which fists flew, guns blazed and punks perished. At no time did he experience, by his surly admission, the slightest desire to break type, to stretch, to try and hold his own with the Method generation. *Let the more earnest Hoffman & Co. act*, he conceded, *and let the quirkier Eastwood experiment*. Bronson remained the self-sufficient small businessman,

In an era when films were about "a guy and his problems," Charles Bronson (left, with Stuart Margolin) and his gun *solved* problems (Paramount/Photofest).

offering modest production companies a tight, nepotistic unit consisting of himself, wife–co-star Jill Ireland (insistently) and select directors in tune with the workaday sensibility he'd developed in Depression-era coal mine country.

The films of Hoffman, Hackman, Nicholson et al. were sometimes referred to, fliply, as movies "about a guy and his problems." The Bronson pictures offered something else: movies about a guy who could *solve* his problems. Bronson's signature silence was not a fit of existential internalization. It was a technical beat foreshadowing the much-anticipated emergence of his .45-caliber problem-solver. It was a facile answer to the universal challenge of righting a dangerously derailed society. But in an age of great proletariat frustration, it worked—and not just, as social critics of these films maintained, for the Nixon-voting, NRA-endorsing silent majority. Bronson's popularity as America's devilish angel soon had him cashing million-dollar paychecks—and this for pictures shot on modest budgets in which all he had to do was squint his steely eyes, show off his impressively sculpted physique, and make good on the odd taciturn threat uttered in his guttural Lithuanian-American basso.

There was also a sorrowful quality to him. The silent human price of the weight of the world and having to personally control its destiny. Some mistook this for acting, but it was inherent, not forced. The heartache of a hardscrabble life, it came to include admitted regrets over the nature of his hard-earned, self-made success. In time, he labeled himself and his films a disappointment. Still, for a long time, he exhibited no shame. He made his movies and his money and stood as proud as the Indian braves or streetwise vigilantes that he played.

That said, in *Breakout*, Bronson sets out to elasticize his talents (a little). It's a typical vehicle for him, a poor man's *Papillon* in which he's a desert rat improbably asked to rescue a middle-aged innocent from a Mexican prison. Yet it allows him to balance his trademark violence with a little comedy and the odd touch of sentimentality. He and Ireland aspire to the Bogart-Hepburn dynamic of John Huston's *The African Queen*, feuding, flirting and forgiving each other their trespasses as she, the victim's wife, insists on spurring him into action.

Huston, in fact, makes a cameo in the film. After the impact the great American auteur made in Roman Polanski's *Chinatown*, the majestically grizzled director enjoyed a sideline as a character actor, doing little more than puffing on panetellas and offering nuggets of jaded wisdom in his wintry baritone. Would that he had cannibalized himself and directed this film (though he had already copped his own *African Queen* with *Heaven Knows, Mr. Allison*) instead of Tom Gries. Still, here, Gries tries. He goes handheld, encourages pushes and otherwise violates TV methodology.

A toupéed Duvall, though co-billed, has a small part as the prisoner. It's a thankless role save for one aspect, when this decent-hearted businessman becomes imbued with the ugly ethos of his circumstance, a notion the film too quickly dispenses with. Still, it was enough for Duvall, a big fan of subversive duality. In an alternate universe, more in keeping with the work of his contemporaries, the picture would have been all his: a character study centered around the psychological and physical effects of unjust incarceration. (Audiences would have to wait for 1978's *Midnight Express* for that.) But this is a Charles Bronson picture. Duvall is largely there to add a little gravitas, a tougher assignment than breaking his character out of prison.

That same year, Duvall would work with another cinematic commodity whose name was synonymous with squibs: Sam Peckinpah. By the mid–'70s, the director's excesses had made him persona non grata with the Hollywood establishment. Deemed, nevertheless, a perfect fit for 1975's *The Killer Elite*, he was hired by producer Mike Medavoy on the proviso that he be a good boy. Perhaps that's why the film punches with kid gloves. Once you take the "Wild" out of *The Wild Bunch*...

Killer Elite's historical distinction is its incorporation of elements from the martial arts genre, one of the first American mainstream releases to do so. Martial arts films had been a staple in China since 1928. The genre's importation to America came after the international success of Chinese American Bruce Lee, through five films produced in Hong Kong between 1971 and 1973 (the year of Lee's premature death at 32). It wasn't simply Lee's lightning-fast exhibitions of Jeet Kun Do (his own variation on the practice) that had won him fans. Like private student Steve McQueen (and *Elite*'s co-scenarist, Stirling Silliphant), Lee was adopted by a younger audience as a counter-culture icon. His anti-heroes were the politically oppressed victims of an Imperialist power, whom he confronted with nunchakus instead of protest signs. Though the films were produced in Hong Kong, their ingression, and Lee's popularity, helped break the long-standing Hollywood stereotyping of Asian Americans. Lee was at his peak in the mid–'70s; his influence had spread to the blaxploitation movement. But the big studios wanted in, too, eager to borrow the younger audience that was attending and re-attending Lee's films.

In '75, two major releases tried it: *The Yakuza* and *The Killer Elite*. The first suffered from the wrong director: the conservative, romantic Sydney Pollack. The second got the right director but at the wrong time. Yes, Peckinpah's name had become synonymous with violence, a convention with which he was eager to do something new. But by '75, he had frittered away his vitality. Further, what remained was straitjacketed by Medavoy, though Peckinpah did come through in the film's final free-for-all, pitting samurai swords against AK-47s.

The film is the fourth pairing of Duvall and ol' pal Caan. They start off playing

Looking to cash in on the cult success of Bruce Lee, Hollywood began to integrate martial arts into its films (Photofest).

on their seasoned *bonhomie*, creating allusions of a buddy picture. Soon, though, their Hope-Crosby act goes dark. They go from being happy, jokey bag men for a shady branch of the CIA to keepers of opposite sides in a soupy war for the protection of a Taiwanese muckamuck. That's as concise as I can make the plot, which critics of the day rightfully admonished for its murkiness. Thematically, the film plays on the post–Kennedy, post–Watergate suspicion of Big Government, a quality it shares with *The Parallax View, Night Moves, The Domino Principle, Three Days of the Condor* and other action thrillers of the era. The grunts, like Duvall and Caan, do the brunt of the killing but the guys in suits, like Arthur Hill and Gig Young, are the *real* bad guys.

Killer Elite wasn't vintage Peckinpah but it's as confessional a work as he ever accomplished. The film is about whoredom: whether 'tis nobler to take the money, do the job, and get a good night's sleep, as does Duvall's character, or be your own man, work from a sense of personal integrity, and maintain a constructive restlessness, like Caan's character. This is clearly Peckinpah expressing his mixed feelings about this transitional stage of his career. No doubt Duvall was attracted to the film's central idea, too: At that time, he also was vacillating between projects he was doing simply to keep his career afloat and those that were worthier of his talents.

By signing on for *Killer Elite*, both Duvall and Caan had hoped to ride Peckinpah's coattails. But despite a rave review from Pauline Kael, one of her few, glaring missteps (unabashedly predicated on her long-standing friendship with the director), cognoscenti and commoners alike could see that this was the work of a once volatile force operating on fumes. (Peckinpah would do so literally in his next film, the indifferently messy *Convoy*, 1977.)

Finally, Duvall was offered a project marked by intelligence and social relevance—*Network*.

For the longest time, the relationship between film and TV had been a tricky one. They started as rivals, evolved into a supplier-customer model, went into production together, and today enjoy a gazillion-dollar symbiosis nobody would have imagined back when that little black-and-white barbarian came pounding at the gate. There was still tension between them, however, in '76. TV had begun to produce made-for-TV movies and mini-series to curb the cost of licensing. The immense popularity of two that were launched in 1976, *Rich Man, Poor Man* and *Roots*, had proven that this financial and artistic intervention was no idle threat.

Despite its aspirations for quality, however, TV continued to suffer much social criticism. By appeasing the lowest common denominator to sell instant coffee and laundry detergent, detractors cited, the small screen had tragically dumbed down the American mind. Lengthy critiques like Jerry Manders' *Four Arguments for the Elimination of Television* were oft-quoted. Another opinionated highbrow was equally jaundiced, and part of his stake was personal: Paddy Chayefsky had made his reputation servicing the medium's more erudite infancy, only to see it debase itself with facile sitcoms and bloated melodramas.

An irrepressible satirist, the disgruntled Chayefsky, coming off a Best Original Screenplay Oscar for his brilliant skewering of the public medical system in *The Hospital*, set his sights on those three, all-pervading networks known as television.

William Holden, Robert Duvall and Peter Finch in *Network* (1976), where Duvall again makes the rules (UA/Photofest).

He devised the story of a veteran news anchor fed up, as most Americans were at the time, with the social ills (Vietnam, corrupt governments, labor strife, runaway inflation, etc.) that had debilitated the country. On-air, this anti–Cronkite announces that he's going to kill himself—live! The network bureaucrats instinctively exploit the situation, encouraging him to rant and rave as long as possible before his final, bloody broadcast.

The film is mostly speeches. Such was Chayefsky's exalted reputation that no one dared push him off his soapbox (plus, contractually, it would have been a bitch). In between is a May–December romance between William Holden, representing Chayefsky's generation, and Faye Dunaway, representing '76's more shallow, greedier breed, and much gnashing and defending of the network's unconscionable actions—hence Duvall as (you guessed it!) the good soldier fighting for the wrong cause. He gives it his all, naturally, but it's hardly his picture. It belongs to Chayefsky, to Dunaway, and to director Sidney Lumet, with his cheeky cinematography and propensity for Grand Guignol.

Ironically, while Duvall benefited from Chayefsky's sourly thunderous take on television, the actor ended up benefiting from playing ball with TV producers. He was later acclaimed for playing war hero cum President Dwight D. Eisenhower in the mini-series *Ike: The War Years* (1979) and for fronting the epic adaptation of Larry McMurtry's Pulitzer Prize–winning *Lonesome Dove* (1989).

Unlike the highly original *Network*, Duvall's next films would mark a return to genre work. One took the traditional route, the other an interesting side road: *The Eagle Has Landed* and *The Seven-Per-Cent Solution* (1976).

The Eagle Has Landed, based on a best-seller by pulp novelist Jack Higgins, was the last film directed by John Sturges. Except for cult and blaxploitation films, American cinema circa '76 was not yet ready to examine the Vietnam conflict, then just winding down. An audience still existed for the old-fashioned war film, in which the aging Hollywood elite, dressed in battle fatigues, mowed down platoon after platoon of goosestepping extras.

In the late '60s, protesters began to picket theaters exhibiting these tired exercises in G.I. Joe-ism, citing the genre's unapologetic promotion of institutionalized violence and subversive endorsement of Johnson and Nixon's duplicitous foreign policy. Nevertheless, big-budget blow-'em-ups like *The Dirty Dozen* and *The Green Berets* (1968) continued to draw a surprisingly healthy, if older, audience. By the mid–'70s, with the slow dissolution of the counterculture, the dissenters stayed home and the World War II adventure stories stayed on screen, reclassified for a less politically charged age as exercises in big-budget nostalgia. They were easier for audiences to swallow, too, if they dealt in defeatism, playing on the lingering post–Vietnam sentiment that war, any war, was a logistical and sanguinary folly (ultimate example: *A Bridge Too Far*). *The Eagle Has Landed*, an action-packed tall tale about a failed assassination attempt on Winston Churchill, fit both bills.

It was intended to check a lot of boxes: an all-star cast, a high quotient of action, a melodramatic love story, an old-fashioned feel. And Britain's greatest showman, Sir Lew Grade, made sure that it did. Higgins' action-packed yarn is as worthy as such predecessors as *The Guns of Navarone* (1961), the aforementioned *Dirty Dozen* and *Where Eagles Dare* (1968).

Like those pillars of the genre, it subscribes to the age-old combat film convention in which a loose-knit unit of rogues is put under the command of a determined disciplinarian who forces them to carry out an improbable mission. In this case, the no-nonsense ringleader is Michael Caine. His co-conspirators include Donald Sutherland and Jean Marsh, with everyone under the ultimate command of Duvall.

It's one of those films in which the Nazis, at least the big ones, speak with British accents—yet there's Duvall, trying his luck with German intonation. But as this (and his turn in that same year's *The Seven-Per-Cent Solution*) demonstrate, he has a limited talent for vocal imitation (despite being prized, in life, as a mimic), going in and out of his Teutonic tonality like the Jeeps weaving throughout the English countryside. Like Hoffman, Nicholson, Pacino and the rest of his contemporaries, Duvall is irrepressibly American, so much so that period pieces are a limited proposition. Made-in-USA genres such as war films, cowboy pictures and film noir were okay, but almost any ring outside that bull's eye carried the risk of outright embarrassment. (For proof, see Duvall in the 1667-set *The Scarlet Letter*, 1995).

That said, he distinguishes himself in the film in other ways. While the rest of the cast, noticeably giddy to be in such forgivably unfashionable fun, throws their weight around and generally snacks on scenery, Duvall cannot be coerced into any violation of his fundamental Duvall-ness. He plays his eye patch–wearing Colonel Max Redl not *à la* von Stroheim, full of starch, Old World defeatism, but as a quiet chess master, moving his pieces around with a logician's aplomb. He is still Tom Hagen, consigliere for a suspect cause, but Hagen as, finally, the mastermind.

And as always, when the folly of his character's ways is made tragically, climatically clear, he's imbued with a gentlemanly sense of self-resignation. Personal tragedy to Duvall's personages is a creeping inevitability, the affirmation of something they had the pleasure of dodging until its inevitable manifestation.

Interestingly, Duvall has an early stand-off in the film with Anthony Quayle. The stuffy Quayle was, throughout his long career, Duvall's British equivalent. Quayle, too, was serially cast as the valuable advisor toiling for misguided bureaucracies, flustered by having his finely tuned insights rebuked in favor of the knee-jerk. Here, in an interesting contrast of approaches, Quayle stiffly rants while Duvall pensively posits.

On to accent #2: *The Seven-Per-Cent Solution*. Like *Eagle*, the film is an all-star British showcase with cross-element aspirations, at once mystery, comedy and swashbuckling adventure. But Nicholas Meyer, on whose best-selling novel the film was based, threw a new element into the mix: the postwar Freudian mindset.

The '70s was the great age of angst, the climax of the neurotic instinct that had been creeping up on people since the uneasy '50s. By the '70s, pop psychology had become a major cultural touchstone, complete with regular re-examinations of Freud. Cleverly, Meyer concocted a goose chase pairing the world's most famous psychoanalyst and its most famous detective. The former is played with hypnotic docility by Alan Arkin and the latter with nervy animation by Nicol Williamson. Though Williamson, a notoriously neurotic performer, was more than qualified for this particular take on an extremely taxed Sherlock Holmes, it's an ironic bit of casting when you consider Arkin's reputation as one of American film's top phobics.

Then there's the equally offbeat casting of Duvall.

Duvall, who was up for the role of Woody Guthrie in Hal Ashby's biopic *Bound for Glory* (1976), showed up for his audition unable to shake the Okie twang he had developed for the role of the famed folk singer. He was smart enough to bring along a tape he had recorded of his shot at an English accent. It worked—at least for the producers, if not, ultimately, the audience.

After he was cast, however, Meyer kept complaining to director Herbert Ross about the staid nature of Duvall's performance. Ross, agreeing, tried to push the actor, who, not unexpectedly, pushed back. Good thing. In his entertaining memoir *The View from the Bridge* (a reference to his contributions as writer-director to the *Star Trek* film franchise), Meyer wrote,

> In the end, Duvall almost steals the movie. What we took to be his static performance, once stitched together, revealed itself to be the most sophisticated film acting. Duvall understood, better than most, how his performance would come together in the cutting room, how gestures so tiny they could not be perceived with the naked eye or indeed in the dailies, once combined, would deliver the cumulative punch. The closer the camera came, the less he knew he needed to do.[4]

Meyer's final analysis speaks to Duvall as one of the American screen's great minimalists, with an innate sense of the camera. Like other such practitioners, including McQueen and Newman, he doesn't need a lot of lines. As further testament, there's his work for Horton Foote, the tight-lipped Texas playwright Duvall satisfactorily serviced throughout his career (*To Kill a Mockingbird, Tomorrow, Tender Mercies*). Much of drama, for Duvall, is in the spaces between the words. He can carry a whole picture with small silences, like his Oscar-winning turn in *Tender Mercies*. Statistically, that role probably has the fewest lines of any Best Actor–garnering performance (excusing Jean Dujardin in 2011's largely silent *The Artist*). But it's a quality that eludes imminent recognition, even to the trained eye.

Duvall returned home to help mythologize an already legendary figure: Muhammad Ali. After the surprise success of the low-budget *Rocky*, it was inevitable that a film be made about the life of the world's most popular boxer. The surprise was that Ali would star in the film himself. Then again, Ali had always been part actor, typecasting himself as a brash, mealy-mouthed showboat with a gift for self-penned verse and socio-spiritual sermonizing. But by '77, when the film adaptation of his autobiography *The Greatest* was filmed, Ali was past peak. He had begun to complain about growing old, was getting away with controversial decisions against his opponents, and had even become a tragic figure to long-time TV cheerleader Howard Cosell. Unbeknownst to most, Ali was in the early stages of Parkinson's, which would coerce him into a belated retirement after humiliating defeats to lesser talents such as Leon Spinks and Larry Holmes.

The rest of the above-the-line talent in the film is a mix. The respected Ring Lardner, Jr., is the screenwriter, but the less-than-respected Tom Gries is the director (he died during post-production). Gries gives the film all he's got but, unlike his star, he's incapable of punching above his weight. That said, while the film never rises above a predictably made-for-TV quality, its central personality does. (For a better film on the champ, see 2001's *Ali*.)

Ali's quintessentially American life was inherently histrionic, a Horatio Alger story with elements of race, prosperity, religion, politics, show business, sports, sex and patriotism. The book and its film adaptation were clearly part of a legacy hunt, an attempt on Ali's behalf to formalize his rise, fall and resurrection(s). The film constituted a different kind of comeback for him, a golden opportunity to relive the highlights of his life. And he's more than up for the challenge, running his mouth, rolling his eyes and rhyming like an ancestral rapper—in short, assuming his public persona, dramatically contextualized.

Such was his stature that actors the caliber of Duvall were happy to participate in the picture, even if Ali concedes the spotlight but little. Duvall, who's in it for all of ten minutes, plays a fiery promoter who gets into a screaming match with the champ over his conversion to Islam. Fittingly, the scene is a sparring match between two equally invested performers. Despite the on-screen friction between the two, it's obvious that Duvall holds great respect for his opponent, whose actions his character eventually endorses. Duvall's a fan playing a foe.

Duvall then reversed course. After helping to tell an American success story, he next assisted in the exploitative dissection of another.

Throughout the '60s and '70s, Harold Robbins, a Hollywood insider, exposed the lurid side of that culture as a best-selling pulp novelist. His *romans a clef*, an unapologetic mix of money, murder and sexual monkeyshines, ultimately earned him the rep of "the dirty old man of American letters."⁵ "Dirty," yes, in the sexual sense, but also "filthy" as in "filthy" rich: For close to half a century, Robbins monopolized supermarket paperback carousels, selling over 750 million books. To critics, intellectuals and discriminating readers, he was a literary whipping boy; to lonely housewives, beach readers and lovers of camp, an irresistible guilty pleasure.

For *The Betsy*, Robbins trades Hollywood for Detroit. He casts his exploitative eye on the Ford family, remaking them as the Hardemans. Their automotive empire, Bethlehem Motors, is expanded to include a talented outsider, Angelo Petrino (the then-rising Tommy Lee Jones, who plays the part as if his character was named "Bobby Joe Hickman"). Car designer and cocksman Petrino helps the family patriarch relive the company's glory days by building the titular Betsy, this while other members of that circle feud, fuck and fire one another.

Canadian Daniel Petrie is this sudsy saga's puppet master. He was no stranger to easy titillation, having supervised two of 1976's biggest made-for-TV movies, *Eleanor and Franklin* and *Sybil*. Dutifully, he delivers all of the ridiculousness Robbins' fanbase expects, creating a big-scale version of the familial soaps then dominating prime-time television: *Dallas* (1978–91), *Knots Landing* (1979–93) and *Dynasty* (1981–89). During the Great Depression, audiences learned to laugh at the eccentricities of the rich; in the inflationary '70s, they learned to pass moral judgment on them.

While much of the film plays as a parody of *The Godfather*, at its essence, it's an elegiac valentine to the American automobile, then in the throes of being towed to the scrapyard. An oil crisis was looming, inaugurating government regulations on gas-guzzling engineering and opening the door to fuel-efficient Japanese imports. On film, the car became both an object of sentiment (as the opening credits of *The Betsy* make clear, the camera poring over every chrome accent of the titular machine to the sound of sentimental strings) and a source of evil, hence horror pictures about runaway sedans like *The Car* (1977).

It's possible that Duvall was intrigued by the relevancy of all of this, despite *The Betsy*'s seriously soapy veneer. But the likelier attractions were probably the contradictions of his character—Duvall remained a sucker for dichotomy—and the opportunity to work with an icon of his craft, Laurence Olivier.

Olivier plays the automotive overlord with a touch of Charles Foster Kane, and in fact, the film's vacillating timeline allows us to see his wily, charismatic despot as both young and old. As the latter, he's an 86-year-old wheelchair-bound capitalist maverick with a turtle's posture and bullfrog's voice—and having, as was characteristic of the actor in that era, a grand time of it. As Olivier aged, he (like Brando) got bored with the art of acting. Increasingly, he had to challenge himself to keep the spark alive. Unlike his American counterpart, though, Olivier was out to make a fool of himself for the good. Acting became not an act of contempt for Olivier but something of a good-natured prank, a shared laugh with his most steadfast admirers. He was out to remain relevant by exercising his schoolboy's mischievousness, goosing audiences by flirting with gross miscasting in insultingly common films. If you don't want to be a has-been, he happily announced, be a ham.

Here he whoops it up over his latest automotive inclination, bangs chambermaids a quarter of his age, and dresses down his successors with a round-toned snap.

At this late stage of his career, he was inserted in films largely to add class and legitimacy to properties sorely short of them—but in almost every case, he acted as if these films were an opportunity to play broad comedy. When he repeatedly goes head-to-head with Duvall, his stylishly sneaky grandson, it's acting's two major schools of the twentieth century in an expository grudge match. In those scenes, and throughout the rest of the film, Duvall conducts his business, both the cold-hearted professional and the uneasy personal, with a diplomatic purr, underlying a fundamental frustration with the social and political protocol by which he's forced to live his life. He's a philistine, boxed in by professional and familial propriety. In every action, regardless of how contained, you can sense his character's itchiness. Occasionally he permits himself to exteriorize his ruthlessness. He uses kid gloves, but they still pack a punch.

In the end, though, the actor inevitably falls to Robbins' melodramatic bidding and struggles to make overblown moments and bad dialogue palatable, a defeat we're unaccustomed to witnessing.

While the picture's about cars, metaphorically, it may have been about the movies. It was released just as big New York–based conglomerates were gobbling up the ailing studios, putting an end to the costly over-the-top shenanigans of the auteur movement by which Duvall had made his name. *Were films guided by personal vision dead?* audiences began to ask themselves, particularly as they watched a talent of Duvall's caliber slum in ones that were clearly beneath him. (Many considered his appearance in *The Betsy* a career nadir.) Yes, they were willing to concede, the man likes to work, appreciates money, and aspires to adulation, as does every actor. Still, they wondered, when will we get to stop asking ourselves, *What's a guy like that doing in a film like this?*

Little did Duvall's fanbase know that at the same time, earnest acts of redemption were in motion. Further, that the quality of these films would erase Duvall's small history with middling material, serve as the climax of his work in the '70s, and restore his status as one of the American cinema's most potent presences.

In '76, Duvall juggled three parts drawing upon his military background: *The Eagle Has Landed*, the biographical TV mini-series *Ike* and, reteaming him with Francis Ford Coppola, *Apocalypse Now*. The same year that *Apocalypse* was released, Duvall enjoyed his first starring role since *The Outfit*, as the title blowhard in *The Great Santini*. Thanks to those last two films, Duvall bagged successive Oscar nominations, first in the supporting category then as Best Actor. Going forward, the supporting parts would be meatier, the star parts more frequent, and the films of a generally higher quality.

Apocalypse Now, Coppola's brilliant transposition of Conrad's *Heart of Darkness* to the messy milieu of the Vietnam War, was released three years after the start of production. Duvall had shot his scenes early in the process, long before the shoot became notoriously plagued with problems. He shows up early in the film, too, as the first eccentric that Martin Sheen's Captain Willard meets on his feverish *Alice in Wonderland* way upriver to assassinate Marlon Brando's Colonel Kurtz, a one-time military hero who has carved out his own genocidal dictatorship within the darkest corner of the conflict.

Duvall's Colonel Kilgore is introduced stepping off a chopper, shot from a very low angle to convey his exalted status and mythomaniacal stance. He's the military ethic incarnate; the universal soldier—and not in the Donovan sense. He wears the cavalry hat of his nineteenth-century Western ancestors and the aviator shades of World War II generals. He barks orders over the din of battle like comic book hero Sgt. Rock and is responsible for the film's first absurdity-atrocity in a picture teeming with them, when he deposits homemade calling cards upon the corpses.

As the ol' song has it (quoted in *Taxi Driver*), he's partly truth and partly fiction. While Duvall subscribed to a number of real-life role models for the part (Colonel John Stockton, General James F. Hollingsworth, and a West Point officer Duvall had known), an element of parody is at work, the same one that *Patton* screenwriter Coppola had relied on to frame the eponymous general as both an exemplary authoritarian and a bloodthirsty clown. Duvall pays due to both aspects of the character, taking charge of the mission and looking out for his men while bemusedly strafing civilians to the Nazi-esque strains of Wagner.

The satirical quality takes on absurdist dimensions when Kilgore reveals his obsession with surfing. And yet, in Kilgore's insistence that his men test the waves in the midst of mass murder, an element of humanity peeks through. In Duvall's subtle hands, the surrealism of recreation-extermination is not just a comment on the absurdity of the war. It's a good man trying to give his boys ("rock'n'rollers with one foot in the grave") a piece of home. He's trying to force them to remember from where they've come, who they remain, and that that world, somewhere, still exists. As always then, though effectively straitjacketed, Duvall, with pinpoint austerity, manages to locate and convey the compassion at the core of the character. There

Robert Duvall plays the title part in *The Great Santini* (1979), arguably his most autobiographical role (Warner Bros./Photofest).

would have been a little more of this had he had his way: a scene in which Kilgore rescues a drowning Vietnamese child. It was shot but cut, much to the actor's dismay. Personally, I side with Coppola, who no doubt recognized that already, Duvall had afforded dimension to his character without having to resort to obviousness or extremism.

Duvall's next film was a far smaller production centering around a character cut largely from the same cloth: *The Great Santini*. That's the title by which we recognize the film today. At the time of its willy-nilly release, it was also known as *The Ace*. Convinced that the film wouldn't make its modest budget back, nervous distributors sold it to fledgling HBO, this while the film's producers were still trying to drum up positive reviews in major markets. The cockeyed battle was won by the latter, who managed to get it into legitimate theaters based on a handful of journalistic encomiums.

Great Santini was truly the culmination of Duvall's work throughout the '70s. It was his first starring role as a known commodity (the obscure *Tomorrow*, *THX 1138* and *The Outfit* don't count); it drew on the major aspects of his life, and earned him the reviews and respect he had only garnered as a character actor.

Throughout the Vietnam War, it was good cinematic sport to lampoon military men. Hits both mainstream, like *Patton*, and cult, like *Harold and Maude*, indulged in the practice. Postwar, satire began to give way to sentiment. By the late '70s, when films examining the legacy of the Asian conflict were becoming a veritable genre, a variety of perspectives on that great, selfless keeper of the American way of life, the soldier, were, well, at war. There was the tried-and-true (*MacArthur*, 1977), the post-traumatic (*Coming Home*, 1978) and, with *The Great Santini*, a mix of both.

Santini, aka William "Bull" Meechum, is a frog-voiced Marine squad commander operating out of Beaufort, South Carolina, in the early '60s, a time of American-Cuban tensions, polarized attitudes over race, and shifts in political and personal attitudes among the young. He's also an incurable braggart, an immature jokester, a closet self-defeatist, and a family irritant—particularly to his sensitive first-born son, whom he burdens with the emotionally crippling expectations of militarily fashioned masculinity. When son bests dad at pick-up basketball in one of the film's best scenes, *Great Santini* takes on other thematic dimensions. Suddenly it's also about the American premium on winning, the waning nature of manhood, and the uphill battle to grow one's own identity from dysfunctional soil.

Much of Meechum came easily to Duvall; it's chockablock with elements suggesting it's the part that he was born to play. The military milieu, the Southern setting and the mixed emotions spawned by both were deeply familiar commodities to him. But this was also a chance for him to break type, for the great recessive actor to become the great explosive actor. We had seen Duvall rage before, but in limited doses only, and either with cool calculation or kneejerk bluster. Here, he unleashes his inner Brando. The sour joke of Meechum's implacable ethic, which runs roughshod over all and sundry, is let down but for one scene: a drunken soliloquy revealing that the only true conflict this career soldier has ever known is the battle within his own soul. The scene vibrates with the prospect of audience disappointment, threatening to convert a taut family drama into a Hallmark production advocating easy reconciliation and sentimental closure. But Duvall, like a good soldier, holds the line, paying due diligence to the moment without allowing the film's foothold to veer too far into soft ground.

Less obvious concessions to the hero's hidden humanity are offered more Duvall-style, via small, doleful close-ups and see-through moments of forced jocularity. Dichotomy, then, a Duvall specialty, on scales both big and small. In Meechum, we get both Bodge as we've never seen him before, and the Bodge with which we've become intimate.

The film is equally divided narratively—and I'm not talking about the too-generous subplot on race relations. Like Pacino's *Dog Day Afternoon*, it's part one-man show, part ensemble. It's Duvall's grand opportunity to claim the spotlight, as well as a chance to function in the group setting by which he is often at his best. The wan Blythe Danner plays Meechum's dutiful wife with bouncy Southern diplomacy and a simple, surprisingly winning fundamentalism; the young Michael O'Keefe, in only his second film role, deftly handles the complicated role of the son; and the rest of the Meechum clan, while given largely thankless roles, come shy of cloying.

Duvall scored some of the best reviews of his life for the role; wrote the respected Vincent Canby in *The New York Times*, "Now it's about time to recognize Robert Duvall as one of the most resourceful, most technically proficient, most remarkable actors in America."[6] He also established a professional precedent: He, too, now joined the other actors of his generation in their collective quest to reframe the traditional American hero through their starring vehicles.

After the military man, it was on to the next archetype: the cowboy. The film, following a few co-billed parts, was *Tender Mercies*. In it, Duvall gives audiences the other side of the Great Santini. Fallen country music legend Mac Sledge is just as respected, just as proud, just as damaging as "Bull" Meechum—only his sober self-inventory extends beyond the sporadic. It's a lifestyle, trapping him in an anguished limbo state between alcoholic egotist and God-fearing everyman. In his own quiet, determined manner, Mac re-pieces his life, settling for the unconditional love of a good woman and her equally amenable child. Pulled, willy-nilly, into a semblance of his old life—unwitting reunions with his complicated ex and his estranged daughter, plus the potential resurrection of his career—he sticks fast to the healing agents of recreational song, Christian fundamentalism and agrarian rituals. With winning vacuity, the film's geographically dwarfed characters thank the heavens for life's salvific second chances, the leaks of light in our otherwise oppressive skies.

It had been a matter of debate among the persnickety as to whether, in his few starring vehicles, Duvall's minimalist style had successfully sustained itself over a full-length narrative. Such arguments were put to rest with his performance as the spiritually recalibrated Sledge. That said, it took the perfect admixture of above-the-line talent to get the job done: the elliptical writer Horton Foote and the sensorial director Bruce Beresford, both sharing Duvall's innate appreciation of the humane isolation of bucolic peoples. While Duvall had long enjoyed a symbiotic relationship with Texan Foote, Beresford, an Australian, was another matter. The Duvall-Beresford relationship was anything but tender, yet their mutual interest in a reverent, realistic look at the marginalized citizenry of the American heartland—then a cultural hot topic thanks to cinematic predecessors *Places in The Heart* (1982) and the top 40 hits of John Cougar Mellencamp—created a lyrical miniature that won over even the most cynical like the simple warmth of Duvall's folksy crooning.

In so doing, Duvall & Co. addressed one of the actor's major bugaboos. Together, they successfully challenged the East-West centricity of the stage and movie industry, giving people from neglected parts of America their representational due. Duvall was out to typify that stock, *his* stock, as honest, worthy people—not just their simple pleasures but their soul-searing pain.

As he once stated, "The center and especially the South of the country have been patronized and made fun of.... If I can do anything at all in my work to show what dignity is in the common man, then that's what my life is really about."[7] Also, "I love those people. I can't learn enough from them. Southerners, Texans, cowboys and country singers.... How tough and loving and vengeful they are, how serious and religious in the best sense of the word."[8]

As noble and novel as that may seem, it's hardly a departure from what he's always strived to bring to any role. As Duvall once put it, "That's what acting is all about. Dignity. Trying to find the dignity in the man. Because the average workingman has dignity that the Hollywood establishment has overlooked."[9] That's exactly how Duvall, himself targeted for being overlooked, garnered notice in the industry.

Robert De Niro

Avenging Angel

There is a lonely quality to Robert De Niro, the ghostly ambling of a dissatisfied urban seeker, trying to make sense of the world, himself, and how the two might live in harmony. His characters are perpetually boarded up in a cave of solitude, a room of rumination, of half-thoughts, of *I-don't-knows* and *yeahs* and *maybes*—much like the answers De Niro the person, a notoriously tricky interview, affords, when he so deems, the press. It has the vibe of a fallen angel, a holy presence sent to Earth to take in humanity, have his heart broken, then come up with his grand plan for man's redemption. On the surface, that's a simple, focused journey from perplexity to primal, mortal anger. He throws off the wings to take on the world on its own ugly terms. Whether he wins or loses (it's the latter, mostly), he's reminded that the only salvation that's truly manageable in the end is his own. And so, a small, personal insight forms, reshaping his character: his wings grow back and he, separated from the effects of his ridiculously self-deluded mission, is born anew. He is finally the angel he mistook himself for in the first place. As the New English Bible quote at the end of *Raging Bull* states, "All I know is this: once I was blind and now I can see."

It's right, it's wrong. It's the nobility of the cowboy mixed with the volatility of the gangster; the strong silent type married to the mealy-mouthed ruffian; Gary Cooper meets Edward G. Robinson. By borrowing from both traditions, De Niro strikes a deep-set chord within movie audiences. They've seen these schticks before, even mixed together in Brando, but until De Niro came along, enveloped in a Zen-like countenance, they had never seen unrest get refined into the irony of calming bloodlust. Siddhartha wearing brass knuckles.

Brute disillusion, introduced in the opening pages of this book, is what De Niro is all about. His parents, like so many of the characters their son would eventually play, had been lost souls: Greenwich Village bohemians whose sexual experimentation had resulted in their only child's birth. Robert De Niro, Sr., had been a painter of some clout, until the Abstract Movement relegated him to the sidelines. He left the family when his son, Robert De Niro, Jr., was young, to devote himself more seriously to his craft and privately exercise his bisexuality. Young Bobby and his father, while estranged, managed to maintain a limited but beneficial relationship. Sr.'s imprint on Jr. was not the result of nurturing but example: From his father,

De Niro Jr. learned to inhabit a private world, one predicated on professional commitment, artistic discipline and a healthy distance from judgmental forces.

While Bobby's mother was also a visual artist (Peggy Guggenheim kept one of her works in her private collection), her primary income came from writing and typing. It was she who urged her young, shy, lonely dependent to try his hand at acting, if for no other reason than to keep him safe from that '50s scourge, juvenile delinquency.

In acting class, De Niro found his second mother: Stella Adler, the strict but nurturing Stanislavskian who had turned another juvie-in-the-making, Brando, into one of De Niro's idols. (De Niro and Brando worked together in the latter's last film, *The Score*, 2001.)

While studying with Adler, De Niro boldly auditioned for all he could. He landed some dinner theater, a few TV ads, and a handful of no- to low-pay films, including a few helmed by some guy named Brian De Palma, who put them into grindhouse distribution. De Niro did a little better when he landed, eighth-billed, in *Bloody Mama* (1970), discount king Roger Corman's cash-in on *Bonnie and Clyde*. Then, like every other Italian-American actor in New York, he was asked to audition for *The Godfather*. Al Pacino got the part, while De Niro got the one slated for Pacino in the mob comedy *The Gang That Couldn't Shoot Straight* (1971), made by the crew that couldn't shoot comedy.

At a dinner party, De Niro met a yappy NYU Film School graduate named Martin Scorsese. The spark between them created a white-hot flame they would set under unsuspecting critics and audiences. Over time, it would emblazon their names over Hollywood skies.

But before the big splash that was *Mean Streets* (1973) came the silent stutter steps of the renegade '60s and early '70s, the embryonic years of the distinguishable De Niro persona.

Long before he set out to out–Hitchcock Hitchcock, the aforementioned De Palma had cut his cinematic chops as a dark, experimental satirist. In this capacity, he became the first film director to showcase the shy, ectomorphic De Niro, featuring him in three little-seen productions.

After the obscure *The Wedding*, shot in '63 but not released until '69, De Palma finally earned a modicum of acclaim with *Greetings* (1968). It's a hippie-era *I Vitelloni* (1953), a loose comic revue chronicling the misadventures of three draft dodgers as they struggle with the cultural playthings of the times: JFK-spawned conspiracy theories, sexual liberation and the prospect of military induction. De Palma's pet theme of voyeurism is in high evidence, taking on a variety of manifestations (including nods to the mega-hit *Blow-Up*, which he would eventually remake as *Blow-out*, 1981). One of them is the arc of De Niro's character, a bookstore clerk who decides to make peep films. While De Palma recognized and encouraged a colloquial, conversational style that well-suited the actor, De Niro the comedian was, at that time, a limited proposition. That didn't deter De Palma. Buoyed by the cult success of *Greetings*, he elaborated on the character with *Hi, Mom!* (1970), a sequel (though few made the link) in which De Niro not only got to again play subversive filmmaker, but guerrilla warrior to boot.

With *Mean Streets* (1973), the struggling Robert De Niro made his presence known (Warner Bros./Photofest).

While De Palma's instinct to prolong the success of *Greetings* was understandable, his insistence that De Niro was poised for big-screen comedy was premature. It was a shaky aspiration still by '77, when the actor, who by then had made his name, was disastrously essayed for the recast Richard Dreyfuss part in Neil Simon's romcom *The Goodbye Girl* (1977).

Dreyfuss, meanwhile, won the Oscar for the part. By that time, he had improbably joined De Niro and company in the pantheon of top male box office commodities. The Brooklyn-born, Los Angeles–raised Dreyfuss perfectly represented both of his geographic stomping grounds: the energetic, wisecracking spirit of New York and the sunny, giddy naivete of Hollywood. On-screen, he was the epitome of chutzpah, clawing his way past all and sundry for the precious attainment of his personal needs (*The Apprenticeship of Duddy Kravitz*, 1974, *The Goodbye Girl*). But he could also play the wide-eyed everyman, humbled by things so much larger than himself that there was nothing to do but to accept his smallness (*Jaws*, *Close Encounters of the Third Kind*, 1977).

The use of "smallness" is not incidental. Except for Hackman, the Method Men of the '70s were, physically, less than intimidating. They ranged in height from 5'4" to 5'10", with Dreyfuss rivaling Hoffman for the least tall. That's another way by which they collectively redefined the traditional male movie hero, the kind of man one

For a few years in the '70s, Richard Dreyfuss—here in *Jaws* (1975)—joined the exalted company of top male screen personalities (Universal/Photofest).

used to literally look up to. Each, too, was palpably propelled by what is today called "short man's energy." (Before that, it was known more grandiosely as Napoleonic Syndrome.) No one had as much of it in the tank as Dreyfuss.

As such, Dreyfuss served as the very personification of America's runaway capitalist spirit. Paired with his propensity for hard-earned humility, both sides of the national character, the greedy and the God-fearing, came into evidence. It was the tug of war between the two that constituted Dreyfuss' winning energy. When it earned him the Oscar (a surprise win over a resurgent Richard Burton), he bested Brando as the youngest actor to procure the honor until that time.

As for De Niro, to score as a comedic presence on the Dreyfussian scale, he would first need to establish a reputation he could translate into self-parody—something that would not happen until the career-altering *Analyze This*.

Till then, though, filmmakers insisted on trying to mine the funny within. The abovementioned *Gang That Couldn't Shoot Straight* was a hopelessly clunky adaptation of New York columnist Jimmy Breslin's comic novel about a messy rivalry between incompetent mobs. The film is a veritable tutorial on how to botch cinematic comedy, as well as an offensive compendium of Italian American stereotypes. As a bicyclist-crook parading as a priest, De Niro, when not asked to play the clown, is afforded his due as a dramatic actor in the film's one redeeming convention: the central love story between himself and the now-forgotten Leigh Taylor-Young.

Even smaller parts in two other brutally reviewed comedies, *Jennifer on My Mind* (1971) and *Born to Win* (1971), followed. Satire was not doing De Niro any favors.

How to graduate from marginal parts in exploitation pictures, starring roles in cult comedies, and episodes of miscasting in commercial releases, he must have been asking.

His prayers were answered in '73. That career-making year saw the simultaneous release of two films, one independent, the other commercial, that would mark him as a genuine up-and-comer.

Since the procurement of pitcher-slugger Babe Ruth from Boston in a fire sale in 1920, the New York Yankees had been baseball's model franchise. From 1923 to 2009, the Bronx-based pinstripers won 27 World Series. There was a serious blip, however, from '65 to '75. Like the city the team had long made proud, the Yankees fell from respectability. Their National League counterparts, the hapless Mets, became the better, and more fun, metaphor for the ineptitude of the Big Apple's civic infrastructure and the equally hapless world that surrounded it. By '69, they were the Miracle Mets, improbable winners of the World Series for a city in dire need of spiritual uplift. The Yankees, meanwhile, were still trying to find their way back to reliability, something they didn't find until 1977 and the complicated importation of Reggie Jackson, a player with Dustin Hoffman's insecurity, Gene Hackman's geniality, Jack Nicholson's showmanship, Al Pacino's volatility, Robert Duvall's cool, and Robert De Niro's resignation.

Bang the Drum Slowly (1973) was shot in both Yankee Stadium and the Mets' Shea Stadium, while the Yanks and Mets were on extended road trips. It was adapted from a fine, delicate novel by Mark Harris; earlier, it had been a teleplay starring Paul Newman. It's part of a quartet of books written in the voice of Henry Wiggen, the reflective, soulful pitcher played in the film by the porously stony Michael Moriarty (as a right-hander, though his literary genesis is a southpaw). Ironically, Moriarty was soon singled out in Tennessee Williams' memoir as the next Marlon Brando, a designation others would eventually affix to De Niro.

The film focuses on the unwitting bond between the battery mates, prompted by Wiggen's catcher's battle with Hodgkin's Disease. As the male gender was being redefined, the "buddy" ethic that had powered Westerns, war films and other exercises in testosterone-based bonding was growing increasingly complex. Now, it was the sports film's turn. The precedent had been set in '71 when James Caan co-starred in the made-for-TV football movie *Brian's Song*, which had conformed to a similar (though real-life) storyline. For years, a subgenre of film had flourished known as "women's weepies." It extended from manipulative melodramas such as *Stella Dallas* (1937) to contemporary Kleenex fodder like *Beaches* (1988). Due to the new, sensitive nature afforded men, now the world had "men's weepies."

Bang the Drum Slowly was De Niro's biggest big-screen challenge to date: a role at odds with every aspect of his personality. He was an unathletic New Yorker with a highly affective demeanor; catcher Bruce Pearson was a baseball-playing Georgian with an agreeably simple disposition.

So the dedicated De Niro went to work. He learned to field and hit and toured the American South to absorb the vibe and drawl. It worked. He swings a credible bat in the film and there's nary a slip into New Yorkese. The toughest part, though, appears to have been the substitution of his perpetually probing expression for Pearson's *tabula rasa* of a face. De Niro's conversion flirts with caricature, threatening to rob the film of much-needed heart. He's rescued, though, by just enough wiggle room to allow him to humanize the character, specifically, when the tragically doomed Pearson experiences the odd bout of sweaty-teary discomfiture. De Niro makes the most of director John Hancock's minimalism, rescuing both the role and the film, which is otherwise a showcase for Vincent Gardenia as the team's troubled manager, a role fitting his neurotic bluster like a well-worn cap.

One has to wonder, though, how much more easily Robert Duvall, with his Southern roots, love of dialect and simpler style, might have fit the part. And how funny is it that the film's sole concession to the over-the-top, a clubhouse-wrecking hissy fit, is conducted by Moriarty instead of his co-star, who would become synonymous with epic exhibits of unleashed rage?

Bang the Drum Slowly was De Niro's first studio release. While it didn't entirely rescue him from the cult and exploitation circuits, it put him on Hollywood's radar. While he was shooting the film, a relationship came along that would pay the dividends alluded to by his multi-picture association with De Palma (though De Niro and De Palma finally made a hit together in '87: the big-screen version of TV's *The Untouchables*). The frustrated director in question, who had both an independent and a commercially distributed failure under his belt, pitched De Niro on his ambitions to capture the tension-filled tenor of their common geography. Borrowing a line from Raymond Chandler, this boldly realistic look at New York's Little Italy would be titled *Mean Streets*.

Mean Streets is many things: a New York movie, a Western, a film noir, a buddy picture, a male character study. Mostly, though, it was the template from which future Martin Scorsese films were wrought. We witness the canonization of the signature conventions that will mark the prolific filmmaker's *oeuvre*: the criminal milieu, the mix of tracking shots, slow-motion sequences and bravura editing, the jukebox-based soundtrack, the colloquial exchanges of dialogue, and the film's central theme: the pull of hedonism over spiritual obeisance. In this, the film borrows most from the venerable Western (whose knockabout humor it mocks by contrasting a fight scene from John Ford's *The Searchers*, 1956, with a much more realistic brawl in a low-lit pool room).

Like the cowboys of yore, the movie's hero, Charlie Cappa (Harvey Keitel), resides in a lawless land. He can go with the criminal flow—in this case, skim from the docks, stiff errant hippies, and deal drugs—or live by a moral code, rooted in the dictates of the Catholic faith. It's the Man-Superman argument, posited as the gun-toting vs. the God-fearing.

Another Biblical question runs throughout the film: Am I my brother's keeper? The brother in question is Johnny Boy Civello, played by De Niro. Johnny, undersized as he is, lives large. He runs his mouth like a car salesman (mostly in funny Abbott and Costello–like exchanges with Charlie), woos women like a lounge lizard, and fights like a rabid Pomeranian. Mostly, though, he ducks shylocks, upsets big shots, and gives his already troubled overseer, the spiritually conflicted Charlie, a bad name. He's a cracked step on Charlie's rise to the top of the ladder, burdening him with that great, Coppola-esque question: What's of greater value, the business or the personal?

In this relationship, as in so many of the films featuring this particular generation of actors, we again see the influence of *On the Waterfront*. Charlie is Scorsese's version of *Waterfront* bag man Rod Steiger (the two characters even share a name), forced to play tough with his ne'er-do-well brother, Brando-DeNiro, in the name of saving his reputation and that of the corrupt regime that holds him dangerously dear.

As Johnny Boy, De Niro remains the skinny, loose-limbed kid we got to know in previous films. And he's just as innocent, playful and vulnerable as those incarnations. But there's a new quality at work here. De Niro's Johnny Boy walks in a loping, defensive strut that, throughout the actor's career, will become imminently recognizable. He's dressed in clothes that'll be appropriated by another proud street hero, Rocky Balboa. And he erupts into kneejerk fits of rage suggesting a foolish fearlessness, a self-destructive quality that will manifest itself again in Travis Bickle, Jake La Motta and other characterizations.

If *Mean Streets* is the film that officially introduced us to Scorsese after a few stutter steps, it's also the film that introduced us, after a few false starts, to De Niro. This is De Niro's first thoroughly confident performance, a certitude that is not simply the product of his cocky character. Like the film itself, it's autobiographical work: De Niro's familiarity with the milieu, its citizenry and his persona oozes authenticity. As much as he considers himself a studious actor, De Niro's Johnny Boy is recognizably the product of a deep-set intuition. Johnny Boy is a living photobomb, the un-squishable fly in everyone's ointment, flesh'n'blood itching powder. He's a victim of his own folly. In the Italian American *patois* of the picture, he's the ultimate "stronzo," the quintessential "mook," the capital J "Jerk-off."

There's little doubt that growing up, De Niro had this guy in his face at least a couple of times. No doubt he shooed him away, but not before absorbing his manner for future use. The rage, too, is real; you can feel it, the same way that the film's violence is real (Scorsese besting, particularly with the climax, Penn and Peckinpah). At last, everything that was buried deep within poor, lonely little Bobby is set free. We feel the personal liberation, the cathartic release of his Freudian anxiety every time he throws his ectomorphic form at some smart-talkin' "fuck-face" twice his size. He'll do it again as Bickle, as La Motta, betraying his Buddhist carapace with bombastic bada-bing.

Mean Streets, a mongrel production shot in New York (for seven days only, incredibly) and L.A. on a catch-as-catch-can budget, caused a veritable sensation. Here was a bold, experimental reinvention of the venerable gangster film, with an unabashed sociological bent and a complex ideological theme. This was Roger Corman methodology, Sam Peckinpah violence, and Bernardo Bertolucci camerawork taking over the fatalistic, pugilistic and hubristic world of Humphrey Bogart, James Cagney and John Garfield. The previous year, *The Godfather* had revised the gangster genre with an exalted sensibility. That film had its moments of grit but on the whole, it was slick, studio-backed stuff. *Mean Streets*, by contrast, was all grit. Yes, there was a Michael Corleone, Harvey Keitel's Charlie, but the rest of the characters, Johnny Boy included, were all Sonnys—no Hagen, no Tessio, no Fat Clemenza. No classicism either, *à la* Coppola. Instead, the technical muscularity of Scorsese, bringing visual virtuosity to pulp, not to class it up but to better expose its organic surrealism, gallows humor and in-your-face–ness.

Mean Streets also introduced us to a new kind of male, one borrowing from the classic archetypes of the past (Charlie lists John Wayne as one of his idols) while suffering the modern ambiguity of the anti-hero. This crisis of identity serves as the basis for his relationship with women: Should they be playthings, like those flirty imports from the Village that Johnny Boy incongruously imports into Little Italy, or someone to whom you expose your greatest vulnerabilities, as Charlie attempts to do with Johnny Boy's confused, epileptic cousin? Admittedly, the neighborhood and the guys are everything to Charlie—or so he claims. But it's a conviction that radiates doubt. In this, Scorsese marks the modern male-female dilemma as a generational phenomenon. In time, other films will come along, including *Saturday Night Fever, Bloodbrothers* (1978) and *The Warriors* (1980), corroborating the contention.

As for De Niro, he collected, despite the perfectly cast Keitel, the lion's share of the acting reviews. The critical cognoscenti familiar with his previous performances acknowledged that at last, the struggling actor might have very well arrived. Where once we had an awkward, aspiring comedian with small suggestions of dramatic depth, we now had a creature capable of an admirable, even shocking sincerity. Nevertheless, the all-important question remained: While the kid had a winning rawness, could he be mannered? Could he be harnessed, challenged, brought to transcend? Was he simply developing a schtick, or was the chameleonic quality of a real actor poised to break out?

The answer came when a completely different De Niro showed up in *The Godfather Part II*. Here, in the burdensome role of a younger version of one of the most iconic screen characters of all time, audiences very visibly saw the work of a dedicated, assiduous craftsman. Method actor does Method actor and out–Method acts him. To wit: De Niro studied Brando's scenes in the first film incessantly, as he put it, "like a scientific problem."[1] His primary interest was the character's signature gestures. De Niro's game plan was to show their origins, the primordial pool from which they had formed. As for the famously hoarse voice, De Niro had himself fitted with a removable implant akin to the one Brando had worn, which reshaped De Niro's face and verbal tenor. He used it to speak in the difficult Sicilian dialect he had learned, the one whose integrity he had tested by traveling to the character's hometown, the Sicilian community of Corleone, to try out.

Our first glimpse of him is familiar from De Niro's first films: a period version of that same skinny, fop-haired nobody, even if this time, he's distinguished by a sharp, set jawline. Then comes that totemically coarse voice, reminding us whose lower face it is he's wearing. This is Vito Corleone in larval form, no doubt about it, in the throes of his silent, watchful apprenticeship. He's new to America, having come over from Sicily, where his mother was murdered by the village Mafioso. Haunted by the crime, he takes it upon himself, after much stewing, to violently end the life of that criminal's American equivalent.

After that, little Vito becomes a big man, prompting more Brando-isms: flourishes of the hands, that pensive stare, the cool egotism. And yet, this is no mere imitation. This is as much De Niro in development as it is Brando. De Niro's Vito Corleone is Travis Bickle, is Jake La Motta, is a score of characterizations since: the outsider who, quietly disgusted by the corruption of his immediate circumstances, takes to violence in the name of ego-boosting order. He's the taciturn, pensive schemer with private, dangerously romantic thoughts of playing public avenger. Don Vito will go after the self-appointed overlords (including, in a return to his homeland, his mother's killer), Travis Bickle the long-haired pimps, Jake La Motta the counterpunching threats to his middleweight crown and sexual plaything.

With the exception of the young La Motta (as opposed to the older, fatter version), De Niro is not built to be a figure of menace. His emaciated body is better suited to the frailty of his previous characters in *Bang the Drum Slowly* and *Mean Streets*. And yet, from his Don Vito forward, he'll become synonymous with it. Almost every one of his characters will ask, in one way or another, "You talkin' to me?" His cocky strut and fed-up, pursy stare, both on display in his Don Vito, will transfer to future roles, becoming such signatures they'll be adopted by TV impressionists. In *The Godfather Part II*, then, mainstream audiences got both a brilliantly imitative actor and a dynamic presence in its own right.

De Niro won the Supporting Actor Oscar for his performance. Overnight, everybody knew his name. He had leaped from little-boy-lost to the latest addition to the Hoffman-Hackman-Nicholson-Pacino-Duvall brotherhood. All audiences had to do to have it affirmed was to wait to see him in starring roles.

They would have to wait a while. Just when De Niro was on the brink of usurping Pacino and Nicholson as the most exciting actor in America, he'd have his wick snuffed out by an unlikely source: the most exciting director in Europe. The popularity of the international *succès de scandale Last Tango in Paris* entitled Bernardo Bertolucci to the amenities of cinematic grand masters Federico Fellini and Ingmar Bergman: a sizable budget, a runaway running time and an all-star cast. He made good on his interest in politics and sex with the much-anticipated *1900* (1976), a chronicle of the epic wrestling match between fascism and Communism that had marked the history of Italy from the film's titular year through to World War II.

Like many an American film at the time, *1900* subscribed to a buddy movie dynamic. The central characters are a pair of brotherly friends, albeit from separate social castes: the well-to-do Alfredo, played by De Niro, and the struggling Olmo, played by France's up-and-comer, Gerard Depardieu. Their fates are crosscut throughout the film's four hours (the European version ran over five) as contrasting vessels of Italy's ideological thrill ride. As history and allegory, this bigger-than-its-art-house-britches *1900* proved a critical disappointment, a small collection of resonant scenes embedded in an overambitious narrative; as a technical achievement, it was lauded for its visual sweep and poetic potency.

There was little division, however, over De Niro's performance—or rather, the lack of it. Bertolucci had taken the most dynamic actor in America and, in importing him into his distinctly Italian conception, rendered him curiously invisible. Ripped from his natural habitat (something De Niro had only experienced for select scenes of *The Godfather Part II*), set to parry with co-stars who did not share his language (each member of the international cast spoke their own), and sidled with a preoccupied director (Bertolucci, working on a far bigger scale than *Last Tango*, could not give De Niro the kind of attention he had given Brando), there was little De Niro could do but appear semi-formed.

That last restriction is significant. De Niro does not do scale. Occasionally, big productions allow him choice moments—see *The Mission* (1987)—but on the whole, they blunt the pugnacious intimacy he uses to foreshorten the distance between actor and audience. In epics, or even ensemble pieces, a quintessence is lost. He appears half-hearted, even baffled. This is not a matter of ego. The intense, dedicated De Niro requires a director's, or a production's, full focus to make a characterization complete. Without a thoroughly invested constructive collaborator, we get a stunted, visibly frustrated edition of him. He either disappears, save for a good scene or two, or walks around in a state of semi-resignation. If he can't go big, he doesn't exactly go home—but you can feel him thinking about it.

The spotlight was all his, though, in *Taxi Driver*—a garishly expressionistic one, exacerbating the druggy vibe of '70s New York after dark. By cruising its stench-ridden byways, De Niro created a complex characterization that still resonates today.

By '76, New Yorkers—indeed, all Americans—had had enough. The dissolution of the idealistic '60s had left that metropolis, and the rest of the country, in tatters. Dramatically rising levels of crime, labor strife, racial tension, drug abuse, sexual promiscuity and runaway inflation, overseen by corrupt and/or indifferent institutions, had made life veritably unlivable.

Robert De Niro and director Martin Scorsese (right) on the set of *Taxi Driver* (1976). Together they crafted one of the most complex characterizations of the '70s (Columbia/Photofest).

The Bicentennial, though, offered the opportunity to subscribe to a new spirit, to "clean up this town" the way that sheriffs in that emblematically American genre, the Western, had. That year, two films suggested bold, controversial pathways to a better, cleaner America. *Network*, a dark satire on the dangerous placidity instilled by television, inspired Americans to turn off their sets, go to their windows and shout "I'm as mad as hell and I'm not gonna *take* this any more!" *Taxi Driver*, borrowing from the urban vigilante genre that had flourished since the start of all this civic unrest, offered, predictably, the Charles Bronson–Clint Eastwood solution. Or did it?

Up until now, the movies had served up the hero and the anti-hero. Now, thanks to Paul Schrader's edgy, complex screenplay, Scorsese's deeply steeped direction and De Niro's brilliantly dualistic performance, both existed in a single persona. The result was the off-putting *Taxi Driver,* a midnight ride through a concrete hell where steam escapes sewers like wisps of hellfire, gangs overrun the avenues like rats, and street corners harbor prostitutes instead of taxi stands—the kind of relentlessly creepy atmosphere that preys upon the mentally askew and converts them into mythomaniacal assassins.

That's the character arc of Travis Bickle, the eponymous hero–anti-hero concocted by De Niro. Described as a "walking contradiction" (in a song snippet borrowed from Kris Kristofferson), Bickle is shy, brash, distanced, sympathetic, dangerous, delicate, childlike and paternal—and in all cases, dangerous. He's a stunted adult, a fully grown pre-adolescent whose peephole perspective on sex negates his genuine ability to charm women.

When he's spurned by a flirty presidential campaign aide (Cybill Shepherd, still at that point American cinema's sexed-up Doris Day), he becomes angrily convinced that there's no transcendence from the ugly world he's been seeing from behind the wheel of his cab. He sublimates his ire by setting out on a self-inflated mission borrowed from a Scorsese (and Schrader) favorite: *The Searchers*. Here, the maiden waiting to be rescued is not a young relative held captive by American Indians but her urban equivalent: an underage prostitute (Jodie Foster) under the thumb of a greasy pimp (Harvey Keitel, with whom De Niro recaptures the chemistry they had in *Mean Streets*). It climaxes with a bloodbath that makes Peckinpah's dust-ups look like pinpricks; Scorsese, on producer's orders, had to tone down its Technicolor vividness.

It's a testament to De Niro's ability to authenticate all parts of Bickle that at once we root for him and revile him. Talking to himself in the mirror as he prepares for the climactic kill ("You talkin' to me?"), we are chilled to the bone; watching him speak with the young prostitute he's scheming to nobly set free, we are awed by the depth of his concern. What buoys actors is the realization that people are not all of a piece. Performers love complexity, contradiction, ambiguity, multi-facedness. Their big, trying job is to keep all of the balls in the air, to create symbiosis from diversity. De Niro, as Bickle, offers a master class in the practice. Alongside Pacino's complete performance in *Dog Day Afternoon* (the two characters share many similarities), it may be the best characterization of the '70s.

Bickle is a product of New York City circa '76 yet crosses space and time. Why else would he, and the film, have retained their relevancy long after the miraculous reinvention of that city? Bickle speaks for every psychotic, political assassin, mass murderer and serial killer in the USA (he even inspired one, who attempted to take out Reagan). America's bizarre mix of Puritanism, civil liberties, easy acclaim and firearms fetishism has propelled many a dysfunctional personality into tragic action. Under President Donald Trump, it was even institutionally encouraged.

On a larger scale, it's difficult today not to observe Bickle's behavior and equate it with the terrorists behind the 9/11 tragedy, who were also out on a messianic mission to whitewash a corrupt America with crimson.

By virtue of De Niro's performance, Travis Bickle became permeated in the American mind. Later, Anthony Hopkins' Hannibal Lecter, via *The Silence of the Lambs* (1991), had the same effect. The bad guy on the side of good, the psychotic serving a sane purpose. Starting in the transitional '70s, heroism had become a fuzzy thing. It was Brando's famous unrest, having graduated from mumbling to mayhem.

Taxi Driver constituted the climax of a lot of subgenres of the early to mid–70s, not just the New York movie and the urban avenger genre (which gave us Eastwood, Bronson and many imitators) but the "man in the room" film (aka the male character study). After *Taxi Driver*, if you excused a small ripple effect (films like *Rolling Thunder*, the screenplay Schrader had written first), the marginalized man was made a cultural hero (*Rocky*), faith was restored in institutions (*…And Justice for All*) and still-troubled New York City was elegiacally romanticized (*Manhattan*, 1979). Further, it took the "new violence" introduced by Penn, popularized by Peckinpah and capitalized upon by Scorsese and elevated that too, such that nobody attempted it again and bloodletting reverted, at least until the '90s, to the pop-gun status of Studio Era fare.

For all of that, *Taxi Driver*, like *Mean Streets*, is essentially a religious film. This single-perspective parable of a fed-up New Yorker, unbalanced by what he witnesses, is out to demonstrate the dark underbelly of America's proud Puritanism. If God appears to have forsaken humanity, then the dirty job of smiting the place for its sins falls to the self-appointed. As mortals, they'll likely lose the war, but they can score a small, important victory or two, allowing them to purge their own burdened souls in the blood-smeared bargain.

On a theological level then, it's about the burden, the folly and the glory of subscribing to the Divine (the same lesson Harvey Keitel's Charlie Cappa learned in *Mean Streets*), made even more shocking, absurd and questionable. As such, the brave, doomed titular persona is both the salvific Jesus and the sadistic Roman who persecuted him. While such mixed feelings about the influence of Christianity had always been a part of Scorsese's work, he found a like sensibility in screenwriter Schrader, a Dutch Calvinist who, like him, was both obeisant and rebellious. As their on-screen muse, De Niro was faced with a daunting challenge: Ease up on Bickle's frustration and self-delusion and you chance making him a modern spokesperson for the NRA; soften his psychosis and the sorriest aspects of society secure the spoils.

While shooting *Taxi Driver*, for which De Niro had prepared by actually driving a cab, he was simultaneously prepping for his next role. The stakes were high. He had made good on his long-simmering potential and had now wowed the world. Plus, other big talents were involved. The project was a mix of Hollywood royalty old and new: an adaptation of F. Scott Fitzgerald's unfinished novel *The Last Tycoon*. Fitzgerald, who had slummed in Hollywood in 1927 and 1931, had recognized another Gatsby in MGM wunderkind Irving Thalberg: dapper, charming, tragic. Fitzgerald's fictionalized account of Thalberg's life offered a look at the day in-day out world of a major studio, including its off-screen politics—plus that Fitzgerald specialty, a central, melodramatic love story.

Monroe Stahr (read: Thalberg) is a brainy, intuitive and respected overlord with an ironclad control over everything ... except love. Throwing himself even deeper into the machinations of his fiefdom to suppress the heartache of the premature death of his actress-wife, he is thrown off course by a sudden infatuation with a British beauty—a dead ringer for his late paramour (shades of *Vertigo*, 1958). When that too comes to naught, Stahr finally sets free the broken soul he has kept in ice, asking audiences to ask themseves, "It is better to have loved and lost…"

As Stahr, De Niro is both cast against type and in keeping with the persona he was fast establishing. On the surface, Stahr is everything De Niro isn't: white-collar, diplomatic, humorous, intellectual, Jewish, Republican, kind. And yet, beneath the rail-thin body (De Niro lost 30 pounds for *Taxi Driver*, and kept them off for *Last Tycoon*), form-fitting tuxedoes, and proudly establishmentarian bearing, all of the De Niro signatures are there: the ticking interiority that will creep silently to the surface; the ill-fated romance that will tear him apart; the climactic purge that will bring him to the brink; the capacity for personal renewal that will permit him to carry on.

De Niro conveys all facets of Stahr with impressive facility. As an audience, we never question why he's never questioned; such is our innate understanding of his deft, unforced authority (a rarity for De Niro, who, when put in this position, usually pushes). And when he breaks down, we mourn for his defenses. What we don't buy, however, is his consuming infatuation for the young extra who is the "reincarnation" of his late wife. Fitzgerald, in his semi-book, and Harold Pinter, in his surprisingly reverent screenplay, have made but a symbol of her. She is an ideal, rarely more, giving poor, Kewpie-dollish Ingrid Boulting little to play but the expression of wan, wandering thoughts.

If you're looking for sparks (and in this staid film, you will be), look to De Niro's scenes with Jack Nicholson. At the time, Nicholson was the cock of the walk. He was coming off a succession of critical and box office smashes, plus a Best Actor Oscar that had sent him to the top of the Hollywood echelon. De Niro, by contrast, was the new blood, out to flush out the old. Their scenes together not only reflect this charged dynamic but also attest to a mutual enjoyment of its existence.

Last Tycoon was directed by the esteemed (if controversial) Elia Kazan. Needless to add, De Niro jumped at the opportunity to work with the man who had helped shape idol Brando. Predictably, Kazan and De Niro fell into a father-son relationship (the latter became another of the former's "twisted boys"). They both worked hard to add subtext and life to Pinter's trademark restraint. But the film is a thin, sluggish affair, characteristic of the vapidity that marks works by aging auteurs. It's redeemed only by De Niro's performance and the spirited back-and-forth between himself and Nicholson.

Looking to pick up where he left off before that disappointing diversion, De Niro threw himself back into the arms of Scorsese. Like De Niro, Marty's star had enjoyed a meteoric ascent. Hollywood had placed him atop their directorial A list. He'd return the favor by paying homage to his new underwriters with a well-intentioned resuscitation of one of their most representative genres: the musical. Just as he had revived the gangster film by affording it contemporary volatility, Scorsese now attempted to do the same for the sunny, splashy song 'n' dance showcases that had buoyed the American spirit throughout the Depression and had unabashedly expressed the renewed *joie de vivre* of the postwar boom years.

Boldly, Scorsese mixed the light with the dark, hoping to recapture the former while integrating the latter. At the same time, he borrowed Hollywood's chutzpah to do his part in a widespread cultural campaign to flag a debilitated, dispirited city. He called this aspirational Valentine *New York New York*.

In '77, a resurgent New York launched the ubiquitous "I Love New York" ad campaign. Corporate benefactors collected donations to give the decaying Statue of Liberty a good scrubbing, and a pair of Broadway veterans came up with a feel-good, sing-along anthem. Though it would become a signature tune for New Jersey-born Frank Sinatra, Liza Minnelli introduced the titular ditty in Scorsese's modern musical. Ultimately, the song achieved a fate that the film had hoped for itself: an enduring monument to the indefatigable spirit of that monolithic, metaphoric metropolis, the odds it threw at you and the booming personal pride and professional acclaim to be found in conquering them. In the film, that battle against oppression also spoke for personal relationships. Under its glitzy exoskeleton, *New York New York* is the autobiographical portrait of two styles of coupling: marriage, as Scorsese's was dissolving at the time, and that of a pair of fellow artists, representing the affair Scorsese was conducting with leading lady Minnelli. If a lot of the film's sensibility belongs to the songwriting team of John Kander and Fred Ebb, authors of the title song, the picture also borrows from George Cukor's version of *A Star Is Born* (1954), the hyperbolic tale of two contrasting careers. (*A Star Is Born*, the last big showcase for Minnelli's mother Judy Garland, had come closest to achieving what Scorsese was attempting.)

Minnelli is Francine Evans, a Big Band "girl singer" in the tradition of Jo Stafford and Martha Tilton. She's pushily charmed by an oily, gum-chewing hipster, sax man Jimmy Doyle—guess who?—in an attraction of opposites torn from the moth-eaten pages of the Studio Era manual on romantic comedy. They hit the road together just as the Big Band era, the musical phenomenon that had dominated the war years, begins to give way to quartets, quintets and crooners. Jimmy's music is out, Francine's is in. It's added tension the couple doesn't need, given their contrasting temperaments, Jimmy's philandering, and the daunting impediment of parenthood.

Had Scorsese stuck fast by the feminist sensibility he applied to his serio-comic *Alice Doesn't Live Here Anymore*, the film would have served, like that one, as an examination of contemporary women's issues, only in pre-feminist dress. "Been there, done that," however, appears to have been his mindset. Equally, that thematic bent might have upset the fireworks promised by the stunt casting of the Old School Minnelli and the New School De Niro.

Acting-wise, an interesting reversal was at work. Historically, it was Minnelli, in films like *The Sterile Cuckoo* (1969) and *Cabaret* (1972), who played the sexualized kook, the offbeat, semi-bawdy, bohemian buttinsky looking to procure affection with her half-crazed manner, free-love physicality, and mile-a-minute mouth. Here, however, she's on the receiving end. It's De Niro, in a gaudy variety of Hawaiian shirts, ocher zoot suits and two-tone shoes, who plays the lecherous, loose-tongued lunatic. His bumptious, braggy Jimmy Doyle is a slick, shiftless clown whose manner and repartee embody the speed and audacity of jazz. In this, the film plays on the absurdist notion of De Niro as a romantic lead, attempting to draw humor from the idea that he's anything but, exempt from that archetype's conventions by virtue of his uncontainable temperament, irrepressible drive and inherent dangerousness.

It's also the first time we see him on screen in an extended relationship with a woman. We learn that it's no deeper than the superficial encounters to which we've become accustomed. De Niro–Jimmy can't live with 'em, can't live without 'em. That's the ultimate pronouncement, on behalf of both sexes, of the film. It's a sensibility born from the bars and pool rooms of *Mean Streets,* a universe to which Scorsese and De Niro returned in subsequent films.

Critical reception to the 1977 release of *New York New York* was, at best, tepid; *The New Yorker*'s Penelope Gilliatt retitled it *Ho Hum, Ho Hum*. But the film is a noble experiment, energized by campy art direction, showy musicianship (including De Niro's warm, edgy tenor sax, dubbed by the man he pestered to learn the fingering, Georgie Auld) and satisfying central performances. Minnelli downplays her neurotic brassiness and wins us over in a whole new way. De Niro is permitted range (he gets to say "I love you" and even cries a little), alleviating the zealous professionalism of his character, a defining trait paralleling his own.

After tangling with women, it was back to the world of men (specifically, Pennsylvania's steel workers) in Hollywood's first big-budget examination of the national military embarrassment that had politicized De Niro's generation.

With the fall of Saigon in '76, the misguided bloodbath that had been Vietnam came to a close. From '64 to '75, almost three million Americans had served, doing the willy-nilly bidding of three secretive, sanguine presidents. While the death toll remains a matter of debate, soldiers who returned from that divisive, debilitating and ultimately doomed conflict endured public scorn and deep-set post-traumatic stress. Close to 60,000 of them committed suicide.

America had tested its men in the worst kind of way. Michael Cimino, a largely unknown writer-director who had made a reputation in TV advertising, cinematically replicated his country's efforts, pitting a coterie of hale, happy, hard-working six-pack guzzlers against a group of Viet Cong sadists in an ad hoc prison camp on the River Kwai. Like another Vietnam film released that year, *Coming Home,* he then logged the effects of the PTSD suffered by these veterans and its unbalancing effect on their community. The film's third act plays as a modern-day (1978) version of *The Best Years of Our Lives* (1946).

Unlike Coppola's *Apocalypse Now,* then still in production, *The Deer Hunter* did not set out to represent the war in toto. It reduced it to a single incident, gambling on conveying its horror and absurdity in a more concentrated manner. The verb "gambling" is not used loosely; we're talking about the famous Russian roulette scene, wherein bets are placed on the savagely coerced American POWs by their captors on which one of them will end up putting a bullet through his head.

Cimino imported the notion from an unproduced thriller by another writer, recognizing that its raw, rattling power could be effectively exacerbated by recontextualization. It worked, and then some. Not only does the scene encapsulate the barbarity and preposterousness of the war, but it also doubles as a vehicle for some of the most demanding and impactful acting of the '70s. The caliber of pain, humiliation, fear and fortitude imparted by De Niro, Christopher Walken and John Savage as the pressured POWS is searingly tangible. That single scene alone excuses the film its sins—over-length, visual staidness, heavy-handed symbolism, a pushy score—and makes it an enduring classic.

In yet another bowdlerizing shapeshift, De Niro converts from the yakky, neurotic Jimmy Doyle to the taciturn, undaunted Mike Vronsky. Jimmy led a band; Mike leads a tight-knit boys' club of working-class heroes, slavish and celebratory Slavic-Americans whose life is soot, slag, sweat and song. A sociologist at heart, Cimino spends the film's first hour chronicling that community's rituals, from an epic wedding (shades of *The Godfather*) to a weekend hunting trip. His conclusion is that this is a functional, harmonic and exemplary America. That, according to Cimino, is what Vietnam destroyed: the defining spirit of red-blooded American endurance.

Robert De Niro headed the cast of *The Deer Hunter* (1978), where his signature persona transitioned from outlier to role model. From left: Christopher Walken, John Cazale, De Niro and George Dzundza (Universal/Photofest).

With Vronsky, De Niro turns back the clock, taking the "anti" out of "anti-hero" to give us the man of fortitude, focus and fraternal concern once embodied by the fatigue-clad figureheads fronting the films of World War II. He's assumed Cassius' "lean and hungry" look and has visibly beefed up his body (he was also prepping to play boxer La Motta in *Raging Bull*) from pencil-thin to tree trunk–hard.

Vronsky is a man of action, the pillar of his community, a guy who leads by example. He operates on a plane above the easy, immediate pleasures of women or the compromised lives of soft-hearted men. When he kills, like the prize deer he so carefully downs, it's done cleanly and with honor—a notion he will have shockingly dispelled when he's imported into the heart of the Asian conflict. While he's hollowed and pacified after his tour of duty, the emotionally mitigated Vronsky soon reclaims his original identity. In yet another homage to *The Searchers*, Vronsky, like *Taxi Driver*'s Bickle, returns to 'Nam to rescue a youngster who's been subsumed by the culture. As it's the last of his brothers in arms, we are again asked to consider *Mean Streets*' "Am I my brother's keeper?" question, only this time, it's a matured De Niro who's the burdened defender, the newbie Walken who's the unruly brother.

De Niro's films operate in a man's world, one akin to the gangster pictures of the '30s and the war films of the '40s. Broaden that hermètic universe—let women or a larger-than-life circumstance encroach upon it—and it must be restored. Stray from it—give it up for marriage and family or professional involvement with a different class of people—and you'll long to return to its protective guardianship.

On the surface, it's a milieu that appears wrong for feminized times. And indeed, De Niro's early films, while devotedly earnest, also play as good-natured parodies of male camaraderie. But that aspect of his catalogue took on new, sober relevance as the decade progressed.

With the return of the "macho man" ethic spawned by the rise of disco culture, a music-based lifestyle displacing the '60s-spawned emphasis on the exploratorily spiritual in favor of the purely physical, the Hemingway-esque hero had been welcomed back. Yes, that long-standing archetype had managed to hold his place, if a smaller one, in the age of the confused, evolving male—characters like Burt Reynolds' implacable outdoorsman in *Deliverance*. Now, though, he was regaining his original status, knocking opponents against the ropes (*Rocky*), strutting his stuff on the dance floor (*Saturday Night Fever*) and offering sexual services to wanting women (*American Gigolo*, 1980). Beginning with *The Deer Hunter*, De Niro had joined this new, austere contingent of the testosterone-based renaissance. He famously took the "macho thing" even further in his succeeding film, Scorsese's artfully barbaric biography of messed-up middleweight La Motta.

Raging Bull, the climax of the '70s male character study, has its visible influences. As Foster Hirsch wrote in his voluminous study of the Actors Studio, *A Method to Their Madness*, "Attempting to beat the masters at their own game, De Niro and Scorsese aim to be more real, more intense, more Method than *On the Waterfront*."[2] De Niro's powerhouse performance, too, is a testament to the picture's lineage. Scorsese classified it as "Jake La Motta playing Marlon Brando playing Terry Malloy!"[3]

And in fact, our first glimpse of De Niro in the film constitutes a transformation as complete as that of Brando's in *The Godfather*. As the middle-aged La Motta,

Director Elia Kazan's *On the Waterfront* (1954): Its elements would reappear throughout '70s cinema (Columbia/Photofest).

De Niro is modified by an expanded waistline, a flattened nose and a punch-drunk manner. Minutes later, it's a whole new De Niro yet again. This time, he's La Motta in his prime, chiseled of body, fleet of foot, free of fear. Would, in *Waterfront*, that we would have seen *that* film's boxer, the better built and equally bothered Brando, in the ring.

By now, you've no doubt noted that this is the umpteenth reference in this book to *On the Waterfront*. Sorry about that—but the imprint of that narrative on American film over the ensuing quarter century must be stressed. Its dramatic arc—a marginalized, complicated lead character motivated into fighting for a public and/or personal cause, only to suffer or die (okay, you can argue that *Casablanca*, 1943, got there first)—becomes *the* story template of the male star vehicle, a monopoly that lasts until the '80s. Then mythologist Joseph Campbell's "hero's journey" takes over. Campbell's approach, on close inspection, is the same storyline, only with a significant alteration: In the end, the lead character is *rewarded* for his hubris. This adjustment fit the less anxious time of Reagan, before gaining added momentum in the ensuing age of parental preening (those uppity "Baby on Board" bumper stickers and the phenomenon of "helicopter parenting") and unearned acclaim afforded by TV talent shows and social media–spawned celebrity.

Meanwhile, just as Terry Malloy–Marlon Brando boxed, Jake La Motta–Robert De Niro boxed. De Niro did it a lot, shadowboxing while shooting *New York*

New York and *The Deer Hunter*, before feeling ready to spar with La Motta himself. Famously, De Niro ate his way through Europe to gain the 80 pounds required to play the fallen version of his subject (scenes, logically, shot first) before putting the production on pause while he lost it all and got himself in fighting trim.

In some of his previous films, Scorsese's characters waffled between conforming to the laws of the streets or those of the church. With *Raging Bull*, the Scoresesian hero at last develops a spiritual equilibrium derived from a strictly personal source (even if it parallels a Biblical contention, quoted in the last frame of the film). Elucidating on the arc of his hero, a happily divorced and cocaine-free Scorsese admitted, "I was able to survive a couple of crazy years and put it into this character and got to the point where Jake was able to sit in front of the mirror and be kind to himself at the end. That was what the lesson of the film was for me."[4] And consequently, for everyone. It's about self-punishment as the route to personal reconciliation. La Motta presents himself as the world's proud punching bag, stopping in between to check out his battered visage in the mirror. When he breaks out into a climactic crying fit during a prison stint, it's Harvey Keitel in Scorsese's *Mean Streets* holding his hand over a flame to come to grips with his frailty, to extricate himself from life's hellfire to learn to live as a self-respecting, God-abiding individual.

Again, we consider the influence of that other generational touchstone *The Searchers*, on both Scorsese (who first started referencing the film in his initial

Director John Ford's *The Searchers* (1956) was another visible influence on male-oriented cinema of the '70s (Warner Bros./Photofest).

feature, *Who's That Knocking at my Door?*, 1967) and De Niro, with its hero setting out into confrontational territory in the name of sacrifice and self-aggrandizement only to find, more valuably, his soul.

The typical Scorsese–De Niro hero, in fact, perfectly matches the character sketch of *The Searchers*' central character, John Wayne's Ethan Edwards, as drawn by novelist Johnathan Lethem: "His persona gathers in one place the allure of violence ... the tortured ambivalence toward women ... the dark pleasure of soured romanticism—all those things that reside unspoken at the center of our sense of what it means to be a man in America."[5] It reminds us that while Scorsese and De Niro spent their careers deeply questioning the unidimensional image of American masculinity embodied by actors like Wayne, in the few films in which that actor was pushed to mess with type, like *Red River* (1948) and *The Searchers*, his otherwise uncomplicated presence suggested the spiritual discombobulation and flirtation with self-destruction that would mark the heroes of the ensuing generation.

Whenever pressed for insight on his approach to acting, De Niro more often than not offered a sincere, reliable response. He spoke of working toward awarding himself "permission to play the part." It's an attitude that comes, by the sound of it, from a deep-set insecurity, a nagging sense of limited worth that forces him to steep himself as deeply as possible in the ways of the Method, to sacrifice body, mind and soul to the task of clearing the high bar of complete characterization. In *Raging Bull*, he took this to its greatest extreme yet, his efforts ultimately classified, like La Motta's actions in the ring, acts of professional masochism. Acting, for De Niro, is often an act of self-admonishment. You get the impression he'd rather reach a place of self-satisfaction through quieter means, but he can't get to Heaven until he puts himself through Hell—a deeply Catholic sentiment he shares with paisano Scorsese. La Motta's "blind," and then he can "see"; De Niro's "blind," and then he can act.

When you subscribe to such methodology, actors admire you, directors are wary of you, and critics and audiences get you some of the time and other times not at all. None of it seems to have remotely affected De Niro, who, like La Motta in his prime, just keeps preparing and attacking.

Defined for years as "an actor's actor," eventually De Niro became something more. Come the '90s and 2000s, he was as much businessman as movie star. He was a formative force behind the conversion of New York's Tribeca area from industrial ghost town to hipster hangout—and New York City real estate does not come cheap. To subsidize this geographic renaissance, De Niro put himself in an endless array of films. Too often, he was the star attraction in otherwise middling material.

After some amusing self-mockery in *Analyze This* and *Analyze That* (2002), he fell back, this time successfully, into comedy. For a little while, with the success of the highly overrated *Meet the Fockers* (2004) franchise, he became, improbably, America's #1 comedy star—the path he had started on, before veering off course. Every forced laugh opened the door for a new boutique, café or shop in the Tribeca area. De Niro established a film festival there too, to showcase the kinds of small, alternative films in which he had kicked off his career. It was a nice way to pass the torch, but at the same time, a painful reminder of how little his current work reflected his chancier roots. That said, the man, still at work, has retained the ability to surprise, reclaiming the integrity by which he's made his name. As evidence, *Silver Linings Playbook* (2012), a rare ensemble piece that bothered to give him his due in which he in turn gave, as of this writing, his last great performance.

A dozen years have passed. The man works less now. Aging and a cancer scare will do that to a person, even to one as driven and implacable as De Niro. There was the Scorsese Reunion *Killers of the Flower Moon* (2023), another remake of *On the Waterfront*, but this time he was the less central Lee J. Cobb character. All fires dissipate, even those we were once thrillingly-frighteningly held over.

1980s–2020s

The Aftermath

We all know what happened to the American film industry after the Golden Age of 1969–1983: money. With the unexpectedly high grosses of *The Godfather, Jaws* and *Star Wars*, the blockbuster mentality formed. The New York financiers behind the studios, hitherto preoccupied with sugar and pork bellies, realized that there was just as much remuneration in popcorn. Film stopped being a director's medium and became, as in days of yore, a producer's.

Besides, the American auteur era was imploding. The egos had gotten too big, the drugs too plentiful, the extravagances too extravagant. Coppola's *Apocalypse Now*, while eventually a hit, and Michael Cimino's *Heaven's Gate* (1980), no such luck, attested that the self-indulgence, logistical challenges and runaway spending that had marked the times had now exceeded von Stroheimian proportions. It was time for the industry to take the asylum back from the lunatics. Exit McMurphy, enter Nurse Ratched.

Besides, the audience had changed. Now they were cutting their hair, buying houses in the 'burbs and voting Republican. Not able to make anything lasting of the cries for social change that had sounded throughout the '60s and early '70s, they settled first for disco, then for domesticity. All being an angry young hippie had gotten you, it then ended up, was a lot of happy, hazy memories and a life like your parents'.

Now these tired sell-outs needed the types of movies that fit their squeaky, complacent new image. So, back to the tried-and-true; goodbye individuality, hello genre. Romantic comedies, action-adventure flicks and family-friendly fare were back; idiosyncratic, director-driven films about outliers, rogues and martyrs were yesterday's news. As Jack Nicholson said about those times in *Rolling Stone,* lamenting the changing of the guard, "I need for someone other than a corporation to be deciding what is germane about a movie and what is not. I need this in order for me to function. And it ain't going that way."[1]

Come the '90s, the industry fractured. Thanks to the homogenization of technology, the common man could make a hit just as well as Francis Ford Coppola. Moviemaking became the new gold mining, a camera and a digital editing system the new shovel and mule. *El Mariachi* (1992), *Clerks* (1994) and *The Blair Witch Project* (1999) were made for budgets that previously, wouldn't have bought lunch for an elevator pitch. And they were all picked up by the studios, who put their vast promotional machines behind them and laughed all the way to the bank. Otherwise, they were countering the DIY movement with large-scale entertainments, films that, like those produced in the '50s, were big on scale and short on character.

The 2000s weren't much better. Appetite for films-by-the-people dried up when aspiring moviemakers settled for an even more low-cost option: the Internet. You didn't even need a script, actors or a crew. Cinema had gone back to its roots: seconds-long excerpts from real life, as if Edison and Ince had been reinstated.

In addition, the comic book generation came of age, just in time for the development of CGI, which the studios used to create endless replicas of Stan Lee's superheroes, formulaically battling some intergalactic despot via a succession of ear-splitting THX-mixed fireballs.

Small wonder Hoffman, Hackman, Nicholson, Pacino, Nicholson, Duvall and De Niro all got lost in the shuffle—or at least, downsized by scale and bluster. Hoffman hung in for as long as he could, sadly settling for supporting roles, some shockingly skimpy (like *Chef*, 2014; fumble for that Jujube you lost under your seat and you'll miss him) and the odd, half-hearted star vehicle made for his now white-haired generation (*Last Chance Harvey*, 2008). Hackman retired in 2004, just before the indignity and inconvenience of Alzheimer's. Nicholson called it quits in 2010, and is now visible only at Lakers games. Pacino's still around, having realized that intelligent, adult content has moved to the streaming services (*Angels in America*, 2003, *Hunters*, 2020–21). Duvall, ever the good soldier, keeps on trudging, though in understandably diminished form (including a mini-reunion with *Apocalypse Now* co-star Martin Sheen in *12 Mighty Orphans,* 2021). De Niro has settled for sending himself up, a practice almost all of this exalted company has indulged in now and then, with the odd turn in something allowing him to genuinely act (*Silver Linings Playbook*, *Killers of the Flower Moon*).

They don't look good in tights and capes, rarely find scripts or directors equal to their talents, and have committed that inevitable industry sin: aging. As one, then, Hoffman-Hackman-Pacino-Nicholson-Duvall-De Niro constitute the lingering stardust of a once blazing meteor. It lit up our skies with an energy, electricity and integrity rarely seen before, in an atmosphere currently so clouded with bombastic banality, it might never make way for anything comparable again.

Postscript

In the event you need further proof of the assertion that concluded the previous chapter—that these actors indeed constitute the greatest assemblage of male screen talent in the history of the medium—consider this comparative study....

Let's start with the Studio Era, back when Hollywood was a factory town and the stars but busy laborers. This prolific period rescued many a New York stage actor and elevated them, largely by volume, to the status of cinematic icon. Almost to a person, they were working-class, hard-nosed outsiders, looking out either for themselves, the proverbial "little guy," or the woman they were sweet on. These Depression-era heroes served as spokespeople for the downtrodden masses. Like them, they felt marginalized, oppressed and emasculated. Life was a mug's game, and the only way around it was to make your own breaks. As such, their habits were often criminal, even cruel—thus, they were due for a Puritan comeuppance. And yet, audiences still walked away admiring them. The fact that they were trapped in cautionary tales mattered little. It wasn't the lesson that was important, it was the indefatigable spirit of their actions. James Cagney, Humphrey Bogart, Edward G. Robinson and John Garfield (America's first Method graduate) became talking cinema's first "men of action," fighting for a new world order that was ideologically Rooseveltian but actively barbarian.

They had the chops—they had earned them on the stage—and indeed, many of their earliest film appearances smacked of the obviousness required for the footlights. But as they continued to grind out films, each actor settled into an itchy naturalism which, while it would eventually pass as mannered, was electric and ingratiating. Nor could the gloss that Hollywood would develop—color, widescreen, surround sound—completely suppress their ruffian roots. Put Cagney in *Tribute to a Bad Man* (1956) or Bogart in *The Caine Mutiny* (1954) and they're the same nervy upstarts from *The Public Enemy* (1931) and *High Sierra*. Their exteriors might have been color, but their souls remained black and white.

Around the end of that period, and tipping into the war years, came the moralists. Like Cagney & Co., they had been products of the stage—but the similarities ended there. These were good boys from good families, and not necessarily from big, bad New York. James Stewart, Henry Fonda, Spencer Tracy, Gary Cooper and Gregory Peck came from a less cosmopolitan America. There's a plebeian decency to them, and a tendency, as such, to impart life lessons veering on the Biblical. They represented America as it wanted to be, not, like the Bogarts or the Garfields, as it was. They offered themselves up as Mr. Smith, Abraham Lincoln, Thomas Edison, Will Kane and Atticus Finch, tall, taciturn men of honor, self-made not by way of criminal behavior but by a deep inner resolve and an unwavering commitment to the tenets of America's formative political agenda.

They were shy instead of showy, reserved instead of romantic, proselytizing instead of pugnacious. Theirs was not the way of the fist or the gun—though when pressed, they could resort to them—but of the inflated speech and the sympathetic word. They were introverts, working in an extrovert's milieu.

As actors, they were figures to be admired. But their innocence seemed infantile, their self-righteousness too thick, their symbolic value too high. As comfortable as we felt in their fatherly company, we missed the companionship of our brothers-in-arms, the proletariat personalities who, while less educated, would be better to have on our side in a brawl. With this new, sanitized generation, a certain fighting spirit, at least on a visceral level, was lost. Thus, these personalities were less cinematic. They moved less and their films moved less. The theaters in which their pictures played became educational auditoriums.

Then came the war. The soldiery required by that historical development made, like the army itself, generic figures out of the most dynamic of men. Edges were rounded, tempers were checked, instincts were suppressed. Actors from the classy, like Cary Grant, to the countrified, like John Wayne, became mere servicemen, and almost all of the films just as functional.

What follows war but post-traumatic stress? With it, a new class of on-screen icon evolved, one battle-weary, cynical and lascivious. They fell into two categories, these actors: veterans, many older than their years, and private eyes, fighting smaller, more personal wars. They remained tough and moral, but their emotional range had gratifyingly expanded. We watched Robert Mitchum fall apart in *The Story of G.I. Joe* (1945), Burt Lancaster anticipate his ignominious fate in *The Killers* (1946) and Alan Ladd throw his (smallish) weight around in *This Gun for Hire* (1942). These were doomed heroes, looking to hold their heads up while they could but acutely aware of the dark, foreboding clouds gathering above them. They brought a new sincerity to American cinema, foreshadowing the ensuing Method generation.

That said, though, they didn't give us very much to root for. True, they would always test themselves against some daunting force or other, but with the shakiest of faiths. Even Brando, as a fatalistic figure, let us know that he/we would somehow survive, that the bruised and bloodied Terry Malloy would eventually stand up.

So, Brando—yes, we have come to him again. Along with Dean and Clift, they collectively embodied the adolescent ambivalence of the '50s. Beneath that decade's squeaky-clean surface, America was changing. Postwar affluence was a Trojan horse, and the weapon inside was existential unrest. A handful of younger, more physically fit actors got hip to this and wore that capacity on their sleeves. Like the postwar generations before them, they too were marked for ignominy but suggested a survival instinct that would see them to a better, if still imperfect, tomorrow. They brought the realism of the Method to the mix and thus complicated Hollywood by violating its precious, long-standing romanticism. Few knew in their time that these actors were paving the way for a new style of domestic cinema, one that would explode in the coming years.

Before that, though, American film entered a period of cool-headedness. Perhaps the influence had been the advent of the Cold War (so, the Cool War?), and the screen's new heroes had simply been emulating JFK's admirable *sangfroid* in the face of Khrushchev and Castro. Suddenly, wait-and-see steeliness was in, modeled by such stars as Paul Newman, Steve McQueen and Sidney Poitier. They were creatures of interiority, minimalists even. It wasn't that they were afraid to act. It was that they did it mostly on the inside, even more than their Brando-esque predecessors. They kept an even, if edgy keel throughout the great cultural tidal waves of the '60s, drowning but occasionally (like poor Cool Hand Luke). As Newman said in *Harper* when pressed about the fact that the title character didn't resemble the traditional looking big screen private eye: "New kind."

Finally, Hoffman, Hackman, Nicholson, Pacino, Duvall and De Niro. In them, at last, we have complete, candid characterizations. By this time, screen acting had officially broken with the cult of personality and committed itself to the premium of authenticity. The studio system had fallen, and with it, their cash cow genres. The actor, once no more than a workman, had finally achieved the status of royalty, able to pick and choose properties at will for inflated salaries. And audiences, fed up with overinflated artifice, were desperate to see their immediate circumstances and personal struggles reflected on screen.

And so, this generation enjoyed a serendipitous advantage: Character studies were in, cutting Hoffman & Co. an extremely wide swath. Filmmaking had changed too, with looser narratives, the addition of improvisation, and franker language and behavior. So unleashed, these actors were freer than any previous generation to show the world what they were made of. They did, of course, marrying the Method with an instinctual sense of showmanship. They called themselves purists and denied that last part, for a while, until it began to take over. In the meantime, though, they offered a new level of performance amalgamating the grit of the Depression-era heroes, the emphatic quality of the Midwestern moralists, the weariness of the post-war existentialists, and the contemptuous sincerity of Brando.

After them, a generation just as well-meaning but almost cubist (or as Isaac Butler calls them in *The Method: How America Learned to Act*, "American Gonzo"[1]): Nicolas Cage, Johnny Depp, Sean Penn; plus, facile, flesh-and-blood action figures: Sylvester Stallone, Arnold Schwarzenegger, Bruce Willis; and a return to the "pretty boy" phenomenon of the Rock Hudson–Tab Hunter–Tony Curtis era: Ben Affleck, Ryan Reynolds, Ryan Gosling.

Need I quote the closing paragraph of the previous chapter of this book again?

Chapter Notes

Introduction

1. Spoto, Donald. 1978. *Camerado: Hollywood and the American Man.* New York: New American Library, p. 82.
2. Spoto, Donald. 1978. *Camerado: Hollywood and the American Man.* New York: New American Library, p. 83.
3. Biskind, Peter. 1998. *Easy Riders, Raging Bulls.* New York: Touchstone, p. 17.
4. Frankel, Glenn. 2021. *Shooting Midnight Cowboy.* New York: Farrar, Strauss, and Giroux, p. 34.
5. Spoto, Donald. 1978. *Camerado: Hollywood and the American Man.* New York: New American Library, p. 83.
6. Haskell, Molly. 1974 (revised 1987). *From Reverence to Rape.* Chicago: University of Chicago Press, p. 374.
7. Haskell, Molly. 1974 (revised 1987). *From Reverence to Rape.* Chicago: University of Chicago Press, p. 377.
8. Brownstein, Ronald. 2022. *Rock Me on the Water.* New York: Harper Paperbacks, p. 65.

Marlon Brando

1. Jordan, Rene. 1973. *Marlon Brando.* New York: Pyramid Communications Inc., p. 15.
2. Farber, Manny. 2009. *Farber on Film.* New York: Penguin Group, p. 369.
3. Strasberg, Lee. 1987. *A Dream of Passion.* New York: Little, Brown & Co., p. 30.
4. Bergan, Ronald. 1993. *Dustin Hoffman.* London: Virgin Books, p. 39.
5. Jordan, Rene. 1973. *Marlon Brando.* New York: Pyramid Communications Inc., p. 68.
6. Jordan, Rene. 1973. *Marlon Brando.* New York: Pyramid Communications Inc., p. 17.
7. Jordan, Rene. 1973. *Marlon Brando.* New York: Pyramid Communications Inc., p. 17.
8. Spoto, Donald. 1978. *Camerado: Hollywood and the American Man.* New York: New American Library, p. 143.
9. Levy, Shaw. 2009. *Paul Newman: A Life.* New York. Harmony Books, p. 376.
10. Levy, Shaw. 2009. *Paul Newman: A Life.* New York. Harmony Books, p. 379.
11. Levy, Shaw. 2009. *Paul Newman: A Life.* New York. Harmony Books, p. 379.
12. Levy, Shaw. 2009. *Paul Newman: A Life.* New York. Harmony Books, p. 380.
13. Levy, Shaw. 2009. *Paul Newman: A Life.* New York. Harmony Books, p. 381.
14. Dowdy, Andrew. 1973. *The Films of the Fifties.* New York: William Morrow and Company, pages 141–142.
15. Mizruchi, Susan L. 2014. *Brando's Smile.* New York: W.W. Norton & Co., p. 73.
16. Sellers, Robert. 2010. *Hollywood Hellraisers.* New York: Skyhorse Publishing, p. 174.
17. Travers, Peter (ed.). 1996. *The Rolling Stone Film Reader.* New York: Simon and Schuster, p. 199.
18. Slawson, Judith. 1985. *Robert Duvall: Hollywood Maverick.* New York: St. Martin's Press, p. 48.
19. Thomson, David. 2009. *Have You Seen…?* New York: Alfred A. Knopf, p. 32.
20. Haskell, Molly. 1974 (revised 1987). *From Reverence to Rape.* Chicago: University of Chicago Press, p. 32.
21. Gerard, Fabien S., Kline, Jefferson T., Sklarew, Bruce (eds). 2000. *Bernardo Bertolucci: Interviews.* Jackson: University of Mississippi Press, p. 94.
22. Sellers, Robert. 2010. *Hollywood Hellraisers.* New York: Skyhorse Publishing, p. 174.
23. Mann, William J. 2019. *The Contender.* New York: Harper, p. 620.

Dustin Hoffman

1. Hofler, Robert. 2023. *The Way They Were*. New York: Citadel Press, p. 18.
2. Bergan, Ronald. 1993. *Dustin Hoffman*. London: Virgin Books, p. 6.
3. Bergan, Ronald. 1993. *Dustin Hoffman*. London: Virgin Books, p. 100.
4. Lenburg, Jeff. 1983. *Dustin Hoffman: Hollywood's Anti-hero*. New York: St. Martin's Press, p. 46.
5. Lalande, Dan. 2023. *The Drop-Dead Funny '70s*. Jefferson, NC: McFarland, p. 17.
6. Fullwood, Neil. 2003. *The Films of Sam Peckinpah*. London: Batsford, p. 159.
7. Kirshner, Johnathan. 2012. *Hollywood's Last Golden Age: Politics, Society, and the 70s Film in America*. Ithaca: Cornell Univeristy Press, p. 18.
8. Haskell, Molly. 1987. *From Reverence to Rape*, 2nd ed. Chicago: Univeristy of Chicago Press, p. 378.
9. Haskell, Molly. 1987. *From Reverence to Rape*, 2nd ed. Chicago: Univeristy of Chicago Press, p. 378.
10. Dworkin, Susan. 1983. *Making Tootsie*. New York: Newmarket Press, p. 2.

Gene Hackman

1. Hunter, Allan. 1987. *Gene Hackman*. New York: St. Martin's Press, p. 5.
2. Giddins, Gary. 2010. *Warning Shadows*. New York : W.W. Norton & Co., p. 319.
3. Hunter, Allan. 1987. *Gene Hackman*. New York: St. Martin's Press, p. 71.
4. Hunter, Allan. 1987. *Gene Hackman*. New York: St. Martin's Press, p. 69.
5. Hunter, Allan. 1987. *Gene Hackman*. New York: St. Martin's Press, p. 76.
6. Phillips, Gene D. 2004. *Godfather: The Intimate Francis Ford Coppola*. Lexington: University Press of Kentucky, p. 82.
7. Gear, Matthew Asprey. 2019. *Moseby Confidential: Arthur Penn's* Night Moves *and the Rise of Neo-Noir*. Portland, Oregon: Jorvik Press, p. 12.
8. Gear, Matthew Asprey. 2019. *Moseby Confidential: Arthur Penn's* Night Moves *and the Rise of Neo-Noir*. Portland, Oregon: Jorvik Press, p. 57.
9. Kael, Pauline. 1980. *When the Lights Go Down*. New York: Holt, Rinehart and Winston, p. 22.
10. Thomson, David. 2010. *The New Biographical Dictionary of Film*, 5th ed., Updated and Expanded. New York: Random House, p. 411.

Jack Nicholson

1. Eliot, Marc. 2013. *Nicholson*. New York: Three Rivers Press, p. 15.
2. Spoto, Donald. 1978. *Camerado: Hollywood and the American Man*. New York: New American Library, p. 157.
3. Travers, Peter (editor). 1996. *The Rolling Stone Film Reader*. New York: Simon and Schuster, p. 23.
4. Sellers, Robert. 2010. *Hollywood Hellraisers*. New York: Skyhorse Publishing, p. 154.
5. Walker, Beverly. 2013. *Jack Nicholson: Anatomy of an Actor*. Paris: Cahiers du Cinema, p. 29.
6. Eliot, Marc. 2013. *Nicholson*. New York: Three Rivers Press, p. 86.
7. Tobias, Scott. 2020. "Five Easy Pieces at 50: A troubling yet thrilling arrival of a new leading man." *The Guardian*, September 12.
8. Kael, Pauline. 1980. *When the Lights Go Down*. New York: Holt, Rinehart and Winston, pp. 87–88.
9. Thomson, David. 2010. *The New Biographical Dictionary of Film*, 5th ed., Updated and Expanded. New York: Random House, p. 28.
10. Kael, Pauline. 1980. *When the Lights Go Down*. New York: Holt, Rinehart and Winston, p. 25.
11. Sellers, Robert. 2010. *Hollywood Hellraisers*. New York: Skyhorse Publishing, p. 195.

Al Pacino

1. Lumet, Sidney. 1996. *Making Movies*. New York: Vintage, p. 67.
2. Grobel, Lawrence. 2008. *Al Pacino*. New York: Gallery Books, p. 145.
3. Yule, Andrew. 1992. *Al Pacino: A Life on the Wire*. New York: S.P.I. Books, p. 34.
4. Hirsch, Foster. 2001. *A Method to Their Madness*. New York: Hachette Book Group, p. 134.
5. Thomson, David. 2008. *Have You Seen...?* London: Alan Lane Paperbacks, p. 231.
6. Kael, Pauline. 1980. *When the Lights Go Down*. New York: Holt, Rinehart and Winston, p. 302.
7. Kael, Pauline. 1980. *When the Lights Go Down*. New York: Holt, Rinehart and Winston, p. 302.
8. Grobel, Lawrence. 2008. *Al Pacino*. New York: Gallery Books, p. 145.
9. Yule, Andrew. 1992. *Al Pacino: A Life on the Wire*. New York: S.P.I. Books, p. 42.

Robert Duvall

1. Slawson, Judith. 1985. *Robert Duvall: Hollywood Maverick*. New York: St. Martin's Press, p. 84.
2. Slawson, Judith. 1985. *Robert Duvall: Hollywood Maverick*. New York: St. Martin's Press, p. 79.
3. *Ibid.*, 80.
4. Meyer, Nicholas. 2009. *The View from the Bridge*. New York: Viking Penguin, p. 55.
5. Callahan, Michael. 2019. "Revisiting Harold Robbins, the Forgotten 'Dirty Old Man of American Letters.'" *Hollywood Reporter*, July 3.
6. Slawson, Judith. 1985. *Robert Duvall: Hollywood Maverick*. New York: St. Martin's Press, p. 104.
7. *Ibid.*, 160.
8. *Ibid.*, 177.
9. *Ibid.*, 160.

Robert De Niro

1. Levy, Shawn. 2014. *De Niro: A Life*. New York: Random House, p. 129.
2. Hirsch, Foster. 2001. *A Method to Their Madness*. New York: Hachette Book Group, p. 311.
3. Christie, Ian and Thompson, David (editors). 2003. *Scorsese on Scorsese*. London: Faber and Faber, p. 77.
4. Dougan, Andy. 1996. *Untouchable*. New York: Thunder's Mouth Press, p. 118.
5. Frankel, Glenn. 2013. *The Searchers: The Making of an American Legend*. New York: Bloomsbury, p. 323.

1980s–2020s

1. Travers, Peter (editor). 1996. *The Rolling Stone Film Reader*. New York: Simon and Schuster, p. 43.

Postscript

1. Butler, Isaac. 2022. *The Method: How the Twentieth Century Learned to Act*. London: Bloomsbury Publishing, p. 202.

Filmographies (1970–79)

Marlon Brando

The Nightcomers, 1971—AVCO Embassy. Director: Michael Winner. Writer: Michael Hastings. Cast: Marlon Brando, Stephanie Beacham, Thora Hird, Harry Andrews. 94 minutes.

The Godfather, 1972—Paramount. Director: Francis Ford Coppola. Writers: Mario Puzo, Francis Ford Coppola. Cast: Marlon Brando, Al Pacino, James Caan, Robert Duvall, Diane Keaton, Richard Castellano, Abe Vigoda, Talia Shire, John Cazale, Sterling Hayden. 175 minutes.

Last Tango in Paris, 1972—United Artists. Director: Bernardo Bertolucci. Writers: Bernardo Bertolucci, Franco Arcalli. Cast: Marlon Brando, Maria Schneider, Jean-Pierre Leaud. 129 minutes.

The Missouri Breaks, 1976—United Artists. Director: Arthur Penn. Writer: Thomas McGuane. Cast: Marlon Brando, Jack Nicholson, Randy Quaid, Kathleen Lloyd. 126 minutes.

Superman, 1978—Warner Bros. Director: Richard Donner. Writers: Mario Puzo, David Newman, Leslie Newman, Robert Benton. Cast: Marlon Brando, Christopher Reeve, Gene Hackman, Valerie Perrine, Ned Beatty. 143 minutes.

Apocalypse Now, 1979—United Artists. Director: Francis Ford Coppola. Writers: John Milius, Francis Ford Coppola, Michael Herr. Cast: Marlon Brando, Martin Sheen, Robert Duvall, Dennis Hopper. 147 minutes.

Dustin Hoffman

Little Big Man, 1970—National General. Director: Arthur Penn. Writer: Calder Willingham, from the novel by Thomas Berger. Cast: Dustin Hoffman, Faye Dunaway, Chief Dan George, Martin Balsam, Jeff Corey, Richard Mulligan. 139 minutes.

Who Is Harry Kellerman and Why Is He Saying Those Terrible Things About Me?, 1971—National General. Director: Ulu Grosbard. Writers: Ulu Grosbard, Herb Gardner. Cast: Dustin Hoffman, Jack Warden, Dom DeLuise, Barbara Harris. 108 minutes.

Straw Dogs, 1971—ABC Pictures. Director: Sam Peckinpah. Writers: Sam Peckinpah, David Zelag Goodman, from the novel *The Siege of Trencher's Farm* by Gordon M. Williams. Cast: Dustin Hoffman, Susan George. 117 minutes.

Alfredo, Alfredo, 1972—Paramount. Director: Pietro Germi. Writers: Pietro Germi, Leonardo Benvenuti, Piero De Bernardi, Tullio Pinelli. Cast: Dustin Hoffman, Stefania Sandrelli. 98 minutes.

Papillon, 1973—Allied Artists. Director: Franklin J. Schaffner. Writers: Dalton Trumbo, Lorenzo Semple, Jr., William Goldman (unbilled), from the book by Henri Charriere. Cast: Steve McQueen, Dustin Hoffman. 150 minutes.

Lenny, 1974—United Artists. Director: Bob Fosse. Writer: Julian Barry. Cast: Dustin Hoffman, Valerie Perrine. 111 minutes.

All the President's Men, 1976—Warner Bros. Director: Alan J. Pakula. Writer: William Goldman. Cast: Robert Redford, Dustin Hoffman, Jason Robards, Martin Balsam, Hal Holbrook, Jack Warden. 138 minutes.

Marathon Man, 1976—Paramount. Director: John Schlesinger. Writer: William Goldman, from his novel. Cast: Dustin Hoffman, Laurence Olivier, Roy Scheider, Marthe Keller, William Devane. 125 minutes.

Straight Time, 1978—Warner Bros. Director: Ulu Grosbard. Writers: Alvin Sargent, Edward Bunker, Jeffrey Boam, from Bunker's book *No Beast So Fierce*. Cast: Dustin Hoffman, Theresa Russell, Gary Busey. 114 minutes.

Agatha, 1979—First Artists. Director: Michael Apted. Writers: Kathleen Tynan, Arthur Hopcraft. Cast: Dustin Hoffman, Vanessa Redgrave. 98 minutes.

Kramer vs. Kramer, 1979—Columbia. Writer-Director: Robert Benton, from the novel by Avery Corman. Cast: Dustin Hoffman, Meryl Streep, Justin Henry. 105 minutes.

Gene Hackman

I Never Sang for My Father, 1970—Columbia. Director: Gilbert Cates. Writer: Robert Anderson. Cast: Melvyn Douglas, Gene Hackman, Estelle Parsons. 92 minutes.

Doctors' Wives, 1971—Columbia. Director: George Schaefer. Writer: Daniel Taradash. Cast: Dyan Cannon, Richard Crenna, Gene Hackman, Carroll O'Connor. 102 minutes.

The Hunting Party, 1971—United Artists. Director: Don Medford. Writer: Gilbert Ralston, William W. Norton, Lou Morheim. Cast: Oliver Reed, Gene Hackman, Candice Bergen. 111 minutes.

Cisco Pike, 1971—Columbia. Writer-Director: Bill L. Norton. Cast: Kris Kristofferson, Gene Hackman, Karen Black. 95 minutes.

The French Connection, 1971—20th Century-Fox. Director: William Friedkin. Writer: Ernest Tidyman. Cast: Gene Hackman, Roy Scheider, Fernando Rey, Tony Lo Bianco. 104 minutes.

The Poseidon Adventure, 1972—20th Century-Fox. Director: Ronald Neame. Writers: Stirling Silliphant, Wendell Mayes, from a novel by Paul Gallico. Cast: Gene Hackman, Shelley Winters, Ernest Borgnine, Red Buttons, Pamela Sue Martin, Jack Albertson. 117 minutes.

Scarecrow, 1973—Warner Bros. Director: Jerry Schatzberg. Writer: Garry Michael White. Cast: Al Pacino, Gene Hackman. 112 minutes.

The Conversation, 1974—Paramount. Writer-Director: Francis Ford Coppola. Cast: Gene Hackman, John Cazale, Allen Garfield, Cindy Williams, Frederic Forrest, Teri Garr. 113 minutes.

Zandy's Bride, 1974—Warner Bros. Director: Jan Troell. Writer: Marc Norman. Cast: Gene Hackman, Liv Ullmann. 97 minutes.

Young Frankenstein, 1974—20th Century-Fox. Director: Mel Brooks. Writers: Gene Wilder, Mel Brooks. Cast: Gene Wilder, Peter Boyle, Madeline Kahn, Teri Garr, Marty Feldman, Gene Hackman (unbilled). 105 minutes.

Night Moves, 1975—Warner Bros. Director: Arthur Penn. Writer: Alan Sharp. Cast: Gene Hackman, Susan Clark, Jennifer Warren, Melanie Griffith. 99 minutes.

Bite the Bullet, 1975—Columbia. Writer-Director: Richard Brooks. Cast: Gene Hackman, Candice Bergen, James Coburn, Jan-Michael Vincent. 131 minutes.

The French Connection II, 1975—20th Century-Fox. Director: John Frankenheimer. Writers: Alexander Jacobs, Robert Dillon, Laurie Dillon. Cast: Gene Hackman, Fernando Rey, Bernard Fresson. 119 minutes.

Lucky Lady, 1975—20th Century-Fox. Director: Stanley Donen. Writers: William Huyck, Gloria Katz. Cast: Liza Minnelli, Burt Reynolds, Gene Hackman. 118 minutes.

The Domino Principle, 1977—AVCO Embassy. Director: Stanley Kramer. Writer: Adam Kennedy, from his novel. Cast: Gene Hackman, Candice Bergen, Mickey Rooney, Richard Widmark. 97 minutes.

A Bridge Too Far, 1977—United Artists. Director: Richard Attenborough. Writer: William Goldman, from the book by Cornelius Ryan. Cast: Sean Connery, Dirk Bogarde, Ryan O'Neal, Robert Redford, Gene Hackman, James Caan, Liv Ullmann, Laurence Olivier. 176 minutes.

March or Die, 1977—Columbia. Director: Dick Richards. Writer: Dick Richards, David Zelag Goodman. Cast: Gene Hackman, Catherine Deneuve, Terence Stamp. 104 minutes.

Superman, 1978—Warner Bros. Director: Richard Donner. Writers: Mario Puzo, David Newman, Leslie Newman, Robert Benton. Cast: Marlon Brando, Christopher Reeve, Gene Hackman, Margot Kidder, Valerie Perrine, Ned Beatty. 143 minutes.

Jack Nicholson

On a Clear Day You Can See Forever, 1970—Paramount. Director: Vincente Minnelli. Writer: Alan Jay Lerner, based on his play. Cast: Barbra Streisand, Yves Montand, Jack Nicholson, Bob Newhart. 129 minutes.

Five Easy Pieces, 1970—Columbia. Director: Bob Rafelson. Writer: Adrien Joyce (Carole Eastman). Cast: Jack Nicholson, Karen Black, Susan Anspach. 98 minutes.

Carnal Knowledge, 1971—AVCO Embassy. Director: Mike Nichols. Writer: Jules Feiffer. Cast: Jack Nicholson, Art Garfunkel, Candice Bergen, Ann-Margret. 97 minutes.

A Safe Place, 1971—Columbia. Writer-Director: Henry Jaglom. Cast: Tuesday Weld, Orson Welles, Jack Nicholson. 94 minutes.

The King of Marvin Gardens, 1972—Columbia. Director: Bob Rafelson. Writer: Jacob Brackman. Cast: Jack Nicholson, Bruce Dern, Ellen Burstyn. 103 minutes.

The Last Detail, 1973—Columbia. Director: Hal Ashby. Writer: Robert Towne, based on the novel by Darryl Ponicsan. Cast: Jack Nicholson, Otis Young, Randy Quaid, Carol Kane, Michael Moriarty. 104 minutes.

Chinatown, 1974—Paramount. Director: Roman Polanski. Writer: Robert Towne. Cast: Jack Nicholson, Faye Dunaway, John Huston, Burt Young. 131 minutes.

One Flew Over the Cuckoo's Nest, 1975—United Artists. Director: Milos Forman. Writers: Laurence

Hauben, Bo Goldman, based on the novel by Ken Kesey. Cast: Jack Nicholson, Louise Fletcher, Will Sampson, William Redfield, Christopher Lloyd, Danny DeVito, Scatman Crothers. 135 minutes.
The Passenger, 1975—MGM. Director: Michelangelo Antonioni. Writers: Michelangelo Antonioni, Mark Peploe, Peter Wollen. Cast: Jack Nicholson, Maria Schneider. 126 minutes.
The Missouri Breaks, 1976—United Artists. Director: Arthur Penn. Writer: Thomas McGuane. Cast: Marlon Brando, Jack Nicholson, Randy Quaid, Kathleen Lloyd. 126 minutes.
The Last Tycoon, 1976—Paramount. Director: Elia Kazan. Writer: Harold Pinter. Cast: Robert De Niro, Ingrid Boulting, Jack Nicholson, Robert Mitchum, Theresa Russell, Donald Pleasence. 123 minutes.
Goin' South, 1978—Paramount. Director: Jack Nicholson. Writers: John Herman Shaner, Al Ramrus, Charles Shyer, Alan Mandel. Cast: Jack Nicholson, Mary Steenburgen, Christopher Lloyd, John Belushi. 105 minutes.

Al Pacino

The Panic in Needle Park, 1971—20th Century–Fox. Director: Jerry Schatzberg. Writers: Joan Didion, John Gregory Dunne. Cast: Al Pacino, Kitty Wynn. 110 minutes.
The Godfather, 1972—Paramount. Director: Francis Ford Coppola. Writers: Mario Puzo, Francis Ford Coppola. Cast: Marlon Brando, Al Pacino, James Caan, Robert Duvall, Diane Keaton, Richard Castellano, Abe Vigoda, Talia Shire, John Cazale, Sterling Hayden. 175 minutes.
Scarecrow, 1973—Warner Bros. Director: Jerry Schatzberg. Writer: Garry Michael White. Cast: Al Pacino, Gene Hackman. 112 minutes.
Serpico, 1973—Paramount. Director: Sidney Lumet. Writers: Waldo Salt, Norman Wexler. Cast: Al Pacino. 130 minutes.
The Godfather Part II, 1974—Paramount. Director: Francis Ford Coppola. Writers: Mario Puzo, Francis Ford Coppola. Cast: Al Pacino, Robert Duvall, Robert De Niro, Diane Keaton, Michael V. Gazzo, Talia Shire, John Cazale, Lee Strasberg. 202 minutes.
Dog Day Afternoon, 1975—Warner Bros. Director: Sidney Lumet. Writer: Frank Pierson. Cast: Al Pacino, John Cazale, Charles Durning, Chris Sarandon. 125 minutes.
Bobby Deerfield, 1977—Columbia. Director: Sydney Pollack. Writer: Alvin Sargent. Cast: Al Pacino, Marthe Keller. 124 minutes.
...And Justice for All, 1979—Columbia. Director: Norman Jewison. Writers: Barry Levinson, Valerie Curtin. Cast: Al Pacino, Jack Warden, John Forsythe, Jeffrey Tambor, Lee Strasberg. 119 minutes.

Robert Duvall

MASH, 1970—20th Century–Fox. Director: Robert Altman. Writer: Ring Lardner, Jr. Cast: Donald Sutherland, Elliott Gould, Robert Duvall, Sally Kellerman, Tom Skerritt. 116 minutes.
The Revolutionary, 1970—United Artists. Director: Paul Williams. Writer: Hans Koning, from his novel. Cast: Jon Voight, Seymour Cassel, Robert Duvall. 100 minutes.
THX 1138, 1971—Warner Bros. Director: George Lucas. Writers: George Lucas, Walter Murch. Cast: Robert Duvall, Donald Pleasence, Maggie McOmie. 88 minutes.
Lawman, 1971—United Artists. Director: Michael Winner. Writer: Gerry Wilson. Cast: Burt Lancaster, Robert Ryan, Lee J. Cobb, Sheree North, Robert Duvall. 99 minutes.
The Godfather, 1972—Paramount. Director: Francis Ford Coppola. Writers: Mario Puzo, Francis Ford Coppola. Cast: Marlon Brando, Al Pacino, James Caan, Robert Duvall, Diane Keaton, Richard Castellano, Abe Vigoda, Talia Shire, John Cazale, Sterling Hayden. 175 minutes.
Tomorrow, 1972—Film Group Productions. Director: Joseph Anthony. Writer: Horton Foote, based on a story by William Faulkner. Cast: Robert Duvall, Olga Bellin. 103 minutes.
The Great Northfield Minnesota Raid, 1972—Universal. Director: Philip Kaufman. Writer: Philip Kaufman. Cast: Cliff Robertson, Robert Duvall, Luke Askew. 91 minutes.
Joe Kidd, 1972—Universal. Director: John Sturges. Writer: Elmore Leonard. Cast: Clint Eastwood, John Saxon, Robert Duvall. 88 minutes.
Lady Ice, 1973—National General. Director: Tom Gries. Writers: Harold Clemens, Harold Trustman. Cast: Donald Sutherland, Jennifer O'Neill, Robert Duvall. 94 minutes.
Badge 373, 1972—Paramount. Director: Howard W. Koch. Writer: Pete Hamill. Cast: Robert Duvall, Verna Bloom, Henry Darrow. 116 minutes.
The Outfit, 1973—MGM. Writer-Director: John Flynn, based on the book by Richard Stark. Cast: Robert Duvall, Karen Black, Joe Don Baker, Robert Ryan. 103 minutes.
The Godfather Part II, 1974—Paramount. Director: Francis Ford Coppola. Writers: Mario Puzo, Francis Ford Coppola. Cast: Al Pacino, Robert Duvall, Robert De Niro, Diane Keaton, Michael V. Gazzo, Talia Shire, John Cazale, Lee Strasberg. 202 minutes.
Breakout, 1975—Columbia. Director: Tom Gries. Writers: Eliot Asinof, Elliott Baker. Cast: Charles Bronson, Jill Ireland, Robert Duvall. 96 minutes.

The Killer Elite, 1975—United Artists. Director: Sam Peckinpah. Writers: Marc Norman, Stirling Silliphant. Cast: James Caan, Robert Duvall, Burt Young, Gig Young, Bo Hopkins. 122 minutes.

The Seven-Per-Cent Solution, 1976—Universal. Director: Herb Ross. Writer: Nicholas Meyer, based on his novel. Cast: Nicol Williamson, Alan Arkin, Laurence Olivier, Robert Duvall, Joel Grey, Vanessa Redgrave. 113 minutes.

Network, 1976—United Artists. Director: Sidney Lumet. Writer: Paddy Chayefsky. Cast: William Holden, Peter Finch, Faye Dunaway, Robert Duvall, Ned Beatty. 121 minutes.

The Eagle Has Landed, 1976—Cinema International Corporation. Director: John Sturges. Writer: Tom Mankiewicz, from the novel by Jack Higgins. Cast: Michael Caine, Robert Duvall, Donald Sutherland, Jenny Agutter. 135 minutes.

The Greatest, 1977—Columbia. Director: Tom Gries. Writer: Ring Lardner, Jr. Cast: Muhammad Ali, Ernest Borgnine, Robert Duvall, John Marley, James Earl Jones. 101 minutes.

The Betsy, 1978—United Artists. Director: Daniel Petrie. Writers: William Bast, Walter Bernstein, from the novel by Harold Robbins. Cast: Laurence Olivier, Robert Duvall, Tommy Lee Jones, Katharine Ross, Jane Alexander. 125 minutes.

Apocalypse Now, 1979—United Artists. Director: Francis Ford Coppola. Writers: John Milius, Francis Ford Coppola, Michael Herr. Cast: Marlon Brando, Martin Sheen, Robert Duvall, Dennis Hopper. 147 minutes.

The Great Santini, 1979—Warner Bros. Writer-Director: Lewis John Carlino, from the novel by Pat Conroy. Cast: Robert Duvall, Blythe Danner, Michael O'Keefe. 115 minutes.

Robert De Niro

Hi, Mom!, 1970—West End Films. Writer-Director: Brian De Palma. Cast: Robert De Niro, Jennifer Salt, Allen Garfield. 87 minutes.

Jennifer on My Mind, 1971—United Artists. Director: Noel Black. Writer: Erich Segal. Cast: Michael Brandon, Tippy Walker, Robert De Niro. 90 minutes.

Born to Win, 1971—United Artists. Director: Ivan Passer. Writers: Ivan Passer, David Scott Milton. Cast: George Segal, Paula Prentiss, Karen Black, Robert De Niro. 88 minutes.

The Gang That Couldn't Shoot Straight, 1971—MGM. Director: James Goldstone. Writer: Waldo Salt, from the book by Jimmy Breslin. Cast: Jerry Orbach, Leigh Taylor-Young, Lionel Stander, Robert De Niro. 96 minutes.

Bang the Drum Slowly, 1973—Paramount. Director: John Hancock. Writer: Mark Harris, based on his novel. Cast: Michael Moriarty, Robert De Niro, Vincent Gardenia. 96 minutes.

Mean Streets, 1973—Warner Bros. Director: Martin Scorsese. Writers: Martin Scorsese, Mardik Martin. Cast: Harvey Keitel, Robert De Niro, Richard Romanus. 112 minutes.

The Godfather Part II, 1974—Paramount. Director: Francis Ford Coppola. Writers: Mario Puzo, Francis Ford Coppola. Cast: Al Pacino, Robert Duvall, Diane Keaton, Michael V. Gazzo, Talia Shire, John Cazale, Lee Strasberg. 202 minutes.

Taxi Driver, 1976—Columbia. Director: Martin Scorsese. Writer: Paul Schrader. Cast: Robert De Niro, Cybill Shepherd, Peter Boyle, Albert Brooks. 114 minutes.

1900, 1976—Paramount. Director: Bernardo Bertolucci. Writers: Franco Arcalli, Giuseppe Bertolucci, Bernardo Bertolucci. Cast: Gerard Depardieu, Robert De Niro, Donald Sutherland, Burt Lancaster. 317 minutes.

The Last Tycoon, 1976—Paramount. Director: Elia Kazan. Writer: Harold Pinter. Cast: Robert De Niro, Ingrid Boulting, Jack Nicholson, Robert Mitchum, Theresa Russell, Donald Pleasence. 123 minutes.

New York New York, 1977—United Artists. Director: Martin Scorsese. Writers: Earl MacRauch, Mardik Martin. Cast: Liza Minnelli, Robert De Niro. 163 minutes.

The Deer Hunter, 1978—Universal. Director: Michael Cimino. Writer: Derek Washburn, Michael Cimino (unbilled). Cast: Robert De Niro, Christopher Walken, John Savage, John Cazale, Meryl Streep. 184 minutes.

Bibliography

Ansen, David. 1978. "Wooly, Not Wild." *Newsweek*, October 9: 94.
Bergan, Ronald. 1991. *Dustin Hoffman*. London: Virgin Books.
Biskin, Peter. 1998. *Easy Riders, Raging Bulls: How the Sex-Drugs-and-Rock 'n' Roll Generation Saved Hollywood*. New York: Simon & Schuster.
Brando, Marlon, with Robert Lindsay. 1994. *Brando: Songs My Mother Taught Me*. New York: Random House.
Brownstein, Ronald. 2022. *Rock Me on the Water: 1974—The Year Los Angeles Transformed Movies, Music, Television and Politics*. New York: Harper Paperbacks.
Bruce, Lenny. 2016. *How to Talk Dirty and Influence People*. Boston: Da Capo Press.
Butler, Isaac. 2022. *The Method: How the Twentieth Century Learned to Act*. London: Bloomsbury Publishing.
Callahan, Michael. 2019. "Revisiting Harold Robbins, the Forgotten 'Dirty Old Man of American Letters.'" *Hollywood Reporter*, July 3.
Callan, Michael Feeney. 2011. *Robert Redford: The Biography*. New York: Random House.
Canby, Vincent. 1980. "Film; 'The Great Santini'; Family Martinet." *New York Times*, July 14: Section S, Page 14.
Christie, Ian, and Thompson, David, eds. 2003. *Scorsese on Scorsese*. London: Faber & Faber.
Ciment, Michel, ed. 1988. *Elia Kazan: An American Odyssey*. London: Bloomsbury.
Cohan, Steven, and Ina Rae Hark, eds. 1992. *Screening the Male: Exploring Masculinities in the Hollywood Cinema*. Routlege: London.
Dougan, Andy. 1996. *Untouchable: A Biography of Robert De Niro*. New York: Thunder's Mouth Press.
Dowdy, Andrew. 1975. *The Films of the Fifties: The American State of Mind*. New York: William Morrow and Co.
Dworkin, Susan. 1983. *Making Tootsie: A Film Study with Dustin Hoffman and Sydney Pollack*. New York: Newmarket Press.
Eaton, Michael. 1997. *Chinatown*. London: British Film Institute.
Eliot, Marc. 2011. *Steve McQueen: A Biography*. New York: Crown Archetype.
_____. 2013. *Nicholson: A Biography*. New York: Three Rivers Press.
_____. 2017. *Charlton Heston: Hollywood's Last Icon*. New York: Dey Street Books.
Evans, Robert. 2013. *The Kid Stays in the Picture*. New York: HarperCollins.
Farber, Manny. 2009. *Farber on Film: The Complete Film Writings of Manny Farber*. New York: Penguin Group.
Forman, Milos. 1994. *Turnaround: A Memoir*. New York: Villard.
Frankel, Glenn. 2013. *The Searchers: The Making of an American Legend*. New York: Bloomsbury.
_____. 2021. *Shooting Midnight Cowboy*. New York: Farrar, Straus and Giroux.
Friedkin, William. 2013. *The Friedkin Connection: A Memoir*. New York: HarperCollins.
Fullwood, Neil. 2003. *The Films of Sam Peckinpah*. London: Batsford.
Gear, Matthew Asprey. 2019. *Moseby Confidential: Arthur Penn's* Night Moves *and the Rise of Neo-Noir*. Portland, OR: Jorvik Press.
Gehring, Wes D. 2016. *Genre-busting Dark Comedies of the 1970s: Twelve American Films*. Jefferson, NC: McFarland.
Gerard, Fabien S., Kline, Jefferson T., Slerew, Bruce, eds. 2000. *Bernardo Bertolucci: Interviews*. Jackson: University of Mississippi Press.
Giddins, Gary. 2010. *Warning Shadows: Home Alone with Classic Cinema*. New York: W.W. Norton & Co.
Gottfried, Martin. 1990. *All His Jazz: The Life and Death of Bob Fosse*. New York: Bantam Books.
Grobel, Lawrence. 2008. *Al Pacino*. New York: Gallery Books.
Hagen, Uta. 1991. *A Challenge for the Actor*. New York: Scribner.
Harris, Mark. 2003. *Bang the Drum Slowly*. Lincoln, NE: Bison Books.
_____. 2008. *Pictures at a Revolution: Five Movies and the Birth of the New Hollywood*. New York: Penguin Press.

Haskell, Molly. 1987. *From Reverence to Rape: The Treatment of Women in the Movies*, 2nd ed. Chicago: University of Chicago Press.
Hirsch, Foster. 2001. *A Method to Their Madness: The History of the Actors Studio*. New York: Hachette Book Group.
Hofler, Robert. 2023. *The Way They Were: How Epic Battles and Bruised Egos Brought a Classic Hollywood Love Story to the Screen*. New York: Citadel Press.
Hogan, Ron. 2005. *The Stewardess is Flying the Plane: American Films of the 1970s*. New York: Bullfinch Press.
Hunter, Allan. 1987. *Gene Hackman*. New York: St. Martin's Press.
Insdorf, Annette. 2012. *Philip Kaufman*. Champaign, Illinois: University of Illinois Press.
Jackson, Kevin, ed. 1990. *Schrader on Schrader*. London: Faber & Faber.
Jacobs, Diane. 1977. *Hollywood Renaissance: Altman, Cassavetes, Coppola, Mazursky, Scorsese and Others*. Cranbury, New Jersey: A.S. Barnes & Co.
Jordan, Rene. 1973. *Marlon Brando*. New York: Pyramid Communications Inc.
Kael, Pauline. 1980. *When the Lights Go Down*. New York: Holt, Rinehart and Winston.
Kanfer, Stefan. 2008. *Somebody: The Reckless Life and Remarkable Career of Marlon Brando*. New York: Knopf.
Kirshner, Johnathan. 2012. *Hollywood's Last Golden Age: Politics, Society, and the '70s Film in America*. Ithaca: Cornell Univeristy Press.
Levy, Shawn. 2009. *Paul Newman: A Life*. New York: Harmony Books.
———. 2014. *De Niro: A Life*. New York: Random House.
Lumet, Sidney. 1996. *Making Movies*. New York: Vintage.
Maas, Peter. 1976. *Serpico*. New York: Bantam Double Day Dell.
MacNab, Geoffrey. 2005. *The Making of Taxi Driver*. London: Unanimous Limited.
Mann, William J. 2019. *The Contender: The Story of Marlon Brando*. New York: Harper.
Manso, Peter. 1994. *Brando: The Biography*. New York: Hyperion Books.
McCabe, John. 1997. *Cagney*. New York: Alfred A. Knopf.
Meyer, Nicholas. 2009. *The View from the Bridge: Memories of* Star Trek *and a Life in Hollywood*. New York: Viking Penguin.
Mizruchi, Susan L. 2014. *Brando's Smile: His Life, Thought, and Work*. New York: W.W. Norton and Co.
Pacino, Al. 2006. *In Conversation with Lawrence Grobel*. New York: Simon & Schuster.
Parker, John. 2017. *Jack Nicholson: The Biography*. London: John Blake.
Phillips, Gene D. 2004. *Godfather: The Intimate Francis Ford Coppola*. Lexington, KY: University Press of Kentucky.
Polanski, Roman. 1985. *Roman by Polanski*. New York: Ballantine Books.
Puzo, Mario. 2022. *The Godfather, 50th Anniversary Edition*. New York: Berkley.
Reynolds, Burt, and Jon Winokur. 2016. *But Enough About Me: A Memoir*. New York: G.P. Putnam's Sons.
Schickel, Richard. 1985. *James Cagney: A Celebration*. New York: Little Brown & Co.
———. 1997. *Clint Eastwood: A Biography*. New York: Vintage.
Sellers, Robert. 2010. *Hollywood Hellraisers: The Wild Lives and Fast Times of Marlon Brando, Dennis Hopper, Warren Beatty, and Jack Nicholson*. New York: Skyhorse Publishing.
Slawson, Judith. 1985. *Robert Duvall: Hollywood Maverick*. New York: St. Martin's Press.
Spoto, Donald. 1978. *Camerado: Hollywood and the American Man*. New York: New American Library.
Staggs, Sam. 2019. *When Blanche Met Brando: The Scandalous Story of* A Streetcar Named Desire. New York: St. Martin's Press.
Strasberg, Lee. 1987. *A Dream of Passion: The Development of the Method*. New York: Little, Brown & Co.
Tarantino, Quentin. 2022. *Cinema Speculation*. New York: HarperCollins.
Thomson, David. 2009. *Have You Seen…?: A Personal Introduction to 1,000 Films*. New York: Alfred A. Knopf.
———. 2010. *The New Biographical Dictionary of Film*, 5th ed., Updated and Expanded. New York: Random House.
———. 2022. *Acting Naturally: The Magic in Great Performances*. New York: Knopf.
Tobias, Scott. 2020. "Five Easy Pieces at 50: A troubling yet thrilling arrival of a new leading man." *The Guardian*, September 12.
Travers, Peter, editor. 1996. *The Rolling Stone Film Reader: The Best Film Writing from Rolling Stone Magazine*. New York: Simon & Schuster.
Wade, Chris. 2019. *Dustin Hoffman: The Classic Performances*. Morrisville, NC: Lulu.com.
Walker, Beverly. 2013. *Jack Nicholson: Anatomy of an Actor*. Paris: Cahiers du Cinema.
Wasson, Sam. 2020. *The Big Goodbye: Chinatown and the Last Years of Hollywood*. New York: Flatiron Books.
Williams, Tennesse. 1975. *Memoirs*. New York: Bantam Doubleday Dell.
Yule, Andrew. 1992. *Al Pacino: A Life on the Wire*. New York: S.P.I. Books.

Index

Numbers in **_bold italics_** indicate pages with illustrations

Actors Studio 14, 38, 108, 169
Adler, Stella 14, 154
Agatha (1979) 59–60
Alfredo, Alfredo (1972) 48–49
Alice Doesn't Live Here Anymore (1974) 8, 116
All the President's Men (film, 1976) 11, 22, 39–40, 54–55, 58, 120
All the President's Men (Woodward and Bernstein, 1974) 54–55
Allen, Woody 7, 75, 112, 118, 129
American dream 16, 40–41, 78, 91, 94
Analyze This (1999) 7, 123, 156, 172
...And Justice for All (1979) 10, 107, 122–123, 164
Ann-Margret 8, 88, 93, 97, 101–102, 105
Antonioni, Michelangelo (director) 72, 102–104, 115
Apocalypse Now (1979) 9–10, 50, 62, 148–149, 167, 174; Brando in 30–31, 34–36, **_35_**
Arkin, Alan 7, 40, 118, 127, 145–146
Ashby, Hal (director) 94, 96, 99, 145

Baby Boomers 17, 52, 79, 85, 87, 129
Badge 373 (1972) 68
Balsam, Martin 43, 56
Bang the Drum Slowly (1973) 157–158, 161
Beatty, Warren 7, 55, 65, 95, **_99_**–100
Benton, Robert (director) 61–62, 65
Bergen, Candice 8, 78, 81, 88, 93, 105
Bergman, Ingmar 74–75, 90, 161
Bertolucci, Bernardo (director) 27, 48, 103, 115, 159, 161

The Betsy (1978) 147–148
Bite the Bullet (1975) 78–79, 81
Black, Karen 8, 88, 92, 101, 105, 129–130, 138
blaxploitation 8, 68, 141, 144
Bobby Deerfield (1977) 54, 107, 120–122
Bogart, Humphrey 5, 50, 76–77, 86, 140, 159, 177
Bonnie and Clyde (1967) 7, 62, 65–66, 71, 76, 95, 100
Born to Win (1971) 156
The Boys from Brazil (1979) 49, 57
Brando, Marlon 13–37, **_16_**, **_24_**, **_29_**, **_35_**, 85–86, **_170_**, 178; *see also* individual titles
Breakout (1975) 139–140, 187
A Bridge Too Far (1977) 18, 55, 79, 82, 144
Broadway/ off-Broadway 14, 38–39, 53, 65–66, 108, 123, 127
Bronson, Charles 6, 57, 113, 134, 138–140, **_139_**, 163–164
Brooks, Mel (director) 74–75
Brooks, Richard (director) 78–79
Bruce, Lenny 11, 13, 52–53
The Bucket List (2007) 9, 106
Bullitt (1968) 43, 67, 69
Burstyn, Ellen 8, 116
Butch Cassidy and the Sundance Kid (1969) 42, 51, 55, 72, 78

Caan, James 80, 109, 114, 127–**_128_**, 131–132, 141–142
Cabaret (1972) 8, 167
Cagney, James 50, 58, 65–66, 68, 71, 177
Camerado: Hollywood and the American Man (Spoto) 5–7, 11, 86
Canby, Vincent (film critic) 5, 103, 151
Cannes Film Festival 72, 74, 96, 109–110

Carnal Knowledge (1971) 21, 88, 91, 93, 95, 97–98
censorship 6, 14, 19, 31, 53, 93
Chandler, Raymond 81, 96–97
Chayefsky, Paddy (screenwriter) 30, 142–143
Chinatown (1974) 21–22, 78, 86–90, 96–99, **_98_**, 105, 116
Cimino, Michael (director) 36, 167–168, 174
cinema verité 41, 112
Cisco Pike (1971) 65, 67
Clift, Montgomery 1, 19, 100, 178
Coburn, James 79, 134
comedies 69, 74–75, 83, 102, 118–120, 128, 154–156, 172; Hoffman in 38–41, 44–46, 48, 62–63
Communism 15, 71, 100, 104, 113–114, 129, 131, 161
Conrad, Joseph 34–35, 148
The Conversation (1974) 9–10, 71, 73–**_74_**, 77–78
"cool" 17–18, 50, 69, 97, 121, 126, 179
Cooper, Gary 134, 153, 177
Coppola, Francis Ford (director) 34–36, 73, 110, 114–116, 127, 148, 167; and Brando 23–26, 30, 36, 97
Corey, Jeff 43, 88–89
Corman, Roger (director) 88, 154
A Countess from Hong Kong (1967) 122
Crimson Tide (1995) 10, 64
critics 13, 66–67, 69, 72, 103–104, 142; *see also* Canby, Vincent; Kael, Pauline

Dean, James 17, 19, 22, 50, 100, 178
The Deer Hunter (1978) 6, 8, 10, 36, 167–171
De Niro, Robert: background

191

Index

153–154; Brando's influence 6, 86, 154, 164, 170; Method acting 160, 164, 167, 171–172; *see also* individual titles
De Palma, Brian (director) 154–155, 158
Dick Tracy (1990) 7, 9, 122
Dirty Harry (1971) 46, 50, 77, 126, 134
Doctors' Wives (1971) 65
Dog Day Afternoon (1975) 23, 54, 107–109, 116, 118–121, **119**, 163
The Domino Principle (1977) 71, 79–80, 83, 142
Douglas, Melvyn 22, 67
Downhill Racer (1969) 65–66, 69
Dreyfuss, Richard 7, 130, 155, **156**
The Drop Dead '70s: American Film Comedy Year by Year (Lalande) 44
A Dry White Season (1989) 36
Dunaway, Faye 2, 8, 21, 43, 88, 96–97, 138, 143
Duvall, Robert: background 10, **125**–126, 152; Brando's influence 86, 150; Method acting 126–127; *see also* individual titles

The Eagle Has Landed (1976) 82, 120, 137, 144–145, 148
Eastman, Carole (screenwriter) 89–91, 94, 99, 102
Eastwood, Clint 75, 78, 134–**135**, 138–139, 163–164
Easy Rider (1969) 7, 72, 86, 88, 90, 95, 112, 127
Easy Riders, Raging Bulls (Biskind) 6
European influence 6, 14, 28, 48–49, 102–103, 120–121, 128

Farber, Manny 13
Farrow, Mia 42–43, 45
fathers/fatherlessness 21–22, 50, 52, 66, 108–109, 116–117
Feiffer, Jules 46, 91
Fellini, Frederico 45, 93, 115, 121, 161
feminism: rise of 2, 7–8, 33, 59–60, 62–63, 88, 167–168; women's roles 21, 28, 47–48, 56, 75, 81, 92–93
film industry (1980s–2020s) 174–175
film noir 77, 96, 98, 144, 158
filmographies (1970–1979) 185–188
Films of the Fifties (Dowdy) 20
Finney, Albert 7, 112

First Artists 49, 58–60, 62
Five Easy Pieces 6, 10, 88–95, **92**, 97, 99, 106
Fletcher, Louise 8, 87, 101, 105, 174
Fonda, Henry 5, 16, 64, 112, 177
Fonda, Jane 8, 116
Fonda, Peter 88–89
Foote, Horton (screenwriter) 127, 133, 146, 151
Ford, John (director) 79, 134–135, 139, 158, **171**, 172
Forman, Milos (director) 100–102
The Formula (1980) 36
The Fortune (1975) 88, 98–100, 105
Fosse, Bob 53
The French Connection (1971) 6, 10, 50, 64, 67–71, **70**
The French Connection II (1975) 76–77, 79
Freud, Sigmund 21–22, 29, 50, 52, 67, 145, 159
Friedkin, William (director) 67–68, 76
From Reverence to Rape (Haskell, 1974,1987) 8, 27, 63, 181

The Gang That Couldn't Shoot Straight (1971) 154, 156
Garfunkel, Art 45, 91–93
genre movies: buddy films 40–42, 72, 78, 91, 142, 157–158, 161; film noir 77, 96, 98, 144, 158; gangster films 6, 32–33, 46, 76, 115, 131, 159, 166; musicals 6, 53, 79, 89, 102, 166; war films 5–6, 30, 46, 82, 84–85, 134, 157; Westerns 31–32, 43–48, 69–70, 74–75, 78–81, 134–135, 158
The Godfather (1972) 6–10, 22–28, **24**, 73–74, 114–117, 159; Brando (Don Corleone) 26–27, 132; Duvall (Tom Hagen) 26, 131–133; Pacino (Michael Corleone) 24–25, 110–111
The Godfather Part II (1974) 7, 15, 97, 114–**117**, 132–133, 161; De Niro as young Vito Corleone 160
Goin' South (1978) 8, 105–106
Goldman, William (screenwriter) 51, 54–55, 57
Goodman, David Zelag (screenwriter) 45, 82
The Graduate 7, 10, 33–34, 38–40, 45, 86, 91
The Great Escape (1963) 50–51
The Great Northfield Minnesota Raid (1972) 135–136

The Great Santini (1979) 2, 6, 10, 125, 133, 148–151, **149**
The Greatest (1977) 146
Greetings (1968) 154–155
Gries, Tom (director) 136–137, 139–140, 146
Grosbard, Ulu 45, 58
The Gypsy Moths 65, 76

Hackman, Gene: background 64, 66; Brando's influence 6, 64–65, 79, 86; Method acting 68; *see also* individual titles
Haskell, Molly 8, 27, 63, 89
Have You Seen ….? (Thomson) 24, 118, 181
Heart of Darkness (Conrad) 34–35, 148
heroes/anti-heroes 15–16, 19–20, 33, 85, 113, 155, 178
Heston, Charlton 129, **130**
Hi, Mom! (1970) 154
High Plains Drifter (1973) 31
Hitchcock, Alfred: influence 57, 68, 70, 73, 111, 154
Hoffman, Dustin: background 38; Brando's influence 6, 62, 86; Method acting 15, 42–43, 53, 55, 58, 61, 63; *see also* individual titles
Holden, William 5, **143**
Hollywood's Last Golden Age: Politics, Society, and the Seventies Film in America (Kirshner) 54
Hopper, Dennis 88–89
The Hunting Party (1971) 65, 81
Huston, John 22, 96–97, 105, 140

I Never Sang for My Father (1970) 22, 66–67
Improvisation 14, 19, 22–23, 60, 96, 120, 179
The Irishman (2019) 9–10

Jaws (1975) 71, 76, 79, 120, 155, **156**, 174
Jennifer on My Mind (1971) 156
Jeremiah Johnson (1971) 55
Joe Kidd (1972) 134–135
John and Mary (1969) 42–43, 45
Jordan, René 13, 16

Kael, Pauline (film critic) 57, 65–66, 84, 101, 106, 121, 131
Kaufman, Philip (director) 135–136
Kaulbars, Rick 118
Kazan, Elia (director) 28, 94, 102, 104, 106, 108, 165; and Brando 6, 14–15, 19–21
Keaton, Diane 8, 21, 110–111

Index

Keitel, Harvey 158–160, 163–164, 171
Kennedy, John F. (U.S. president 1961–1963) 6, 55, 77, 98, 142, 154
Kerouac, Jack 13, 86–88, 90
The Killer Elite (1975) 141–142
The King of Marvin Gardens (1972) 91, 93, 97
Klute (1971) 8, 116
Kramer, Stanley (director) 80–81
Kramer vs. Kramer (1979) 2, 8, 11, 21, 47, 60–63, **61**
Kubrick, Stanley (director) 87, 102, 105, 129

Lady Ice (1973) 136–137
Lancaster, Burt 129, 178
Lange, Jessica 63, 88
The Last Detail (1973) 8, 10, 86–87, 90, 93–94, 97
Last Tango in Paris (1972) 21, 23, 27–**29**, 32–33, 36, 103–104, 161
The Last Tycoon (1976) 9, 54, 104, 120, 165
Lawman (1971) 187
Lee, Bruce 141, **141**
Lemmon, Jack 7, 43
Lenny (1974) 11, 15, 19, 43, 52–53
Leone, Sergio 48, 134
Levy, Shawn 17, 19
The Little Big Man (1970) 15, 43–**44**
Lloyd, Kathleen 8, 33, 104
Loose Cannons (1990) 7
Lucas, George 8, 24, 128–131
Lucky Lady (1975) 74, 79–**81**, 120
Lumet, Sidney (director) 23, 107, 110–114, 116–119, 121, 143

Malden, Karl 16, 22
male identity/masculinity: in buddy films 40–42, 72, 78, 91, 142, 157–158, 161; and patriarchal model 2, 21, 24–26; as the rebel 16, 20–22, 64, 85, 112–113, 136–137; in revenge films 46–48, 57, 68, 111, 134, 139; in screen violence 25, 32, 36, 46–47, 118, 140–141, 159–161; as stereotypes 8, 16, 21–22, 32, 78, 82, 141; in struggles with authority 19, 22–24, 50, 52, 65–67, 128–129
Marathon Man (1976) 48, **57**, 58, 120
March or Die (1977) 10, 54, 64, 79, 82
Marvin, Lee 69–70

MASH (1970) 128–129, 137
McGuane, Tom (screenwriter) 31, 104
McQueen, Steve 18, 39, 49–52, 69, 134, 141, 145, 179
Mean Streets (1973) 7, 15, 154–**155**, 158–161, 163–164, 169, 171
Meet the Fockers (2004) 7, 9, 172
Meisner, Sanford 14, 50, 126; see also Method acting
The Men (1950) 13, 22
Method acting 5, 68, 100, 138–140, 160, 172, 177–179; Brando and 14–17, 22, 27, 30, 32, 42, 122, 169; Hoffman and 42, 61–63; Russian-influenced 1, 6, 14
A Method to Their Madness (Hirsch) 169
Midnight Cowboy (1969) 7, 11, 38, 40–44, 51, 72, 108
military service 14, 64, 71, 91, 94–95, 126, 148–150
Minnelli, Liza 8, 79, 166–167
The Missouri Breaks (1976) 23, 30–34, 104
Mitchum, Robert 5–6, 129, 178
Muni, Paul 5, 85
musicals 6, 53, 79, 89, 102, 166

naturalism 1, 6–7, 14–15, 120, 177; see also Method acting
Network (1976) 95, 120, 142, **143**, 163
The New York movie 6, 15, 22, 91, 158–159, 174; NY location in 1970s film 63–65, 67–69, 76, 108–113, 118–122, 162–164; Office of Film, Theatre and Broadcasting 40–41; stage 14–15, 30, 53, 72, 120, 152, 177; see also Actors Studio; Broadway
New York New York (1977) 6, 10, 166–167, 170–171
Newman, Paul 1, 17–19, **18**, 39, 49–50, 179
Nichols, Mike (director) 7, 38, 86, 94
Nicholson, Jack: background 87–88; Brando's influence 6, 85–86, 91, 94, 104; *Night Moves* (1975), 8, 10, 67, 76–79, 81, 142; see also individual titles
The Nightcomers (1971) 23, 32
1900 (nineteen hundred) 48, 161
Nixon, Richard (U.S. president 1969–1974) 33, 48, 54–55, 77, 116, 140, 144

Of Mice and Men (1992) 42, 72
Olivier, Laurence 30, **58**, 147

On a Clear Day You Can See Forever (1970) 89
On the Waterfront (1954) 15–**16**, 20–22, 25–26, 94, 116, 159, 169–**170**
One-Eyed Jacks (1963) 22
One Flew Over the Cuckoo's Nest (1975) 19, 76, 86–87, 90, 100–**101**, 103–104
The Outfit (1973) 125–126, 129, 138–139, 148, 150

Pacino, Al: background 107–108; Brando's influence 6, 86, 107, 110, 113; Method acting 107, 123; see also individual titles
Pakula, Alan J. (director) 39, 55–56, 78
The Panic in Needle Park (1971) 72, 109–112, 114, 121
Papillon (1973) 49–52, 59, 140
The Parallax View 1974, 56, 78, 142
Parsons, Estelle 8, 67
The Passenger (1975) 20, 102–104
Patton (1970) 30, 49, 67, 149–150
Paul Newman: A Life (Levy) 17, 19
Peck, Gregory 5, 177
Peckinpah, Sam (director) 32, 45–48, 141–142, 159, 163–164
Penn, Arthur (director) 30–33, 43–**44**, 65, 76–77, **99**, 104, 164
Poitier, Sidney 8, 49, 179
Polanski, Roman 98, 105, 140
Pollack, Sydney (director) 39, 120–121, 141
Portnoy's Complaint (Roth) 45, 91
The Poseidon Adventure (1972) 19, 64, 71–72
The Postman Always Rings Twice (1982) 88, 93
Presley, Elvis 13, 27, 86
press and critics 13, 29, 66–67, 69, 72, 107, 153
Prime Cut (1972) 69–71
Prizzi's Honor (1985) 87–88
Puzo, Mario 114, 116

Rafelson, Bob (director) 88, 93–94
Raging Bull (1980) 6, 9, 153, 160, 169–172
Rain Man (1988) 52
The Rain People (1969) 126–127, 129–131
Reagan, Ronald (U.S. President 1981–1989) 87, 164, 170

Index

Rebel Without a Cause (1955) 22
Redford, Robert 7, 11, 18, 62, 64–65, 82, 99; in *All the President's Men* 39–40, 55–56
revenge films 46–48, 57, 68, 111, 134, 139
Reynolds, Burt 7, 59, 80–*81*, 122
Richards, Dick (director) 81–82
Righteous Kill (2008) 9
Ritchie, Michael (director) 65–66, 69–70, 136
Robbins, Harold 146–148
Robinson, Edward G. 5, 177
Rocky (1976) 33–34, 82, 146, 159, 164
Runaway Jury (2003) 9

A Safe Place (1971) 93, 186
Salt, Waldo (screenwriter) 41, 113
Sarris, Andrew (critic) 40, 66
Saturday Night Fever (1977) 113, 160, 169
Scarecrow (1973) 9, 71–72, 111–112
Scarface (1983) 123
The Scarlet Letter (1995) 144
Schaffner, Franklin D. (director) 49–50
Schatzberg, Jerry (director) 72, 109, 111–112, 114
Scheider, Roy 67–68
Schisgal, Murray (screenwriter) 38
Schlesinger, John (director) 40–41, 57
Schneider, Maria 21, 27–29, 103
Scorsese, Martin (director) 116, 154, 158–160, *162*–164, 166–172
Scott, George C. 30–*31*, 36
Segal, George 7, 40, 112
Serpico (1973) 10, 56–57, 77, 107, *109*–110, 112–114
The Seven-Per-Cent Solution (1976) 120, 144–145
The Shining (1980) 87, 102, 106
Simon, Neil (playwright) 55, 118, 155
Simone (2002) 7

Smokey and the Bandit (1977) 80, 122, 126
Spielberg, Steven 8, 57, 79
Spoto, Donald 5–7, 11, 86
Stage 14–15, 30, 53, 72, 120, 152, 177; *see also* Actors Studio; Broadway
Stanislavski, Konstantin 14–15, 126, 154; *see also* Method acting
Star Wars (1977) 34, 129–130, 174
Steenburgen, Mary 8, 105
stereotypes 8, 16, 21–22, 32, 43, 67, 78, 141, 156
Stewart, James 5, 16, 177
The Sting (1973) 11, *18*, 99
Straight Time (1978) 58–60
Strasberg, Lee 14–15, 17, 108, 116–117, 177
Straw Dogs (1971) 9–10, 45–47, 57–58, 82
Streep, Meryl 8, 21, 62
A Streetcar Named Desire 13, 21, 87
Streisand, Barbara 8, 49, 89
Sturges, John (director) 134–135, 137, 144
Superman (1978) 7, 9–10, 31, 33–34, 75, 79, 83
Sutherland, Donald 7, *137*–138, 144

Tarantino, Quentin 46, 138
Taxi Driver (1976) 8–10, 19, 116, 138, 149, *162*–165, 169
Tender Mercies (1983) 125–126, 146, 151
Terms of Endearment (1983) 87, 106
Three Days of the Condor (1976) 11, 55, 142
THX 1138 (1971) 128, 130–131, 150
To Kill a Mockingbird (1962) 127, 131, 133, 146
Tomorrow (1972) 123, 133, 138, 150
Tootsie (1983) 11, 38, 43–44, 47, 49, 62–63
Towne, Robert (screenwriter) 87, 94–99, 102

Tracy, Spencer 22, 66, 177
Travolta, John 59, 96
TV 50, 71, 88, 119, 122, 138, 142–143, 147, 158
Tynan, Kathleen 59–60

The Ugly American 19, 47, 55, 76
Uncommon Valor (1983) 64, 84
The Unforgiven (1992) 10, 75, 84

Vietnam War 6, 49, 62, 78–79, 143–144; in *Apocalypse Now* 35–36, 126, 148–149; in *Deer Hunter* 6, 36, 167–169; in *MASH* 128
vigilantism 46, 56, 68–69, 108, 134–*135*, 140, 163
Viva Zapata! (1952) 20, 87
Voight, John 7, 38, 41–42, 51

Wag the Dog (1997) 7, 9
war films 5–6, 30, 46, 82, 84–85, 134, 157; *see also* Vietnam
Warner Bros. 5, 50, 55, 78
Washington Post 55–56
Watergate scandal 53, 73, 98, 113, 142; *see also* All the President's Men; Nixon, Richard
Wayne, John 41, 50, 69, 129, 134, 172, 178
Westerns 31–32, 43–48, 69–70, 74–75, 78–81, 134–135, 158
Who Is Harry Kellerman and Why Is He Saying Those Terrible Things About Me? (1971) 43–45, 58
The Wild Bunch (1969) 31, 46, 79, 141
The Wild One (1953) 20–21, 87
Wilder, Gene 72, 118
The Witches of Eastwick (1987) 88
World War II 15, 30, 48, 82, 129, 144, 149, 161, 169

Young Frankenstein (1974) 7, 73–74, 83

Zandy's Bride (1974) 8, 73–75, 78, 80